Women in the Professions, Politics and Philanthropy 1840-1940

Edited by Katherine Bradley and Helen Sweet

Front cover illustrations by Lyn Selwood. Back cover photograph of the National Union for Women's Suffrage Societies Pilgrimage marching down Cornmarket St., Oxford, July 1913, courtesy: Centre for Oxfordshire Studies, Oxford.

Order this book online at www.trafford.com
or email orders@trafford.com

Most Trafford titles are also available at major online book retailers.

Note for Librarians: A cataloguing record for this book is available from Library and Archives Canada at www.collectionscanada.ca/amicus/index-e.html

Printed in Victoria, BC, Canada.

ISBN: 978-1-4269-1187-3

Our mission is to efficiently provide the world's finest, most comprehensive book publishing service, enabling every author to experience success. To find out how to publish your book, your way, and have it available worldwide, visit us online at www.trafford.com

Trafford rev. 10/2/2009

 www.trafford.com

North America & international
toll-free: 1 888 232 4444 (USA & Canada)
phone: 250 383 6864 ♦ fax: 812 355 4082

Contents

List of Contributors

Dr Katherine Bradley is an Associate Lecturer at the Open University (since 1985) where she is currently teaching courses on social policy and history. She is also a tutor at Denman College (Women's Institute College) where she teaches courses on women's history and was until recently a co-ordinator of the International Oxford Women's Festival. She is a social science graduate (Brunel University), has MAs in politics (Essex University) and in history (Oxford Polytechnic) and completed her PhD: 'Faith, Perseverance and Patience, the History of the Suffrage and Anti-suffrage Movements, 1870-1930', at Oxford Brookes University in 1998.

Katherine has a long experience in teaching in further and higher education including, until recently, Oxford Brookes University. Her publications include: *Job Evaluation: Theory and Practice.* British Institute of Management, 1979; Johnson, Daphne et al (as co-author) *Secondary Schools and the Welfare Network.* Allen and Unwin, 1980; *Women on the March. A Suffrage Walk around Oxford City Centre.* Oxford City Council, 1996; 'Women's Suffrage Souvenirs.' In: Michael Hitchcock (ed.) *Souvenirs: The Material Culture of Tourism.* Ashgate, 2000; *Friends and Visitors: A First History of the Women's Suffrage Movement in Cornwall, 1870-1914.* The Patten Press, Penzance, Cornwall, 2000; "*If the Vote is Good for Jack, Why Not for Jill?*" *The Women's Suffrage Movement in Cornwall, 1870-1914.* Cornish Studies Eight, 2000.

Dr Gina Burrows was until recently PA to a professor of Social Anthropology in the University of Oxford where her experience in achieving a PhD proved at least as useful as her historical researches in giving reassurance and guidance to graduate students. Trained as a mature student at Berkshire College of Education (Bulmershe), majoring in Religious Studies, she taught in primary schools in Berkshire and Oxfordshire until she took early retirement in 1995. While teaching in Oxfordshire she began her interest in women's history through a part-time MA at Oxford Brookes University. Her research into the concepts of love and duty and the demands on clergy families to lead exemplary lifestyles led from work on eighteenth century clerical families to a PhD thesis on 'Images and Perceptions of Wives and Daughters of the Victorian Clergy'.

Since graduation she has continued to work full time but is looking forward to retirement when she can engage in her next project which is to write a biography of Catharine Tait, (wife of nineteenth century Archbishop Tait), one of the three principal subjects of her doctoral research, whom she believes deserves a fresh visit. She continues to embrace politics, as a town councillor and formerly as Town Mayor where even in the 21st century the image of women in an exemplary position can become an issue.

Professor Anne Digby's research ranges widely over the landscape of British social history from the eighteenth to twentieth centuries: from schooling and society to the New Poor Law, agrarian society in the nineteenth century to welfare policy in the twentieth. However, her primary interest is in the social history of medicine. Areas of research include: South African medicine, medical markets and healthcare systems; history of social policy and welfare; and the history of psychiatry.

Her main research interest is the medical history of South Africa, focusing particularly – though not exclusively – on the social history of medicine in the Cape. She is especially interested in medical pluralism and interactions between western and indigenous medicine in South Africa. Her book, *Diversity and Division in Medicine: Health Care in South Africa from the 1800s*, was recently published by Peter Lang. Professor Digby is currently working with historians from the University of Cape Town on the history of Groote Schuur Hospital, funded by a Wellcome Trust International Collaborative Award.

Anne is author of a considerable number of edited volumes, historical handbooks, chapters and journal articles. Monographs include: *From*

York Lunatic Asylum to Bootham Park Hospital (Borthwick Paper, York, 1986); *Pauper Palaces: the Economy and Poor Law of Nineteenth-Century Norfolk* (Routledge, 1978); *Children, School and Society in Nineteenth-Century England* (Macmillan, 1981), with P. Searby; *Madness, Morality and Medicine: a Study of the York Retreat, 1796-1914* (Cambridge History of Medicine Series, Cambridge University Press, 1985); *Making a Medical Living. Doctors and Patients in the Market for Medicine in England, 1720-1914* (Cambridge Studies in Population, Economy and Society in Past Time, Cambridge University Press, Hardback edition, 1994. Paperback edition June, 2002); *The Evolution of British General Practice, 1850-1948* (Oxford University Press, 1999); *Division and Diversity in Medicine: Health care in South Africa from the 1800s* (Peter Lang, 2006).

Dr Anne Keene is Fellow and Director of Development at Linacre College, Oxford University, a graduate college, where she works with alumni from over 130 countries. She has an MA in French and German from the University of Edinburgh, a PGCE and an MSc in Educational Studies from the University of Oxford and a PhD in History from Oxford Brookes University, for which her thesis was 'The Role of the Principal of an Oxford Women's College 1879-1925'. She is the author of *Oxford; The American Connection* (1990), is a *Dictionary of National Biography* contributor ('Barbara Gwyer', 2004), Editor-in-chief of *First Person* (2005), and has contributed papers to the *CASE International Journal of Educational Advancement*. In her early professional life, over a period of ten years she taught French, German, and English as a Foreign Language, to children and adults in schools and businesses in Oxfordshire, and also worked for seven years as a Blue Badge Oxford Guild of Guides Lecturer.

Dr Caroline Morrell completed her PhD on Housing and the Women's Movement, 1860-1914 at Oxford Brookes University in 1999. Her first degree was in Comparative History, obtained at Essex University in 1979; her second degree, an MSc in Applied Social Sciences, was obtained at Oxford University in 1987. Caroline has taught history at Oxford Brookes University and at Ruskin College and social sciences with the Open University. Her other research interests include housing and homelessness and she has written a distance learning course on homelessness for the University of Wales and taken part in national evaluation of tenant management organisations for the Office of the Deputy Prime Minister. More recently, she was commissioned in 2006 to carry out an evaluation of community garden projects in Bosnia and Herzegovina for their funding body, the American Friends Service Committee.

Publications: *Black Friday: Violence against women in the suffragette movement*, Women's Research and Resources Centre Publications, 1981; 'Octavia Hill and women's networks in housing' in Anne Digby and John Stewart, (eds.), *Gender, Health and Welfare in Britain 1850-1950*, Routledge, 1996; with Karen Kuehne, 'Single women and homelessness in Oxford, 1880s and 1990s' in Jane Darke, Sue Ledwith and Roberta Woods, (eds.), *Women and the City: Visibility and voice in urban space*, Palgrave, 2000; Liz Cairncross, Caroline Morrell, Jane Darke and Sue Brownill, *Tenants Managing: an Evaluation of Tenant Management Organisations in England* Office of the Deputy Prime Minister, 2002; *Working with the Homeless*, Department of Voluntary Sector Studies, University of Wales, Lampeter, 2003; 'Rachel Barrett, Suffragette', entry in the *Dictionary of National Biography* Oxford University Press, 2004.

Dr Gwen Searle Born in Australia, and obtaining her first degree there, Gwen Searle worked on a voluntary basis with the Care Committee after she came to London, and subsequently as a social worker in special schools with the Inner London Education Authority. Moving to Oxfordshire in the early 1970s, she was employed as a senior Psychiatric Social Worker in Family and Child Guidance in the Education Department of Oxfordshire County Council, dealing with developmental problems of children and their families. After retirement, she obtained her M.A. in social history, and her Ph.D from Oxford Brookes University in 2004, researching child emigration to Canada in the late nineteenth and early twentieth centuries. She is currently taking part in researching the history of the village in which she lives.

Dr. Helen Sweet is Research Associate at the Wellcome Unit, University of Oxford where she is currently undertaking post-doctoral research studying the role of mission hospitals which served the rural communities of KwaZulu Natal, South Africa during the twentieth century. She has worked on two previous Wellcome-funded research projects. The first focused on the historical development of general practice medicine in Great Britain from the Medical Registration Act of 1851 to the NHS Act of 1948, whilst the second explored the concept of medical pluralism in the South African Cape, from the early nineteenth to mid-twentieth centuries.

Helen's PhD was on the '*History of district nursing within the context of the development of the community care team, c. 1919-1979*'. She is also a registered nurse and midwife and has a particular interest in nursing history. Her publications include a number of book chapters and journal articles. She is author (with Dr R. Dougal) of: *Community nursing and primary healthcare in Twentieth Century Britain* (Routledge: 2007); co-editor with Mark Harrison, Margaret Jones, *From Western Medicine to Global Medicine* (Orient Longman, 2009); and is currently preparing a second monograph for publication in 2010: '*Medicine with a Mission: The Role and Development of Missionary Nursing and Medicine in KwaZulu Natal: c1920-1980.*'

Mrs Lesley Wade is a lecturer at the University of Manchester within the school of nursing, midwifery and social work. As both an academic and practitioner, she has written extensively on promoting change within health care and effected change both nationally and internationally. The author of the first book on gerontological nursing within the UK she continues to practice within this field. In 2001, she was jointly awarded a grant from her university to undertake a study on the history of occupational health within the Lancashire cotton towns. A member of the United Kingdom Centre for History of Nursing and Midwifery, she is also forum committee member and magazine editor of the Royal College of Nursing's History of Nursing Society. She has written on the history of nurse leadership and recruitment and on the history of provincial childcare.   Presently she is working on a biography of an early twentieth century nurse leader, Charlotte Seymour Yapp.

List of Figures

Fig. 3.1 Catharine Tait - the engraving used for the frontispiece of her biography written by her husband after her death

Fig. 4.1 'The historic five' reproduced by kind permission of GFS Platform

Fig. 4.2 'GFS Catechism' from Friendly Leaves, 1884, reproduced by kind permission of GFS Platform

Fig. 4.3 Picture of Mary Higgs, reproduced by kind permission of Oldham Public Library

Fig. 4.4 Exterior of a common lodging house

Fig. 6.1 Back-to-back housing and mills in Bacup, 1898.

Fig. 6.2 Map of Bacup (From O.S. Map c 1890)

Fig. 6.3 District nursing cases attended annually, Bacup (1920s)

Fig. 6.4 District Nurse's annual total visits, Bacup (1920s)

Fig. 6.5 Bacup district cases nursed on monthly basis (5 yearly, 1915-1940)

Fig. 6.6 QVJIN Nurse-Doctor Message Sheet

Fig. 7.1 Millicent Fawcett, President of the National Union of Women's Suffrage Societies addresses the Oxford Union in November, 1908. The first woman to address the Oxford Union. (*Illustrated London News*, November 20, 1908)

Fig. 7.2 The Oxford Women's Suffrage Society Banner illustrating St. Frideswide (patron saint of Oxford) 'bearing the sword of justice, but surrounded with the thorns of prejudice'. (A line drawing, *Oxford Times*, June, 29, 1908)

Fig. 7.3 Oxford Women's Suffrage Society: Rules, Election Paper and Membership Card. (author's own collection)

Figure 7.4 Oxford Women's Suffrage Society office, 35, Holywell Street, Oxford. (Drawing: Lyn Selwood)

Figure 7.5 Oxfordshire, Buckinghamshire and Berkshire Federation of Suffrage Societies, banner, 1912. (a 1990s postcard reproduction)

Figure 7.6 Poster advertising an Oxford Women's Suffrage Society meeting, March 9, 1912. (Centre for Oxfordshire Studies, Oxford)

Figure 7.7 National Union of Women's Suffrage Pilgrims marching in Oxford High Street. July 21, 1913 (author's own collection)

Figure 7.8 The Oxford Suffrage Summer School, August 11-18, 1913. (*Common Cause*, August 22, 1913)

Figure 7.9 Oxford Women's Students' Suffrage Society banner, 1911. (reprinted from a 1912 postcard and sold by the Bodleian shop in the 1990s)

Preface

During the nineteenth and early twentieth centuries women were expected to conform to certain class- and gender-based behavioural norms, which defined the boundaries between the public and private spheres. However, there is a growing body of research which illustrates that these boundaries were either adapted to existing circumstances or contravened. Through a series of essays, the book analyses this discourse by examining the influence of gender and class issues; how women adapted and in some cases changed their lives together with the lives of others; and by focusing on their role in such areas as work, education, health, politics, housing and religion. The women featured throughout the book did groundbreaking work in their spheres, and were significant figures in opening up many areas of life for women of subsequent generations.

The book covers a period of change brought about by increasing urbanisation and industrialisation and by associated developments in agricultural and rural life. These changes influenced women's social, political, cultural and religious ideas. Thus the authors consider the manner in which key issues were socially and politically constructed, together with the specific consequences of these constructions. By dividing the book thematically the philanthropic, professional and political roles adopted by women are highlighted, revealing the development of ideas and responses to issues in ways that are important for gaining a greater understanding and perspective of the period. All are connected by being situated on the margins of history, in the sense that they have been neglected by historians, even within the field of women's history. Some endeavoured to change their traditional role, others worked in behalf of marginal groups and yet others invented strategies for survival in a male-dominated world. The book's fundamental premise is that not only are such marginal groups and individuals intrinsically interesting, but that they throw significant light on women's lives both in the public and private spheres.

The book incorporates the following sub-themes:

a) *Gender*: how the boundaries between the private and public spheres were broken down or adapted by women.

b) *Class*: inter-class relationships.

c) *Employment*: the boundary between professional and voluntary work, and paid and unpaid work.

d) *Local and National*: the relationship between these in terms of ideas, issues and activities.

An additional unifying theme is that all the chapters are based on a variety of biographical materials. Thus some chapters concentrate on the lives of specific individuals, whilst other analyse the role of groups of people, either within pressure groups or by examining their working and personal lives. All the chapters are based on both qualitative and / or quantitative analysis.

DEDICATION

To Anne with love and thanks.

CHAPTER 1

Introduction: Women in the Professions, Politics and
Philanthropy, 1840–1940

Anne Digby

This book focuses both on the achievements of notable individuals and the dilemmas that faced them as women during a fast-changing century. It discusses whether they challenged or conformed, whether they were reformists or revolutionaries, how they discerned the limits of the possible (and the acceptable) and, crucially, how they extended those boundaries within a borderland between the private and public spheres. The three areas chosen to illustrate this are philanthropy, the professions and politics, although their porous frontiers mean the existence of dynamic and interesting interconnections between them. For example, Catharine Tait (the subject of chapter 3) hosted a significant Lambeth Palace meeting that contributed to the founding of the Girls' Friendly Society (whose housing work is discussed in chapter 4), while the activities of Oxford student suffragists (described in chapter 7) encountered the hostility of college principals (whose burdens are examined in chapter 5.)

This collection of case studies also shows the impossibility of separating individuals and their personal experiences from the social and political contexts in which their lives were lived, and their contributions made. The confluence of different forms of agency is revealed in these studies

1

of 'movers and shakers' whose evolving forms of empowerment and legitimacy are illustrated through diverse but complementary case studies. No single trajectory unites or defines these women; instead their diverse lives – spanning class, generation and nationality – confound simplistic assumptions. But what emerges in striking fashion is fluidity of role and its definition in an age of social transition for women. As Gwen Searle aptly remarks: 'the profession of a lady in mid-century was philanthropy'. And the kind of case work that she describes Caroline Chisholm and Maria Rye using in their charitable endeavours to assist girls and women in emigrating would develop into a basic tool of the later profession of social work. Similarly, the lady principals who headed the charitable collegiate foundations for women in Oxford would not have described themselves as politicians, yet in their quasi-ambassadorial functions they utilised political skills. In the absence of appropriate professional templates, women constructed standards of behaviour and built up self-belief in their own talents. Catherine Tait, for example, had a pronounced ability in bookkeeping and, although this was a stereotypically Victorian masculine occupation, she used it to good effect both in her household accounts as well as those of Rugby School.

Few, if any, of the women discussed here are remembered today. The names of Caroline Chisholm, Maria Rye, Mary Higgs, Catharine Tait and other pioneering women are hardly household names. Like many other female agents of change, their achievements did not receive the acclaim accorded their male counterparts. Some received minor public recognition: for example, Higgs was called to give evidence before a Departmental Committee on Vagrancy while both Rye and Chisholm received pensions from the Civil List. That they were not fêted by contemporaries or remembered as notable historical figures may be attributed in part to the specifically female fields they chose to work in, such as the emigration of women and children, the housing of women, women's suffrage, or the higher education of female students. It is also linked inextricably to the demeanour and values of ladylike behaviour many adopted since they would have eschewed personal publicity as unbecoming to their status. Also germane to the hidden qualities of some of their work were its local dimensions, as was the case particularly for district nurses and for those working for the Women's Institute. Their endeavours had a community rather than national focus that was outside the spotlight of metropolitan publicity. Yet these were innovative women whose work is deserving of historical analysis and record. Using a variety of documentation, knowledge of locality and oral interview, the contributors to this volume have helped liberate these individuals from past obscurity.

The subjects of the following chapters were part of the first women's movement and its aftermath. Prominent in their work was the moral dimension so conspicuous in the first, and largely invisible in the second women's movement. As Gwen Searle shows in her analysis of Rye and Chisholm's emigration endeavours, and Caroline Morrell also highlights in her chapter on Higgs and others engaged in the housing movement, the desire to save girls and women from potential sexual exploitation, and consequent moral downfall or pauperisation, was prominent. Moral ideals thus drove the highly practical and hands-on interventions that characterised both the socially conservative Girls Friendly Society and the campaigning coordination of the National Association of Women's Lodging Houses. Evident amongst the individuals who make up this group biography was an implicit but strong belief in women's moral duties, again evident in the values of the first women's movement. Gina Burrows's empathetic portrait of Catharine Tait exemplified this with her description of her all-encompassing religious world view. However, a rights-based ethos also developed to a lesser extent (being evident in the National Association of Women's Lodging Houses, for example) and this grew to become a key characteristic of the second feminist movement in the twentieth century. Some women examined in this volume – such as Higgs or Rye – were clearly feminist, but other individuals, such as some in the Girls' Friendly Society, held anti-feminist views.

The biographical focus so evident in most chapters facilitates an understanding of some of the key qualities of these notable women. Physical energy was an important asset, enabling Catharine Tait, for example, to lead from the front in her many charitable endeavours, but it was not an essential element since the Oxford women principals managed to head their colleges despite the frailty highlighted in Anne Keene's analysis. Physical courage was prominent in some who, like Chisholm or Rye, were even prepared to travel in the outback of Australia or New Zealand to find homes for their emigrants. Assumption of path-breaking roles frequently led to performance pressure to excel, so that persistence, determination, diligence and independence were amongst gritty qualities they conspicuously developed in their work. Many were ladies, but of course these were not stereotypical ladylike qualities and so serve as a useful corrective to simplistic typecasting. Admittedly, these were women who were challenging contemporary views as to what was personally feasible or socially acceptable, thus extending the frontiers of female activity from the private to public spheres. In doing so, these individuals were willing to challenge their own physical limitations through overwork in a range of activities; not least by a heroic balancing of the considerable private demands of home and family with those of their public duties.

An interesting dimension of this book is that it shows the complex framework of voluntary and official agencies in which women worked, whether in membership of the ladies' committees of workhouses, school boards, district nursing societies or other philanthropic organisations. Women learned by doing and so acquired the necessary skills of organisation, whether this was fundraising for their cause, arguing their case in a committee, holding a public meeting, or lobbying influential people. A notable example of the latter was Caroline Chisholm's interview with the colonial governor, Sir George Gipps, that successfully gained his backing for an Emigrant Home for women. Less conspicuous but equally valuable was the mobilisation of the community by district nurses, or the bridging of disparate groups in order to unite for a common aim in women's institutes. In addition a growing sophistication and differentiation in approach might become evident, as is shown in Katherine Bradley's description of the contrast between the militancy of the suffragettes (motto: 'Deeds not Words') and the moderation of the suffragists (motto: 'Faith, Perseverance and Patience').

That these path breakers were disinterested was helpful; these women were not working for themselves but for others. The first women's movement was for many years characterised by middle-class women (or occasionally upper-class ones) working to improve the conditions or status of their working-class sisters. This type of effort is conspicuous in this volume in chapters 2 and 4 discussing emigration or housing. And the examination of the charitable endeavours of Catharine Tait in chapter 3 makes clear that it was her eminent status that gave her an entrée to so many field of philanthropic endeavour. Another dimension is provided in chapter 5 which, in focusing on the first and second generations of Oxford women principals, shows that college staff and students each came from an elevated social status. Chapter 7 indicates that by the early twentieth century class-bound activity was breaking down into a broader social solidarity mobilised behind the single campaigning issue of the female vote, but one viewed as a means to influence women's rights more generally. Helen's Sweet's depiction of the Bacup district nurse in chapter 6 shows the nurse's recruitment from a working or lower middle-class background, with supervision vested partly in the amateur ladies' committee of a district nursing society.

On a more individualistic basis these biographical studies throw light on a different dimension of the public and the private in hinting at the personal self-doubts that could afflict women who assumed demanding roles outside the home. One could surmise that path-breaking women might counter their own inner lack of confidence by appearing articulate and informed in their public roles and by learning to combine a ladylike demeanour with steely assertiveness. Mary Higgs's decision to assume the position of a vagrant woman may have tested her courage in making her face the threatening rigours not only of the open road but of the workhouse's casual ward in order to experience at first hand its punitive conditions, and later to record them. In a very different context the early female principals of Oxford women's colleges had to face a hostile ideological climate, navigate the intricacies of the university bureaucracy, tackle difficult issues in college management and understand complexities of institutional accounts. As token women in an emerging female professional world they faced unreasonable demands, looked in vain for role models or support networks, and so found their exposed position stressful, insecure and lonely, having to fall back on the support of relatives and friends.

As the women's movement consolidated, however, so female networks and organised support mechanisms were built up, as the account of the suffrage movement makes clear in locating local activity within a broader national context. And by the early to mid- twentieth century, the study of the Bacup District Nursing Society shows a more developed professional situation. Here qualified district nurses had recourse to the Queen's Nursing Institute for professional legitimacy, whilst contact with other professionals such as general practitioners provided support within the community. Similarly, Lesley Wade's examination of the early years of the Federation of Women's Institutes indicates how the demeaning stereotype of 'jam and Jerusalem' was wide of the mark, in that this was a proactive, politicised, and self-confident organisation that operated across social divides and national frontiers.

These studies discuss both the opportunities and the pressures of women operating within a world with few occupational templates. Whether in philanthropy, the professions or politics women found freedom to improvise and create credentials through their own success but, at the same time, by challenging and extending the boundaries of social conformity, some encountered mental stress and physical strain. Illustrating both commonalities and contrasts in individual lives and achievements, these studies thus provide fresh perspectives and unusual insights on female agency through investigating the varied and ground-breaking work of a group of pioneering women.

Section One: Women in Philanthropy

These three chapters look at the charitable work undertaken by middle and upper-class ladies over the latter half of the nineteenth and early twentieth centuries. These women took extraordinary steps to tackle the problems with which they and society were faced. Mrs Chisholm and Miss Rye, whose work is described in Chapter Two, made it their mission to help young women emigrating to the Colonies find employment and accommodation; the ladies of the Girls' Friendly Society and Mary Higgs of the National Association for Women's Lodging Homes who feature in Chapter Three, worked on a national scale to provide decent housing to vulnerable women and Catharine Tait, the subject of Chapter Four, combined the role and duties of a senior clergy wife with wider philanthropic and social concerns. All were married with the exception of Miss Rye. To pursue their ends, women in philanthropic work generally had male support, and accepted help from men, making use of male patronage and skills where available. However, their activities had both costs and benefits to the women involved, and to their families, and it might be asked what motivated them to undertake onerous and often distressing tasks.

There are many reasons why people become involved in philanthropic work, other than simple human kindness, but benevolence is generally offered by the more privileged to the more dependent, whether based on social, political or economic conditions. For generations before the industrial revolution, the upper classes had provided almshouses, hospitals and schools for the poor, in addition to charitable giving and visiting the sick. From the early seventeenth century, it was the duty of the parish to provide for the orphan, widow and the destitute, the word 'charity' signifying the relief given to the destitute poor and hungry who relied on casual almsgiving. The premise of the Poor Law Act of 1834 that destitution stemmed from moral failing of the individual, introduced the concept of non-eligibility, and the harsh provisions of the Act left the workhouse as the last resort the state offered to the poor unable to earn their own living. Much philanthropic activity of the nineteenth century was driven by the principle that voluntary action was preferable to state provision. This is unsurprising at a time of *laissez-faire* when intervention by the state was seen as interference and individuals were held to be responsible for themselves. However, the widespread distress caused by the effects of industrialisation and urbanization was undeniable and gave rise to an upsurge in humanitarian activities.

The Evangelical movement, with its insistence on the Christian obligation to help the poor and needy, was a powerful influence on nineteenth century society, and every denomination became involved in charitable work. From an early age, children of the more privileged classes were taught to include the poor in their prayers and encouraged to give up their pennies to help poor children. But here was no real egalitarian feeling and much philanthropic activity was based on the idea that the working classes, like children, needed the supervision and guidance of their betters. There was also unease about the perceived gulf between the classes, both physical and moral. Much of the philanthropic activity of the period was aimed at bridging that gulf and there was a great emphasis upon improving the poor through the agency of personal relationships, a sphere in which women were held to have a special role.

Women were at the forefront of the philanthropic movement and it has been estimated that by 1893 there were half a million women working continuously and semi-professionally in philanthropy.[1] This huge mobilisation of women coincided with, and can be seen as part of, the early women's movement. Ray Strachey commented that it was the exposure of middle-class women to the sufferings of the poor, together with the realisation that they as women could do nothing to affect the causes of poverty, that provided 'the illumination' from which the women's movement sprang.[2] Involvement in philanthropic activities opened women's eyes to the injustices and exploitation to which their sex in particular was exposed and it is notable that the women discussed in this section were especially exercised by the vulnerability of young women to prostitution. Such involvement also enabled women to work with other women and importantly, to cross, or blur, the boundaries between private and public spheres, and voluntary and professional roles at the same time as fitting comfortably within conventional expectations of a woman's role.

Marriage, family and the domestic sphere, although not realistic for all, were supposed to be at the centre of a woman's life. An acceptable adjunct to this was engagement in neighbourhood activities, the offering of help to the poor, the sick and the aged. Provided for by their men-folk, ladies of the middle and upper classes were not expected to undertake employment outside the close confines of family life. Charitable undertakings fulfilled a 'mothering role' and the desire of many nineteenth century ladies who wished for a purpose beyond the home. But the women in these three chapters went beyond this and dedicated their lives to the causes for which they worked. Mrs. Tait, who in many ways personified the ideal of the Victorian lady, supported her husband in his work while engaging in her own charitable pursuits. Throughout her life she maintained regular visiting of the sick, of prisons and workhouses and established support groups or clubs necessary to meet the current need. She was also able to use her position as a Bishop's wife to create the Ladies' Diocesan Association from the willing and the wealthy, not only to raise funds but also to work among the needy and the victims of disease and disaster. Greater challenges, such as the 1860s cholera epidemic, involved her in increased organizational efforts and the need to see through a tragedy to its end caused her to establish a home for its female orphans.

These women responded to their tasks with a 'hands-on' approach to which they brought imagination, organizational skills and vigour. They had both extraordinary strength of character and physical courage. Mrs. Tait risked her life visiting the sick during various epidemics, and indeed lost five of her children to scarlet fever, Mrs. Higgs of the National Association for Women's Lodging Homes undertook expeditions into the underworld of the homeless, Mrs. Chisholm led parties of girls to find positions in the outback of New South Wales and Miss Rye personally accompanied emigrants on their voyages to Australia and New Zealand. Although, with the exception of Mrs. Higgs, they would not have described themselves as feminists, and indeed talked more in terms of women's duties than of women's rights, by their very example they were breaking new boundaries for women.

While recognised and honoured for their achievements in their own lifetimes, these pioneering women are largely forgotten or ignored in the historical record. However, their activities provided the foundations for women's increasing participation in public life and helped many to move into work of more professional status.

Endnotes

1. Julia Parker, *Women and Welfare: Ten Victorian Women in Public Social Service*, (Macmillan Press, 1988) p. 20.

2. Ray Strachey, The Cause: a Short History of the Women's Movement in Britain, (Virago, 1978) p.44

CHAPTER 2

Movers and Shakers: Women In Female Emigration To
Australia 1840–1870

Gwen Searle

This chapter considers the undertakings of two mid-Victorian middle-class ladies in the field of female emigration to the colony of Australia. This era was the height of the British Empire when the role of women as wife and mother within the setting of the home was generally accepted. However, both these women moved away from this setting in seeking to improve conditions for the less fortunate girl needing employment. Mrs Caroline Chisholm (1810–1877) responded to the situation she found when she arrived in Sydney with her husband and children, where young emigrant girls from England were stranded on the wharf after their arrival there, with no plans made for their reception. Miss Maria Rye (1829–1903) also spent her life in the work of emigration. Her concern for young educated girls from the middle classes who were unable to earn their living in Britain led her to seek opportunities for them as governesses through emigration to Australasia. Later she turned to taking working-class girls to become domestic servants. Both these women began at an early age to undertake charitable work, and both expected the girls they helped to make the best of themselves, following the ethos of the time that each man or woman was responsible for their life and living. Despite the fact that both women moved away from their home role, they nevertheless undertook a 'mothering' role in their work for the young girls. Both women were good at making known their intentions, when asking for practical and material help to further their work. To achieve their projects they made use of patronage, Miss Rye through Shaftesbury and Mrs Chisholm by appealing to Governor Gipps in Sydney and Lord Grey in London. They were in tune with much of the mid-century attitude that members of the population were expected to help themselves, but that help was nevertheless necessary for the poor and the destitute. Thus the prime focus of this chapter is on a recognition of class differences between the emigrating girls, the methods of the work undertaken by these two middle-class Victorian ladies and their achievement.

Australia was set up as a penal settlement in the late eighteenth century, and emigration to the newly discovered and developing colony became of considerable importance until the discovery of gold there in the early 1850s. With the ending of transportation and the despatch of convict women to Sydney in the 1840s, girls of working-class background were sent through government-subsidised passage to become servants- in the 1860s some attempt was made through private philanthropy to send young ladies and widows to be governesses. Two middle-class ladies set out to improve both the situation and the prospects in the colony for these young women. After her arrival in Australia in 1838 with her husband, an officer in the East India Company, Mrs Caroline Chisholm reacted to the conditions she found on the Sydney docks: her time in that town led her to devote herself for the rest of her life to the whole question of colonial emigration to Australia. The relevance of emigration to Australia for Miss Maria Susan Rye lay in her belief that there were greater opportunities in Australia for the more educated girl forced to earn her own living. This led her to initiate in England a voluntary scheme to find employment in Australia for women and girls who found themselves in this situation.

The enthusiasm for the new colonies led Mrs Chisholm and later Miss Rye to turn their attention to encouraging emigration and to introduce facilities for the protection of young women and their reception on arrival at the colonial ports. Both women aimed at enabling girls to settle into situations where they could earn their own living. Mrs Chisholm herself led single girls into the outback country to place them in situations with families. Miss Rye initially sent young women to Australia, and subsequently, from 1869, widened the scope of her work by taking women to Canada with the same aim in mind, together with girls under the age of 14 either to be adopted, or to be trained in Canadian families for domestic service.

An Irishwoman, Mrs E.L. Blanchard, concerned about the distress of Irish women, also believed that emigration might be a solution to their poverty. Learning of the work of Mrs Chisholm, she went to London and appealed to Miss Rye, and subsequently led a party of emigrant women and girls to New Zealand, where she married and remained for some years. On her return to Ireland, she was in the 1870s appointed by the New Zealand government as their accredited agent in London to select women from Ireland for emigration. She regularly took emigrant parties to their port of departure, entrusting them to the captain of the ship, and claimed to have been responsible for sending 12,000 emigrants to New Zealand and Australia.[1]

Captain Cook's discovery and annexation of New South Wales for Britain in 1770 came at an opportune time for the government, as the American War of Independence had meant the loss of that colony as an outlet for Britain's convicted prisoners. Although little was known about the extent of the unexplored Australian continent, the decision was made to use the new colony of New South Wales as a convict settlement. The First Fleet with its cargo of over 700 convicts was despatched under the command of Captain Arthur Phillip, arriving in Botany Bay in 1788 after a voyage of eight months. More than half of the 188 women convicts[2] were domestic servants, and of a wide range of ages. The convicts of the First Fleet were neither political prisoners nor dangerous criminals: although some had been convicted of highway robbery or robbery with violence, in many cases their convictions were for minor thefts. In 1790, eleven months after setting out from Plymouth, the *Lady Juliana* of the Second Fleet arrived in New South Wales, bringing among her complement 222 women convicts,[3] mostly of marriageable age.

Owing to the great shortage of women in the colony, especially those of marriageable age, Governor Phillip asked for more female convicts as wives for the men. He hoped for the development of agriculture, and wanted free settlers to be encouraged to emigrate. For the first three decades of the nineteenth century New South Wales was a mixed community, consisting of convicts, either in gaols or working as forced labour along the roads or on farms, and ticket-of-leave men, who after four years of good behaviour in a seven-year sentence, could acquire land and farms of their own, or work and eventually earn their passage home. In the uncultivated colony of New South Wales the government granted land to enable emancipists to become small farmers with the help of convicts; if successful, they could become independent. Among the free settlers were men who had gone out to the new colony to seek their fortune, including younger sons of prosperous families in Britain. In addition there were government administrators, army personnel and [the Emancipists who having completed their seven-year sentence could elect to stay on to make a new life in the colony]. It is no supposition that transported women would find it difficult, if not impossible, to earn their fare to return to England. Many would have had children who, having been born in Australia, were born free. Wives and families of emancipated convicts had initially been brought from England at government expense, but after 1839 this was discontinued on the grounds that no further convict ships were travelling to New South Wales.

Among the middle classes of mid-nineteenth century England, it was traditional for women to be the home-makers. The expectation of both men and women was that all young girls should make a good marriage. A woman without a husband was regarded as a failure, someone to be pitied or even despised. In such a family-orientated society, with marriage and home-making representing a woman's basic career, a middle-class woman could lose her social position if the death or financial failure of her male protector faced her with the necessity of earning her own living. For the girl whose birth and education defined her as a lady, but who was threatened with destitution, the only option acceptable to respectable society was to become a writer or a governess. While it was fashionable for middle-class families to have a governess, the governess herself was accorded less respectability and could be cast aside during her mid to late thirties. Governesses and domestics alike needed a character reference to obtain a post, and without one, the workhouse was the terrifying prospect for a governess, bringing with it the loss of respectability. There were some 25,000 governesses in England during the period 1840–1860, and their plight became a subject of public concern.

For daughters of the working class facing the workhouse the choice lay between becoming a domestic or a prostitute. The fact that, according to the census of 1851, young women outnumbered young men by upwards of half a million,[4] only exacerbated the situation, and the question of the 'redundant woman' was much written about and discussed in mid-century. It was the women in the upper and educated sections of the community who were 'redundant' – those who were not, generally speaking, adaptable enough to emigrate to a new colony. The men these women might have expected, and be expected, to marry were in the Army, the Royal Navy and the Merchant Navy, or had emigrated to the new colonies of Britain's expanding empire.

Yet this was also the time when it was recognised that education for girls was required in order to meet the demands of the country's expanding economy. Women were moving out into the community to take up a more positive role in charitable and public affairs. However, for girls with some education who needed to earn their own living, suitable employment was not available, and 1859 saw the formation of the Society for Promoting Employment of Women with the Earl of Shaftesbury as President. Miss Rye believed that greater opportunities existed in Australia for the more educated girls forced to earn their own living, rather than training them in new trades at home. She therefore initiated in England a voluntary scheme to find employment in Australia for those women and girls who found themselves in this situation. Subsequently, she widened her original aim by taking respectable girls from the working class to do domestic work in Australia, and later by taking working-class women to Canada for the same purpose. From 1869 she spent her life in taking girls under the age of fourteen to Canada either to be adopted, or to be trained in Canadian families for domestic service.

By the 1830s there was a chronic shortage of skilled male labour in the colony. To increase the supply of labourers the only option was to set up a system of free emigration – transportation had come to be recognised as socially degrading and was having a deterrent effect on emigration. Influenced by the ideas of Edward Gibbon Wakefield, who had proposed to colonise Australia by enabling free settlers to acquire land at reasonable rates, the British government had by 1831 introduced a scheme of assisted passages with the intention of settling young families on the land. The aim was to bring about a more equal distribution of men and women, in the hope that this would lead to a better mix of age, sex and social status in the colony. Before the Molesworth Committee, established in the mid 1830s to inquire into the system of transportation, had presented its report to the House of Commons, the decision had already been taken to introduce free emigration. By 1840, opposition to transportation came not only from the more numerous free labourers and skilled artisans in Australia, but from the increasingly humanitarian climate of opinion in Britain.

The bounty system approved by the Colonial Office in 1837 gave £30 to every able-bodied emigrating couple aged under 30 years, and £5 for each child, although the number of children permitted was limited; single men were sponsored by settlers and underwritten by the sum of £10; and respectable unmarried working-class girls aged between 15 and 30 years, wanted as domestics or wives, received £15 if they accompanied a married couple. For women without education to emigrate to an unknown country required not a little courage, and meant the loss of family ties and loyalties. If they were not able to cut down trees, clear the land and plough it, there was not much opportunity for them other than to be wives or servants. Although it was laid down that the girls had to produce a character reference, and travel under the chaperonage of a family, these rules were often disregarded, especially if girls only met their chaperones on arrival at the ship. In these situations moral abuses on the long voyage from England might be expected.

In instituting emigration using money derived from the sale of public lands, the government endeavoured to send those who would be useful for the development of the colony. Within a few years 18,000 free emigrants had arrived in New South Wales through the scheme, and over 40,000 had made their own way.[5] Their arrival changed the social structure of the colony. By the 1840s there were over 87,000 men to almost 43,500 women in the colony.[6] By 1846 the total population of New South Wales was 187,000, of whom fewer than 11,000 were convicts still under sentence.[7] From 1847–49, during England's economic depression, a surge of emigration occurred, with 30,000 people sailing for Australia. At the time, letters to *The Times*[8] testified to the shortage of labour and the wish for servants in the colony, in addition to the need for shepherds and farm workers. Women could expect to receive £25–£30 a year and would be almost assured of work on landing, as servants were in short supply in the outback. In the twenty years between 1831 and 1850 over 200,000 emigrated to the Australian colonies under the government bounty scheme.[9]

In the decade 1830–1840 some 7,700 female convicts sailed from England and Ireland. The hope was that if they became wives/cohabitees in the Australian bush their presence would provide a civilising element in that untamed country. Although English middle-class opinion regarded prostitution as morally reprehensible, it was not in itself a transportable offence, and women's crimes were usually regarded as of minor importance – women were seen as the accomplices of crime rather than as actual criminals. When the women arrived in Sydney, demoralised, their helplessness and poverty forced them into cohabiting or surviving by prostitution. The policy of transporting women of marriageable age meant that when the convict ships dropped anchor at Sydney, their upper decks acquired the appearance of a slave market, with men choosing women on sight.[10] Since becoming a servant or cohabiting (which was in many cases synonymous) were the only means of women gaining a living, most women in the colony cohabited with men as the settlers wanted female servants. Hughes maintains that, although 'doubtless some were' actual whores, many others were treated as whores. However, Anne Summers contends that until 1840 almost all women in the colony, whether convict or not, were classed as whores.[11] Official policy encouraged marriage, but the poverty of the small settlers and uncertain nature of the Emancipist workers' life in the colony did not encourage matrimony; although some stable relationships existed.

Caroline Chisholm

Born Caroline Jones in Northampton in 1808, the youngest of a large and devout Church of England family of influential yeoman background,[12] Mrs Chisholm was one of the earliest of Victorian philanthropic women. Her father died while she was still a child, and she was brought up by her mother to regard philanthropic work as part of everyday life. From an early age she was interested in the colonies: she later claimed that, as a seven-year-old child, she began 'playing at emigrants in a wash hand basin with boats made out of broad beans'.[13] Aged twenty-two she married Captain Archibald Chisholm, an officer serving with the East India Company, and followed her husband to India in 1832. Described as a tall, shy, quiet and pretty woman with penetrating grey eyes, she knew what she wanted and was decisive in achieving it. Concerned at the lack of any organisation in the barracks in India, where children and orphans ran wild, she established a Female School of Industry where the pupils were taught general knowledge and housekeeping, including keeping accounts, and some instruction on food and methods of cooking, based no doubt on her own middle-class background. For reasons of her husband's health she accompanied him to Australia, arriving in Sydney in 1838.

In 1831, with the introduction of assisted female emigration, matrons were appointed to care for the girls on the voyage to the Australian colonies, but their duties were ill defined and often selection was inadequate. Mrs Chisholm, who regarded the lack of protection and the consequent moral downfall of these girls as one of the great evils of emigrant ships, argued for a better type of matron. It was left to private contractors to carry emigrants, a bounty being paid to shippers according to the number of emigrants who arrived alive in Sydney Harbour. Assisted emigration involved prepaid passages, loans for fares or for passages and removal expenses. Irksome regulations were laid down as to age and number of children: families with more than two children under seven, or more than three under ten, were unacceptable for assisted passages. Although the scheme did not permit the separation from parents of children under the age of 18, this safeguard could not be enforced and was often disregarded. Parents with large families who could not meet the conditions laid down were induced by the contractors to leave their children behind with relatives or in the workhouse,[14] leading inevitably to the break-up of families.

In 1850 the average length of the voyage to Eastern Australia was quoted as 112 days,[15] although this improved over the next 20 years. Overcrowding on the emigrant ships, meagre provisions and lack of adequate ventilation led to fevers and death on the voyage from England, with an increase in child mortality. There were no steamers on the England/Australia run, only windjammers, until the P & O *Chusan* reached Port Jackson in August 1852.[16] Although emigrants continued to travel by sailing ships, the introduction of steamers led to improvements in sailing conditions generally, and thus had an indirect effect on conditions on board the sailing ships. Information regarding the colony was available to emigrants at the point of embarkation in London, but no plan existed for placing them once they had arrived. The British Government did not accept responsibility for emigration, which was left to individuals and families themselves, and to philanthropic endeavour. Owing to this lack of any plan for distribution, or for the welfare of emigrants arriving in Sydney, Mrs Chisholm found that, in addition to other destitute emigrants, homeless and friendless young girls wandered about the streets of the city, a prey to abuse and corruption.

When her husband returned to active service in India, Mrs Chisholm remained in Sydney because of her concern at the plight of the young single girls arriving in Australia. She was deeply critical of girls being engaged directly during the time they remained on the ship, fearing that they could be recruited for brothels.[17] She confronted the governor of the colony, Sir George Gipps, arguing the case for a centre to support young single women until she was able to find situations for them. He had not expected to find 'a handsome and stately young woman', who reasoned with him about what she saw as necessary for the young women migrants, and was perhaps more surprised when he recognised that 'she thought her experience and reason' were as valuable as his.[18] He provided her with a government building close to the docks as an emigrant home, with the stipulation that there should be no expense to the government. Leaving her own children in the care of a nanny, she moved into the building to care for the girls who had nowhere to go. One incident that indicated her personal courage and determination occurred when she moved into the centre on the docks before accepting any of the emigrant girls. Woken by a noise on the first night and lighting a candle, she was confronted with the sight of a number of rats running about her cubicle. Intimidated but feeling she could not give up before she had begun, she laid plans for the following night. Setting out food laced with poison, she waited for the invasion which duly came. Hence, before accepting any girls, she had found the means of overcoming the rat problem. Within a year she could close the home as she was able to find situations for her girls.

Mrs Chisholm met every emigrant ship that arrived in Sydney for the next six years, and after the last landing of convicts in Sydney at the end of 1840, she worked to improve conditions for young single girls on their arrival. Although she began by providing accommodation and help for the single girl to find employment, she was equally concerned to settle all emigrants and to this end she opened a central registry, establishing depots in several country towns to find employment for all new arrivals, including farm labourers.[19] She set out forms of agreement, which were accepted by master and employee in the interests of both.

In order to discover where there was a need for labour, and who would employ the immigrants in their district, she wrote to all those whom she thought would know best, including small farmers and police magistrates. On the first occasion when she took young immigrant girls into the country to establish them on the land or to place them with families, Mrs Chisholm led the party on her own. Subsequently she always travelled with men in the party, because of local bushrangers. She also led immigrant families, encouraging and including the hesitant to move out of the town into the outback country districts. She made many journeys inland in the bush, riding from homestead to homestead and from farm to farm, seeking suitable places for her protégées. She herself wrote of 'wandering for hundreds of miles in search of suitable homes and eligible employment for the emigrant families and ticket-of-leave men'.[20] Travelling on horseback or by bullock dray, she braved the appalling roads in the country, confronting the threats of ex-convict bushrangers who had no respect for men, women or children. When placing single girls as servants or teachers, she personally inspected the homes of families in districts where young women were most wanted to become wives. The government of the colony supported her, as did the *Sydney Herald,* which urged donations of food and money for her emigrants. By placing young married families in the bush, she was then able to send single girls who could be protected as members of the family until they married the local bachelors. She pleaded for 'a respectable system of female emigration', but saw sending 'abandoned women' to the colonies as cruelty towards them, as few would be regarded as desirable or eligible to become wives, nor would they be accepted as servants by respectable families.[21]

Her husband having retired the previous year, Mrs Chisholm returned to England in April 1846. On her return she was instrumental in arranging for two shiploads of the children who had been left behind in workhouses at the time of their parents' emigration to rejoin their parents in New South Wales. Women in English workhouses whose husbands were ex-convicts were also enabled to join their menfolk through her efforts.[22] She helped to set up the Family Colonisation Loan Society[23] in 1849 in order to help emigrants to save up small instalments for their passage money. Underwritten by Coutts Bank through Baroness Burdett Coutts, the Society provided small loans to be repaid through a Board of London Merchants; her husband lent the first money to an emigrant before the official establishment of the Society.[24]

Mrs Chisholm's husband returned to Australia in 1851 for a further 12 years to run the Australian end of the Family Colonisation Society. In a letter to *The Times*[25] she explained that once the Society was formed her husband saw the need for someone 'devoted to the work' to go to Australia. Their concern was that there were no channels through which English migrants to Australia could cheaply and safely send their small savings to families in England. Her husband had therefore gone to collect the loans of the Society's emigrants, and to remit these to Britain. Mrs Chisholm followed her husband to Melbourne two years later.

Her ideas were clearly set out in *Emigration and Transportation,* her pamphlet addressed in 1847 to Earl Grey, then Secretary of State for the Colonies. She deplored the burden on the state of the existing poverty in England and argued for help for the poor to emigrate to the colonies, contrasting the starving poor of Britain with good wheat rotting in the ground of the colonies for lack of labourers to harvest it. As it was accepted that she spoke from knowledge and with authority, her advice was sought by many of those enquiring about emigration.

Her aim was to encourage impoverished families to emigrate together, as she regarded the separation of families as 'one of the greatest evils connected with our present system of emigration'.[26] She argued that the duty of the state was to protect the child, not letting it become an obstacle to the emigration of the whole family. Believing that the family was the natural basis of society and, like most women of her time, accepting that a woman's place was in the home, Mrs Chisholm was concerned to keep families together, and to strengthen their independence. In this, she was influenced by the Victorians' strong belief in the importance of the family as well as the changing attitude of the nineteenth century towards children and childhood. She wanted a sound and humane system of colonisation, stipulating that consideration be given to the social needs of families. She was against free emigration, seeing this as pauperising the recipients.

By the early 1850s Mrs Chisholm was recognised by press and public in both England and Australia, and continued until her death in 1877 to give advice to those applying to her, and to those interested in emigration, and attending meetings in her Islington home. On her return to England in 1866 she was granted a Civil List pension of £100. She travelled about the country lecturing on emigration, addressing public meetings and stressing the need for labour in the colony. In addition to the pamphlets she published, her letters to *The Times* made her ideas on conditions and opportunities in the Australian colonies known to both the government and the public. Her stated aim was to turn the paupers of England into respectable and responsible citizens who would become producers for the good of all, rather than being a burden on England. The interests of the colony would be advanced, she believed, by attracting emigrants, who saw the colony as a land of plenty. Although distance made the cost of emigration to Australia greater than that to Canada, she pointed out that the value of the market for British produce was greater in the Australian colonies than in any other part of the world. In this she was perhaps ahead of her time in recognising clearly the value of the colony as an integral part of the Empire, not only as a consumer of British-made goods but also as a producer. She believed that consumers who then became producers would become contented citizens. She claimed to have been responsible for settling 11,000 migrants to Australia.[27] Yet writing in 1916 G. Elliot Anstruther remarked that her name was scarcely remembered.[28]

The Passenger Act of 1852[29] set out instructions for emigrant passengers regarding times for rising, meals and lights out, as well as the duties of sweeping the decks and spaces under the berths, washing and attending Sunday morning church parades. By 1855 the owners of vessels had increased responsibility to provide new equipment and material comforts for their passengers. Provision was made for light and ventilation, more space was allowed and efforts were to be made to keep the vessel clean and in a sanitary condition.[30] In addition, food was provided, which although perhaps coarse, was plentiful. Following Mrs Chisholm's concerns about the inadequacy of the care of young girls on emigrant ships, the London Female Emigration Society had begun in the spring of 1850 to pay the passage of matrons selected to watch over the needs of the single women emigrants. Their duty was to travel to North America and Australia on those ships that carried unmarried women and girls among the passengers, but did not carry stewardesses. The matrons were expected to give the girls religious instruction, to provide occupations (such as needlework) to prevent idleness on the voyage and, if necessary, to teach them reading and writing. By the time Miss Rye was sending young women to Australia in the early 1860s conditions on board were considerably improved. The ship was divided into three departments: poop deck for single women, main deck for the married couples and fore deck for the single men.

Maria Susan Rye

Born in London in 1829, the eldest of nine children, Maria Susan Rye was the daughter of a Protestant professional family – her father and brothers were solicitors. Brought up by a governess, she also enjoyed the resources of her father's extensive library, and had experience teaching in a Sunday school and among the poor. As she was constantly approached by young women wanting employment, she took over the running of the Society for Promoting the Employment of Women in the late 1850s. She sought to promote for middle-class girls the semi-mechanical and profitable activities of working the telegraph, printing and law copying. At one point she managed a law stationer's business/law copying firm and, finding that the number of women applying for employment was far greater than the enterprise could take on, she looked further afield for more employment opportunities for young women who had some education. She came to believe that colonisation was an effective method of improving the condition of women,[31] providing more opportunities for them, as in general the professions and work in government were not open to them. In the early 1860s Miss Rye set out to help young ladies emigrate to become governesses in Britain's colonies. Like Mrs Chisholm, of whose work she knew, she was a firm believer in self-help, but she recognised that these young women lacked knowledge of the opportunities the colony might offer and were inhibited by lack of funds. She felt that emigration had received a bad name with 'respectable persons' because 'such a disreputable set of women' had for years 'formed the bulk of emigrants'.[32] In an 1860 article on assisted emigration in the *English Woman's Journal*,[33] she wrote enthusiastically of England's 'magnificent colonies', although she believed the subject was regarded with apathy in England. No free or assisted passage to any colony existed for the educated woman but only for household servants from the labouring classes. As women were usually unable to pay the costs of emigration and were seldom familiar with the procedures involved, Miss Rye set out to acquire information from those with knowledge of the colonies. She wrote to colonists in Australia and New Zealand asking about opportunities for employment there for middle-class women, and was advised that the need was for domestic servants. However, she was convinced that opportunities also existed for her young governesses.

She put her belief in emigration into practice by sending several small parties of educated young women to be governesses, and in 1862 publicly appealed to *The Times*[34] for funds for the Female Middle Class Emigration Society (FMCES) for those young women, superior in birth to most of the young women previously sent to the colonies, and for those wishing to emigrate to Australia. She recognised that these young women lacked knowledge of opportunities the colony might offer and were inhibited by lack of funds. She felt that emigration had received a bad name with 'respectable persons' because such a disreputable set of women 'had for years' formed the bulk of emigrants.[35] She wrote that, having privately raised £800, she had already sent 38 governesses. Miss Rye set up the society with her friend Miss Jane Lewin, and the Earl of Shaftesbury – known to be an enthusiastic supporter of colonial emigration – became the first President. The rules of the society stipulated that prospective emigrants had to provide the names of four referees, of whom two had to be personal references, together with the sum of not less than £25, which included the cost of the passage and all requisite cabin fittings.[36] Young ladies wishing to emigrate were required to raise as much of their own fare as possible from relatives and friends. By raising money in Britain, Miss Rye furnished the balance, as a loan to be repaid by the emigrants within two years and four months. Believing that the careful selection of the young ladies to become governesses was a necessary factor in the success of the enterprise, she sent only a few at a time – six to New Zealand in 1860, and 14 to Australia and five to other colonies in 1861.[37] She recognised the importance of having ladies available in the principal ports of Sydney and Melbourne who would be prepared to provide protection for the young emigrants on their arrival in Australia, receiving them and making arrangements for their accommodation until the girls found a post. Although this appeared to be a good plan, and Miss Rye had the help of well-connected friends, it was not effectively carried out. She wanted emigration to be regarded not as banishment for bad behaviour but as a reward for good conduct.[38]

In 1862 Stephen Walcott of the Government Emigration Board in London wrote a letter to *The Times*[39] stating that colonial authorities were of the opinion that there was no demand for governesses and educated women in the colony. This was confirmed by a subsequent short report from Melbourne in the same paper stressing the demand for first-class servants, but confirming the lack of demand for the superior class of female emigrant such as governesses and milliners.[40] Miss Rye, however, did not accept that there would be problems for the young ladies she sent. Letters from individuals to the *English Woman's Journal*[41] noting that too few competent teachers were available in the colony confirmed her belief in the need for educated girls. She believed that the mere presence of these young women would improve the morals of the colony. It was her firm belief that her emigrants, whether governesses or domestics, should be of good health and impeccable moral character. Miss Rye also insisted on training and sound qualifications for the girls she sent. In a letter to a friend[42] she made it clear that women who disliked work and were, as she put it, 'not very steady in their principles' were better off in England rather than the colonies. However, Australia's need was less for governesses to teach French, Italian, dancing, music and embroidery – as required in the homes of the middle classes in England – than for capable women to live and work in the outback. Miss Rye recognised that the young women needed initiative, self-reliance and the ability to accept a different kind of life, hence her practice of sending only small parties at a time in order for them to find a satisfactory situation. Many of the women keen to emigrate were governesses not qualified to teach or carry out what was required of them in a new country, and because of their lack of recognisable qualifications were unsuitable for emigration. Concerned as she was with the interests of women – in particular with those women unable to help themselves – Miss Rye also found that many young women were unwilling to take the step of emigrating. Girls brought up as young ladies had no expectation of paid employment and viewed marriage as their role in life, and therefore only the courageous or the desperate could face emigration to a colony on the other side of the world.

Difficulties of communication often meant that there was no accurate knowledge available of existing conditions: Miss Rye received contradictory advice from people already in the colonies as to the need for her governesses and the opportunities of employment for all women. Having ensured that her governesses had obtained posts, Miss Rye in November 1862 entrusted the work of the FMCES to her co-worker and successor Miss Lewin and accepted the request of the Otago government to lead a party of 100 young women, including eight governesses, to be domestic servants in New Zealand. She felt it was imperative for her to see for herself the conditions obtaining there and in Australia. She sailed out in November and was away from England for over three and a half years, initially visiting various towns of New Zealand, and thence travelling on to Australia. From the latter part of 1862 she was responsible for sending parties of working women, including at any one time dressmakers and superior domestic servants but only a few governesses.

She complained about the inadequate food, water and bedding provided for the group on board the ship to New Zealand, and was horrified at the lack of preparation for the reception of immigrants when they docked at Dunedin in the South Island of New Zealand. In a letter to *The Times*[43] advising the safe arrival of the ship, she repeated her assertion that 'it is certain destruction to ship off unsteady girls', recognising, as Mrs Chisholm had done some twenty years earlier, that sending unsuitable women would not find them marriage partners, and that respectable families would refuse to have them as servants. Miss Rye organised local ladies to raise money to set up a Servants' Home, and induced the authorities to provide 'decent accommodation for decent women'.[44] A strong and indomitable woman, she remonstrated with the authorities at Dunedin, and her efforts met with some success. She spent almost two years looking at the social conditions in the country, and assessing the need for female labour. In addition she sought to form reception committees to meet the female immigrants, visiting Wellington, Nelson, Picton and Hawkes Bay to make the necessary arrangements.

She then went on to Australia and was even more trenchant in her condemnation of the conditions she found there, visiting Queensland, New South Wales, Victoria and Tasmania. In her writings in 1860 and 1861 she had pointed out that government emigration meant recognised and responsible agents in Britain using the money voted for emigration to provide free or assisted passages, but only for members of the labouring classes and for women who were household servants. Her aim was to send girls who were of a higher class than those qualified for domestic service, and who were therefore not provided with assisted passages. She argued on behalf of educated girls of limited means who, she believed, could find employment in the towns of Australia and would provide wives for the large number of single men. She recognised that many farmers, the owners of sheep runs and large properties, were marrying beneath them, as there were no educated women from whom to select a wife – a matter of concern to a lady of the upper middle classes.[45]

In the absence of Miss Rye, Miss Lewin, a gentle but strong character, was left to assume much of the work on behalf of the governesses of the FMCES, which was based at 12 Portugal Street. Also at this address was the Society for Promoting the Employment of Women, the National Association for the Promotion of Social Science and the *English Woman's Journal*. Interested in all these movements, Miss Lewin acted as a focus for the women emigrants, offering support, advice and encouragement. When Miss Rye widened the scope of her work, Miss Lewin, as Honorary Secretary, carried on the work of the FMCES until her retirement in 1881.[46]

By the time she returned to England in 1866, Miss Rye was a public figure, and the government recognised her services to the cause of female emigration by awarding her a pension of £70 a year. Despite the improvement in conditions on emigrant ships, her suggestion that the selection of emigrant women might be put into the hands of women was not heeded. Over the next three years, she recruited some hundreds of women and family groups to send to the colonies, including Canada. She appealed for funds to take working girls, both orphans and the totally friendless, as she felt that they could never have the opportunity to become respectable members of society in Britain.[47] Miss Rye was always a resourceful woman: on one occasion she travelled to Liverpool by the midnight train only to discover that the berths she had expected for the party of 100 girls to travel to Australia had not been allocated. Such was her reputation that she was able to persuade a ship-owner she knew to take the girls without payment; she then sent a letter to the Victorian government explaining the circumstances and asking them to reimburse the ship-owner.

As distinct from Mrs Chisholm's actions to assist the family to emigrate as a unit, Miss Rye's interest in emigration stemmed from her feminist approach to the conditions specifically affecting women of the middle classes in the mid-nineteenth century. Although there was a surplus of women in England, it was felt that middle-class women should not work, which led to a lack of suitable employment for those forced to earn a living. In many cases, this was due to women's lack of adequate education, not to mention their lack of political power. A group of middle-class women known as the Ladies of Langham Place had established the *English Woman's Journal* to discuss such questions and bring them more clearly to public attention. While some saw employment other than in the home as a temporary measure, philanthropists believed that in order for these women to avoid starvation, the alternative was emigration.[48] Given the imbalance between the sexes in the colonies, particularly in Australia, emigration proved a powerful argument. Yet the Letter Book of the FMCES contains many intimations that whereas domestic servants continued to be required throughout the 1860s, openings for governesses were limited unless they were very well qualified, able to teach music and languages, and aged under 35. It was pointed out that governesses should not go on emigrant ships but should travel first class.

As a condition of sending working-class women to become domestics in Australasia in the mid 1860s, Miss Rye insisted on the use of government ships with their improved arrangements. As we have seen, in her three and a half month voyage to New Zealand and Australia, she discovered for herself the conditions under which the young women travelled. All were qualified for a higher form of domestic service than the average domestic servant in Britain. She wished to select them herself, and to place them in the care of a qualified matron on the ship. At the end of the voyage they were to be received in an Emigrants' Home until respectable employers were found for them.[49] By 1870 she had been responsible for the emigration of some 1500 women. Nevertheless she was criticised on the grounds of the unsuitability of some of the women sent. It became clear to her that governesses were not in demand, apart from some individual cases, as education was generally available to children in Australia. Australians needing only domestic servants were suspicious of female emigration such as that undertaken by Miss Rye.

By 1869 she had decided that she would be helping the women she most wanted to help – the distressed needlewomen (including milliner's apprentices), and the daughters of poor curates or clerks who needed employment – by taking children to Canada. Orphaned, destitute and abandoned little girls, the so-called 'gutter children',[50] would be adopted into good homes with settled and comfortable Canadian families, learning domestic duties alongside Canadian housewives, and would thus be assimilated into the Canadian way of life. This would enable them to grow up with better employment opportunities and marriage prospects than they could expect to have in Britain. In that year she began by taking a party of little orphan girls and setting up a Home in the Niagara area from which to place them in families.

The profession of a lady in the mid-nineteenth century was philanthropy: to care for those unable to care for themselves. Mrs Chisholm and Miss Rye were both strong characters from the middle classes, brought up to assume the duty of philanthropy and to undertake charitable works from an early age. Their family background and social position depended on their class, and their personal commitment stemmed from the strength of their religious upbringing and their own beliefs. Neither was interested in committee work for a fashionable cause, and both spoke at meetings to advance their work, Mrs Chisholm in addition addressing large rallies. Mrs Chisholm was married with children and as a good wife of the time followed her husband to where his career and livelihood took him, but she had warned him before marriage that she had to follow her philanthropic work. Miss Rye, unmarried, earned money from her writing and, as a feminist, wanted more education for women to provide them with better opportunities to earn their own living. Both believed in marriage and home life for women, yet both subscribed to the important concept in Victorian Britain of self-help. Poverty, accepted as a fact of life, did not affect the concept of the individual's responsibility for his or her own life, from which arose the emphasis on independence and the emigrant's responsibility for his/her own fate. Although dissimilar in personality, both women could be assertive – a necessary characteristic for women in Victorian England engaged in undertakings outside the accepted domestic sphere.

The importance of Caroline Chisholm lay in her activities on behalf of the young women and families arriving in Sydney and her subsequent encouragement of personal saving to enable a whole family to emigrate; her strength lay in her integrity, spirit, energy and practical common-sense. Although not original in her thinking, she was essentially a woman of action,[51] championing the rights of the emigrants whatever their class or creed. She put her work in emigration before all other considerations, sacrificing her own personal comfort and family. Kiddle asserts that from the beginning Mrs Chisholm's intention was to help all immigrants to New South Wales, not only young women,[52] although her initial efforts were directed towards the girls she observed wandering on the streets of Sydney. Not satisfied with government specifications to ship-owners and the unsatisfactory conditions on board that led to infant deaths and the corruption of female morals, she was influential in the passing of a new Passenger Act ensuring certain minimum standards regarding shipping. She was neither a revolutionary nor a reformer but was influential in her endeavours to help the distressed and poor to emigrate, in her encouragement of the reuniting of families, and in her advocacy of the importance of emigration for the whole family. She claimed that her strong desire was to advance the interests of the poor and to improve their condition.[53] Her concern was also to encourage emigrants to Australia in the interests of the colony, seeing good and virtuous women, wives and little children as a stabilising influence and in Summers's assertion of them, as 'God's police'.[54] Making a significant contribution to the colony, Mrs Chisholm was greatly helped by the local settlers in that, once interested in her work, they met her expenses through public subscription. In England she appealed to the public for support and was encouraged by many eminent men and middle-class ladies who supported her.

Miss Rye was concerned to improve the lives of educated young women and to obtain positions for ladies, and subsequently for girls of good character in domestic service. She wanted girls who would be good colonists: she too recognised the needs of Australia. She realised that the young women she sent had to be prepared for conditions in the bush, where most of the vacancies existed, but believed that these women could, by using their social skills, make a useful contribution to the developing colony. She was criticised in the colonies for her authoritarian manner and her perceived lack of knowledge of local conditions. She was critical of institutions in Brisbane, and begged the Queensland government for a building to house thirty orphaned children whom she found in a Brisbane hospital, their parents having died on the voyage to Australia. Obtaining a shelter, she transferred the children and as a first task washed them herself. She raised money and established a local committee, leaving it to run the orphanage when she moved south to New South Wales, where she battled with the local medical establishment. She was nevertheless able to gain some cooperation for her work in New Zealand as well as Australia, stating in a letter to *The Times*[55] that the Melbourne papers promised to help in her endeavours. She was officially advised that the colony did not require governesses of the type she wished to send. Women she had helped to emigrate, as well as others, wrote that although people were wanted in Australia, there were not the openings for governesses that she had supposed.[56] This advice influenced her decision to accept the offer of the New Zealand government in 1862 to lead a party of girls to learn for herself the actual conditions.

Letters received in London from the women themselves conveyed their distress and disappointment that the arrangements had been inadequate, although Miss Rye had endeavoured to ensure that representatives were on hand to meet the young governesses on arrival and to make some provision for them. One representative writing in 1864 disclaimed all responsibility for meeting the emigrants sent by the FMCES at the ship and for providing accommodation, saying that the most she could do was to provide a letter confirming she had heard of them from Miss Rye and leaving the young women to find their own situations.[57] Whether Miss Rye was over-optimistic in her expectations, and in her public comments, or whether this correspondent was guilty of a misunderstanding, is a matter of conjecture. Another correspondent reported in 1868 that the Home established in Melbourne for governesses and servants had no applications on its books for governesses, although she suggested that needlewomen could do well.[58] Despite Miss Rye's efforts, letters from the young women (often including part-repayment of loans extended by Miss Rye or Miss Lewin of the FMCES) were frequently critical of the conditions under which they travelled, and the conditions they found on arrival. Though Miss Rye had some success, her settlement of governesses in Australia could not be said to have been entirely successful. However, many women, despite unhappiness over the loss of their life in Britain, seemed determined to make something of the decision they had taken to emigrate.

Whereas Mrs Chisholm could better be described as a philanthropist, whose intention from the beginning of her work was not only to help girls to obtain employment in New South Wales, but to help all arriving emigrants and those with families of young children,[59] Miss Rye might be regarded as a feminist in as much as her prime concern was with finding employment for young women and girls with some education, and she looked to emigration as a means of achieving this.[60] Her sympathies turned increasingly towards the establishment of a scheme by which educated women might safely emigrate to the colonies rather than commence new trades in England.[61]

Mrs Chisholm and Miss Rye were innovative in their activities to protect and care for emigrant women and young girls. To a large extent, each worked on her own, until able to obtain financial support from the public. Mrs Chisholm responded at once to a situation which confronted her on the Sydney docks; Miss Rye was an innovator in her work for the 'redundant' woman with some education. Coming from the middle classes, these women focused generally on girls and young women from a lower social background; there was no real egalitarian feeling for the poorer classes in Victorian England. Although caring and concern for women and children were regarded as suitable interests for women in the nineteenth century, Mrs Chisholm and Miss Rye stepped out of the generally accepted mid-Victorian stereotype of a woman's role within the home. Both exhibited great courage, Mrs Chisholm in facing the unknown of the Australian bush, and Miss Rye in setting off on her long travels to, and within, Australia and New Zealand. In addition, both recognised the social benefits of their work as not only affecting the individual girl, but also as strengthening the ties of the colonies to Britain. However, it was not until later in the century that the true value of the colonies in economic and political terms was to be generally appreciated. For their work in emigration these two women were recognised by Queen Victoria and received a Civil List Pension.

Acknowledgements

My thanks to the many staff of the following libraries and archives who willingly gave their time and helped me in the research for this chapter: the British Library, the National Archives, the Department of Special Collections and Archives, University of Liverpool Library, and the Women's Library.

Endnotes

1   Pratt, Edwin A. *Pioneer Women in Victoria's Reign being Short Histories of Great Movements*. London: George Newnes Limited, 1897, pp 62, 67.

2   Hughes, Robert. *The Fatal Shore*. London: Collins Harvill, 1987, p 2. Summers, Anne. *Damned Whores and God's Police*. Australia: Penguin Books, 1994, p 313 (gives the figure as 192).

3   Hughes, p 105.

4   *English Woman's Journal* ,vol 5, March 1860, p 4.

5   Hughes, p 497.

6   Kiddle, Margaret. *Caroline Chisholm*. Melbourne: Melbourne University Press, 1950, p 25.

7   Hughes, p 554.

8   20 and 24 May 1848.

9   Clark, Manning. *A Short History of Australia*. London: Heinemann, 1969, p 76.

10   Hughes, pp 252–3.

11   Hughes, p 71; Summers, p 313.

12   She converted to Catholicism on her marriage.

13   Darton, J.M. 'Caroline Chisholm', in *Famous Girls who have become Illustrious Women of our Time* (quoted), 21st edn, London: Marshall Brothers, p 263.

14 *What has Mrs Chisholm done for the Colony of New South Wales.* Sydney: James Cole, 1862, p 4.

15 11th *General Report Colonial Land and Emigration Commissioners.* CO/384/86, The National Archives (NA).

16 Fitzpatrick, Brian. *The Australian People 1788–1945.* Melbourne: Melbourne University Press, 1946, pp 162,163.

17 Kiddle, p 55.

18 Darton quoting Sir George Gipps, pp 267–8.

19 Kiddle, pp 44, 60.

20 Chisholm, Caroline. *Emigration and Transportation Relatively Considered. In a letter, Dedicated by Permission to Earl Grey, by Mrs Chisholm.* 3rd edn, London: John Ollivier, 1847.

21 Chisholm, pp 16, 17.

22 Anstruther, G. Elliot. *The Emigrant's Friend.* London: Catholic Truth Society, 1916, p 16.

23 The word 'Loan' was subsequently dropped.

24 *What has Mrs Chisholm done for the Colony of New South Wales.* Sydney: James Cole, 1862, p 6.

25 16 August 1852.

26 Chisholm, pp 10, 20.

27 Mackenzie, Eneas. *Memoirs of Mrs Caroline Chisholm, and Sketches of her Philanthropic Labours in India, Australia and England.* London: Webb Millington & Co, 1852, p 61.

28 Anstruther, p 2.

29   CO 384/89 NA.

30   Rye, Maria S. 'Emigrant Ship Matrons' in *English Woman's Journal* (EWJ), vol V, March 1860, pp 26–7.

31   Rye, Maria S. 'Female Middle Class Emigration Society'. Paper read at the meeting of the Association for the Promotion of Social Science in London, June1862, reprinted in *EWJ*, vol X, September 1862, p 21.

32   Rye's letter to *The Times*, 29 April 1862.

33   vol V, June 1860, pp 235–40.

34   7 April 1862.

36   Female Middle Class Emigration Society (FMCES). *First Report 1861.* GB106/1/FME 1/1 Women's Library.

37   Rye, Maria S. 'The Colonies and their Requirements'. Paper read at the meeting of the Association for the Promotion of Social Science held at Dublin, August 1861, reprinted in *EWJ*, vol VIII, November 1861, p 171.

38   *The Times*, 25 December 1866.

39   26 April 1862.

40   *The Times*, 5 September 1862.

41   vol VII, July 1861, p 351; Vol VIII, February 1861, p 241.

42   20 May 1865, Women's Library.

43   14 April 1863.

44   Letter from Miss Rye to Miss Nightingale from Sydney, 21 September 1865. 1865 Miss Rye letters ADD 45799 ff 178-207 NA.

45   Rye, Maria S. 'On Assisted Emigration' in *English Woman's Journal*, vol V, June 1860, p 236.

46 Monk, Una. *New Horizons:100 Years of Women's Migration*, London: HM Stationery Office, 1963, p 6.

47 *The Times*, 3 April 1868.

48 *EWJ*, vol I, August 1858.

49 *Victoria Magazine,* vol VII, October 1866, pp 562–4.

50 It is not known who first used this description, but this heading appeared above the letter Rye wrote to *The Times* in March 1869 advising of her desire to take little orphan girls to Canada to enable them to have a start in life within the framework a family.

51 Copland, Douglas. Foreword in Kiddle, p 6.

52 Kiddle, p 41.

53 *Emigration and Transportation,* p 7.

54 Summers, p 347

55 7 April 1862.

56 *Letter Book* FMCES.

57 Ibid, 22 December 1864.

58 Ibid, 28 January 1868.

59 Kiddle, p 41

60 She did not support votes for women.

61 Rye, Maria S. 'The Colonies and their Requirements'. Paper read at the meeting of the Association for the promotion of Social Science, held at Dublin, August 1861, reprinted in the *EWJ*, vol VIII, November 1861, pp 235–40.

CHAPTER 3

Fram'd and Fashion'd: Married love and Christian duty
in the life of Catharine Tait (1819-1878)

Gina Burrows

> Q: Will you be diligent to frame and fashion your own
> selves, and your families, according to the doctrine of
> Christ; and to make both yourselves and them, as much
> as in you lieth, wholesome examples and patterns to the
> flock of Christ?
>
> A: I will apply myself thereto, the Lord being my helper.[1]

So every priest at his ordination makes a promise not only for himself, but
for his wife and his family. It is a great undertaking, for it is assumed that
he may answer for them. He is declaring himself not alone in the tasks set
before him . . . not alone, because the Lord is his helper, but also, in this
exemplary life he is about to undertake, he is declaring a commitment
to a way of living on behalf of a woman he may not even yet have met,
and for any number of children not yet born. To be the wife of a priest in
the Church of England implies vows additional to those of the marriage
service, a commitment to serve God as well as a husband. To be the child
of such a man brings with it a commitment acquired through accident of
birth.

It is the aspect of 'framing and fashioning' by a clergyman of his wife and children that interests me. The words are picturesque and illuminating in the manner of the seventeenth-century English used in the prayer book. 'Framing', perhaps within the constraining structure of the church and its expectations, limiting the extent of that which is contained, defining clearly the boundaries. 'Fashioning' has an altogether different image: one that involves not restriction but nurture, encouragement, development; maybe the moulding of a raw material, the transformation of something simple into something more complex; and the product of this activity – a blueprint, a template, an example to be learned from and followed. The one is about the appearance, the perceptions, the image: the other about activity, personal qualities, achievements, outreach, the soul. I want to look at how these two forces of framing and fashioning manifested themselves within the family of Archibald Tait and most particularly in the life of his wife Catharine, for, with his own words, Tait acknowledges the importance of these forces: 'It is impossible to judge rightly of the character of my dear wife without considering the influences which surrounded her early days.'[2]

While a study of images and perceptions of wives and daughters of the Victorian clergy may be viewed in the light of such 'framing and fashioning', the particular life of Catharine Tait (clergy daughter whose husband ultimately became Archbishop of Canterbury) does test this view. Here we encounter the challenges and opportunities of the clerical upbringing taken to much greater lengths, and therefore my question is whether it is upbringing as well as commitment which can enable a woman to face extraordinary circumstances, or whether there is something additional in the form of personal faith or character which is the determining factor.

Handbooks and books of guidance for the clergy in the nineteenth century address themselves to clergymen, but only occasionally to their wives and families. In 1828, the Reverend Leigh Richmond wrote a letter to his daughter on the eve of her marriage to a clergyman:

> Study your own and your husband's dispositions, that you may cultivate true conjugal peace and love. Ever be ready to open your heart to him on things spiritual as well as temporal. Disappoint him not herein, for he will watch over your soul, as one that must give account. A minister's

public labours are intimately connected with his private
and domestic consolations.[3]

The Reverend Leigh saw the resolution of such questions in terms of
obedience. A simple matter: 'If you and your husband happen to differ in
opinion and feeling upon any point remember whom you have promised
to love, honour and obey. This will settle all things.'[4] When Catharine
Spooner married Archibald Tait at the parish church of Elmdon in
Warwickshire in 1843, it is almost certain that she promised to obey him.
It was the standard wording of the Prayer Book service. However, in his
journal on the eve of his marriage Archie Tait wrote:

> Almighty God, this is the most important day of my life I
> pray thy infinite mercy . . . let this day be the beginning
> of a new life of holiness. If it is not I have but inclosed
> [sic] an innocent and holy being in misery. O Lord may I
> learn from her to give my life to thee. May we be united
> in thy faith and fear, she is one to live to thee. Save us O
> lord from my hard evil heart and make me with her thy
> servant for ever.[5]

This is not a man seeking obedience or subjection from his wife but one
who, in all humility, seeks to be worthy of her and to learn from her.

Catharine Spooner was born in 1819, the youngest daughter of William
Spooner, Rector of Elmdon and Archdeacon of Coventry. With her sisters,
she gained her education at home, in the firm tradition of clergy daughters
learning from their mothers and conversing with their fathers, with
constant access to a well-stocked library and stirred on and stimulated by
conversation with older brothers during school and university vacations.
She was an avid reader, always wanting to share books, to have them read
aloud during meals, to recommend them to others. Her husband was able
to describe her life:

> Her daily routine was to read some interesting book of
> history, philosophy or theology all the morning, to teach
> in the Sunday school, to visit the cottagers and help them
> in their difficulties and almost every evening towards
> dusk, to take a long walk through the parish with the

much loved father, to tend the somewhat failing health of
the dear mother who was a perfect model of a Christian
lady, directing all around her by the gentlest influences.[6]

Her father was a leading evangelical and his visitors reflected this
inclination, but the connections of his sons and daughters brought other
theological perspectives into the house. Also his brothers, and her mother's
family – Irish landed gentry at a time of immense religious and political
upheaval in Ireland – brought to the Spooner household a richness of
opinion and diversity which more than compensated for its rural and
isolated situation and the physically limited horizons of Catharine's early
life.

Although Catharine Tait was never the wife of a simple country clergyman,
she was herself familiar with such lives, having grown up in a country
rectory. This firm footing in the heart of the English rural community is
fulsomely described in an article in a publication called *The Clerical World*
(A Paper for the Pulpit and the Pew) (1882):

> When Hall and parsonage chime well together, this form
> of government has a mellow goodness worthy of the
> golden age, and fragrant as the golden pippins under the
> fruit-wall of old years gone by . . . It is not to be believed
> that any better school than such a parsonage can ripen the
> character of 'a perfect woman, nobly planned' and such a
> one was Catharine Spooner. [7]

Catharine, I suspect, would have found such a description remarkably
pious and stuffy. She was possessed of an intellectual curiosity, an
understanding and an informed mind that prepared her well for the life
she was to know. As part of a large family she was accustomed to meeting
the variety of visitors, clerical and other, who came to see her father. She
was widely read and strongly self-disciplined, two attributes which were
also to stand her in good stead, as was knowledge of the schisms within
the church and the passions which drove men to express their love of God
in very different ways.

Within the district lived Lord and Lady Wake, and Charlotte, Lady Wake's
brother was Archibald Campbell Tait, a young Oxford don. It is Lady

Wake who chronicles in her *Reminiscences* the first meeting of her brother Archie and the fifteen-year-old Kitty Spooner (as she was known in her childhood). While they 'suited each other exceedingly well', their paths were not to cross again for several years. Meanwhile her sisters married and left home, her brothers took up their orders and Catharine appeared to be happy to remain as the daughter at home, supporting her father and tending her mother.

Into the world of this young woman came not only the evangelical clergy friends of her father, and the friends and associates of her brothers and sisters, but also the diverse clerical attachments of her mother's family. From a cocktail of religious influences, there was much for a person of strong faith and lively mind to draw upon, but it was this last influence that was to prove the most potent. Her husband in later life was to cite her ambition, at the time, to become a schoolmistress in a village where her brother-in-law, the young priest Edward Fortescue, much enthused by Newman and the Oxford Movement, was in residence. The requirement for personal holiness accorded well with Catharine's vision, but it would be remarkable if the young Catharine were not totally confused or overwhelmed by so many powerful and opposing influences. It is possible, however, that her nurturing in the faith had been so implicit in all her upbringing that it could transcend difference and, while choosing a path that accorded with her own feelings, she could nevertheless hold on to her own personal position within the Church of England at her father's side.

It is clear, though, that she did not move from one to another of these quite diverse manifestations of the Christian Church without feeling some pain or concern. In a letter to her fiancé, she describes the feelings she experienced when, having seen another way than that favoured and promoted by her evangelically inclined father, she continued as his dutiful daughter in her parish activities:

> My father wishes me to go to the meeting. I always
> accompany him at home and there was a time when I
> fancied nothing could equal either the benefit or delight
> of attending these meetings – most fully can I enter into
> my then feelings, at the same time that so entire a change
> has come over my mind that the pain of going is greater
> than the pleasure ever was. [8]

It would have been interesting to know to what extent Catharine discussed her changed and changing feelings with her father. If her morning readings of theology and philosophy came from his library shelves, then it may have been stimulating for them both to discuss such texts; she with her enquiring mind and concern to travel productively the pilgrim's way along which her Christian life would seem to lead her, and he glad of the opportunity to further 'frame and fashion' his intelligent and questing daughter. There is certainly no indication in any of her correspondence with Archie of any conflict between her and her father other than in the quote above, and we are left to conjecture whether she kept her own counsel, or whether her father was aware of her difficulties but understood and tolerated them. Because of the immense diversity of religious allegiance represented by the whole Spooner and O'Brien families, it is likely that a deep sense of tolerance did prevail and that for Archdeacon Spooner, the importance of their shared faith and Christian commitment outweighed, ultimately, any theological differences. Archibald Tait had, in later life, reason to be grateful for this steeping of his wife in the works of English theology:

> I have always liked to think that her eager study of these thoroughly English and practical and devotional works left an impression on her mind which time never effaced, and was one of the means that kept her heart ever loyal to that church into which she had been baptised. [9]

Tait's life plan was to be a clergyman in a parish, but given his considerable academic ability, a life within the confines of the university would be more likely. He fulfilled both of these plans . . . his abilities were sought after as a teacher and he became a fellow of Balliol but, after his ordination, he chose to be attached to the parish of Baldon, outside Oxford, and to learn the ways and life of a parish priest. His was not going to be a quiet life, however, for matters of moment, the birth of the Oxford Movement, the contentions between high and low church and the consequent passionate representation of different religious views, brought him into the public arena. In 1841 his letter to *Essays and Reviews*, strongly criticising Tract 90 and Newman's moving towards Rome, was published and to those who read and concerned themselves with the high politics of the Church of England, this was a clear statement of position from a young man who was beginning to be known.

Circumstances can change very swiftly, however, and the death of Thomas Arnold, celebrated headmaster of Rugby School, found colleagues encouraging the 29-year-old don to put in an application. He had no experience of teaching children or of running a boarding house. He was contested by strong and experienced candidates but, to the amazement of many, he was appointed. His sister Charlotte was delighted but also aware that it would be a difficult task to take on for a young bachelor used to life in an Oxford college. She had an inspiration, made enquiries about her continued availability and then sent him a letter, reminding him of the young woman he had met some years before, and living in a direct route along the turnpike on the other side of Coventry. He replied with a telegram: 'I have received your testimonial in favour of Miss Catharine Spooner which shall receive due consideration.' His next communication with her, some time later, contained only one line: 'Hurrah, I have proposed and been accepted.'[10]

It could be suggested that, since he needed a wife in order to better accomplish the task of running Rugby School, that Catharine Spooner was conveniently available and, fortuitously, she was amenable to the match. Indeed that this was a marriage of convenience organised by sympathetic but managing relatives and friends on behalf of a man who had, practically speaking, very little time to seek out an appropriate partner himself. Undoubtedly Charlotte, Lady Wake played a very strong part in this, and if one were to build a picture of the coming together of this couple simply on her testimony it would appear a very straightforward and simple matter. Fortunately, we have more material from which to establish an image of the preparation for marriage of two people who took the whole business very seriously, and it is their views about what marriage could and should mean that are essential to my study of this woman both as clergy wife and daughter.

The journey for the young clergyman from Rugby to Elmdon would have been by horse or stagecoach. Consequently, much of their courtship was carried on by post. As lovers do, they sustained themselves between meetings with an affectionate correspondence, full of gentle endearments, regrets at the time and distance put between them, explanations of misunderstandings, pressures of work (his) and self-reproach for asking too much (hers). Yet even within this tender exchange of love, passion and daily triviality, there is already a glimmer, from both sides, of an aspect of their future life together that would demand more than anything they had yet encountered. Catharine writes that 'being blessed and happy ourselves must make us more conscious than ever to do all we can for others.'[11] She was deeply concerned about her future role as his wife – at that time as the wife of a headmaster. She seemed to see, even then, that she was entering into a partnership every bit as vocational as any other calling. So, after a very brief period, their troth was plighted; part of a letter from Catharine a fortnight after their engagement sets the tone for their relationship and her understanding of what it would mean:

> This day as being the day of our betrothal, my thoughts are with you, in fact I have been as it were going over this day fortnight again . . . I went alone into the garden and thought of all you said and all I replied and felt again the overwhelming feelings of that hour, only so much more happy, such a full assurance and deep thankfulness for the feelings that we both had been guided aright, that it is not so much our own doing as the very portion which was chosen for us, given to us and how if strength is but given us to use our blessings aright I feel sure that every day will give us greater cause for thankfulness.[12]

In a later letter she continues this theme:

> How blessed a thing it is, to trace a ruling hand in all our earthly portion, to feel that it is given us, and we are prepared and made fit to meet it, in all that it offers to us, quite a new life both of happiness and trial and danger.[13]

It is hard, with hindsight, not to reflect on the importance of this view given the nature of the challenges that were before them.

The young clergyman Archibald Tait, newly appointed Headmaster of Rugby School, courted Catharine Spooner during the spring of 1843. His letters, beginning as they do 'my dearest darling love', look to her as 'a partner who will share my cares and difficulties in a Christian spirit'.[14] But in his journal, as we have seen, written on the morning of their wedding, he indicates his belief in her not just as a partner but as an influence for good, someone whose faith and goodness he considers much greater than his own. If one considers how she was spending the very moment that he was making such an entry in his journal:

> On her wedding morning she did not omit as usual to go to her mother's room to read to her the psalms and lessons of the day, (just as), in the busy midst of Rugby, she attended the morning service in the Parish Church before the labours of the day began; in her ordinary life and throughout all her sorrows the same high influence sustained her. [15]

then it is evident that her influence for good was couched in such a sense of self-discipline and that she would, indeed, be a good example. At the same time, however, she was aware of something additional and different which, now, she must add to her role: 'to always be with you and to share as far as possible all with you and to try and cheer you after the toil and labour of the day.'[16]

If this was Catharine's perception of the duties and demands of her forthcoming marriage, it is clear also that such a view of duty and calling was in the mind of her father too. She had fulfilled a very considerable role in his life, the last 'daughter at home' and his help and support, given the frailty of his never robust wife. After her marriage he felt her loss as he set out in a letter to her:

> My dearest Catharine,
>
> It is so long since I have written to you that I must now tell you, for fear you should forget it, that I do love you a little bit – that I do often as I sit solitary many hours in the Deanery rooms, miss you a little bit . . . but at all these times I can think of you as happy, as usefully fulfilling the duties of that station of life to which it has pleased God to call you and cheering the heart and home of an affectionate . . . husband and then all selfish feeling vanishes.[17]

It is not clear from this whether the notion of 'calling' was that of wife or of wife of a clergyman, and from the perspective of one so deeply versed in the 'rectory culture' of his day, it was probably hard to see any difference, but he too puts emphasis on the 'cheering' aspect of wifely duty which was clearly in Catharine's mind and which Archie Tait also looked forward to: 'This lovely spring day I have longed for you. But I am happy thinking of you and the time when, God willing, we shall be joined for ever.'[18]

Joined they were in July 1843 at Elmdon, and Catharine took on the extended family which a boarding school headmaster brings with him. These next early years of their marriage were, in her husband's view, the happiest of all their life together. There was no question that the headmaster's new wife fitted well into the part. It was a new environment for her, having lived all her life in a parsonage, but she had a household to manage and a husband in a demanding job to care for. Almost at once she had stepped beyond these boundaries and established new ones, bringing the kind of charm and caring concern she had exercised in her father's parish to her husband's flock of boys, young men and masters, as well as to the community outside the school.

> God gave her wonderfully good health, and a buoyant, cheerful nature . . . At Rugby, a beautiful house of their own, with a pleasant garden, the green grass of the Close, and the old elms overshadowing it, congenial society, ample means, abundant occupation – all these outward circumstances were added to the charm of the freshness of her early married independence.[19]

Although her sister-in-law describes her as having no part in the management of Tait's boarding house, nevertheless the pastoral care and concern for the boys of the house was within her remit and indeed she enjoyed the youthful company with which she was surrounded. The boys, in later life, retained happy memories of their headmaster's wife:

> I am one of those whose memory retains very vividly impressions received in the beginning of 1843 when your Grace's happiness was so fresh and when as sixth-form boys – at least I can speak for myself – gained a most delightful experience of the exquisite kindness with which the wife of our Headmaster could second and support his constant efforts to befriend and help us in all

ways open to him. We knew how bright and winning a
presence was that which presided over the School House
hospitality . . .[20]

Almost at once in their married life, Archibald Tait handed over the
household accounts to his wife, quickly followed by those of his school
house, and ultimately his general school accounts. She had a great ability
in this field, which constantly confounded the various men who were to
audit or handle financial matters in the many areas of the Archbishop and
his wife's activities. While her husband had no problem with entrusting a
woman with matters of finance, the same could not be said of other men
of the time. Her brother-in-law, Sir Charles Wake, Tait describes as having
a 'preconceived feeling that a lady's habits of business were not much
to be trusted'. [21] As Tait's own career developed and his affairs became
more complex, she was still able to render this service, adding to it her
own enterprises, such as the St Peter's orphanage which she founded, and
which, at her death, was to reveal everything entirely in order and up to
date to the day of her departure from Lambeth a fortnight before. Even at
Carlisle, when departing after the most tragic and traumatic few weeks of
their lives, she was able to sit down and:

> . . . quietly took in hand the arrangement of the affairs
> of the poor women whose subscriptions to the Mothers'
> Club were in her keeping; she went through them all,
> placing every one's money with each little account to the
> proper name, so that there might be no mistake or loss.[22]

It might at this point be appropriate to consider the provenance of much
of the material that supports this research. Inevitably in biographies of
recently departed people written by those closest to them there is, on the
one hand, the possibility of much personal detail and insight not available
to a more distant (in time or proximity) biographer. The counter-argument
to this is that such accounts are unlikely to be objective in their treatment
of the subject and that distance (again in time or relationship) will afford
a more clear and honest view. Much of the material about Catharine
Tait is found in the writings of her widower, her family, both immediate
and extended, and those employed by her husband as biographer and
chaplain. It is clear that there is unlikely to be total objectivity in any of
their accounts, and she has had no comprehensive biography since then.

[More recent historical or analytical commentaries on her life, such as Michael Wheeler's consideration of her Carlisle narrative in *Heaven, Hell and the Victorians*,[23] or the more distant (though still family) accounts in which she is a less prominent figure in Swinton and Sitwell's 1940 *Two Generations*,[24] though looking more critically, as in Wheeler, or less clouded by past tragedy in Swinton and Sitwell, do not, I think, change the perception given in the contemporary biographies.] I would contend that there is a problem here, that in trying too hard to dismantle an image, one can lose the picture entirely. Catharine Tait was a good woman who suffered considerable tragedy in her life, but who nevertheless lived a full and impressive existence, both as a private individual in her own spiritual life, but also as a public figure as the wife of a prominent churchman.

It was three years after their marriage that their first child, Catty, was born, and then followed almost at once the serious illness of her husband, struck down with rheumatic fever: 'one of those quick-gathering dark clouds which, at intervals, God has sent to overshadow my bright life.'[25] Here was the first call to uphold a loved one in time of sickness, ready to pray with him and aid his recovery with helpful texts and hymns. To maintain her own strength she called upon the words in Isaiah 1:10: 'Who is among you that feareth the Lord, that obeyed the voice of His servant, that walketh in darkness, and hath no light?'[26] But for Archie Tait the light was Catharine and she made sure hers shone, thereby concealing her anxiety and willing her weakened husband to greater strength and recovery. An extensive holiday did much to restore him. The births of their second and third children, May and Craufurd, followed, and then came Lord John Russell's offer of the Deanery at Carlisle.

This first step up the ladder of preferment within the Church brought with it the kind of challenges Catharine may have had in mind when she spoke, during her courtship, of 'future trial and danger'. Carlisle was a rough place, an impoverished garrison town. The influence of the previous Dean had not penetrated much into the vice and misery which surrounded the comfortable seclusion of the Deanery.[27] This was not the Taits' way. The new Dean took his first clerical appointment very seriously and his wife balanced the demands of a growing family with the requirements of a clergy wife, working among the poor, setting up schemes for their help and improvement, keeping abreast of her own reading and above all supporting and taking an interest in the work her husband had undertaken, the 'Mary' in her sitting at his feet while the 'Martha' made sure that visitors to the Deanery were well cared for. She was being all she had set out to be and he, in turn, was receiving all that he could have asked. However, something more was to be asked of them – a call upon their inner resources of greater magnitude than they could have imagined, made all the more awful by the possibility that the sickness that proceeded to wipe out five of their seven children may have been brought into the family by themselves as they continued their round of sick visiting in the city. Indeed, in her own narrative she commented on the dangers they were aware of even as they first arrived in the city:

> We went (to Carlisle) with rather anxious hearts, as we heard that scarlet fever was bad in the town; still it was the path of duty, and we felt we ought not to shrink from it.[28]

Scarlet fever was rife in Carlisle, and through the autumn of 1855 the Dean and his wife worked hard to bring comfort to the distressed. They were then called to Ireland and returned just before Christmas to be reunited with their young family and to await the birth of their seventh child in the spring. Much of Catharine's time was taken up in the rearing and educating of her children, but she did have the addition of a nurse, Mrs Peach, and her assistant, Miss Golding, to help her and, with the assistance of Catty, the eldest daughter, the daily routines of the nursery had been established. Catharine describes her plans for how Catty's role would have developed: 'this dear girl who we had fondly hoped would so soon have taken her place beside us in all the duties and business of our life.'[29] But, notwithstanding this aspiration for what might seem heavy responsibility at a very young age, her sister-in-law, Lady Wake, is full of praise for the manner in which her nephew and nieces were brought up: 'Mrs Tait has the talent of thus blending the children's life with that of their parents and their friends without making them little bores.'[30]

For children being brought up in a clergy family, the offices and routines of the Church year were part of an understanding of daily life, just as family worship was a feature of many Victorian middle-class homes. The children had a good repertoire of favourite hymns and a collection of books and pictures. Their familiarity with the Prayer Book as well as the Bible was inevitable, but its importance was underlined as the children called upon these resources when this dark period came upon them.

The first child to suffer was Chatty, whose symptoms followed immediately after the birth of their new sister, Lucy, in February. This was a double torment for Mrs Tait, torn between the need to nurse her baby and the desire to tend her sick daughter. Reassured that the baby would be safe from the contagion, her mother confided Lucy to the care of a young nursery maid, returning to her only to feed her and then going back to the bedside of her daughters. The sickness was unremitting. Each of the girls, in turn, suffered the fever, the nausea and the indignity of having their long hair shorn. Always there was the hope that the others might escape, that their own illness might not prove fatal, that even yet they might recover. Baby Lucy's baptism they followed from the Prayer Book and gazed from the tall windows of the Deanery. Here began the 'first dark days of nothingness'. After Susan's death came the tenth birthday of Catty, the eldest child, like every event in this terrible calendar celebrated with all the pain and poignancy imaginable. Although she was only ten years old, all the descriptions are of an older child, a rock and comfort to her parents and the onset of whose sickness was the heaviest burden to bear.

It was Easter and they followed the Easter services, remembering how in previous years they had celebrated Palm Sunday and Easter Day together. They were now grateful for the uplifting and comforting routine of the liturgy as the days passed on, bringing more inevitable suffering. They were, by this time, living life in four separate camps: the Dean carrying on with his work and attending, one by one, the funerals of his daughters, their son Craufurd removed to the care of friends, Catharine nursing her baby and returning to the ever-diminishing company of the nursery with their faithful attendants, each bearing the twin burdens of sadness and fear. The bedside vigils brought great tiredness and the additional agony of witnessing each other's pain. Catty herself tried to comfort her grieving parents, and Catharine tried to protect her from the pain of seeing her father cry. What is so evident, and probably not remarkable, is their constant reference to the sustaining support of the Everlasting Arms and their looking to a great reunion with those sisters gone before. Because the progress of the illness was unrelenting, and the demands of the newborn baby unavoidable, the routine of daily life was maintained where possible, but when May died on 8 April there only remained seven-year-old Craufurd to be reunited with his mother and to greet his newborn sister.

We know of this catalogue of sad events because Catharine set them down almost immediately afterwards. It was her way of dealing with such a tragedy. It would have made very hard reading at any time. It is a moving and inspiring narrative, but there is no bitterness in it. It records events, fears, hopes and sadness, but it also carries a strong commitment to the belief in the afterlife and a firm conviction that the life to come is not to be feared, but to be rejoiced in. In writing to a friend, Mrs Wordsworth, she comments:

> As yet we hardly realise their exceeding blessedness, our agony is too deep for that, and consequently, deadens our faith; but in His own good time God will strengthen us if we wait upon Him, as we will strive to do.[31]

Archie, in his own prayer diary, reflects: 'Oh, Lord, thou hast dealt very mysteriously with us.' [32] It would appear to have been Catharine's intention to keep this account to herself during her lifetime, except that it might prove comforting to some in similar circumstances – it was certainly not published until after her death 18 years later. What we do know is that she did not read it to her husband until a year after the tragedy when she comments: 'he seemed able to bear it and though it was full of agony to us both, it seemed a comfort.'[33]

The terrible irony was that it was the publicity surrounding the death of their daughters that had prompted Queen Victoria to recommend Tait being given the See of London. That Catharine supported him in all his ventures was never in doubt, but it is to be wondered to what extent she was aware that in his private writings he yearned for high office. He does half-acknowledge that her view might be different from his: 'like my dear wife, I hope I have no wishes but that Thy Holy Will may be fulfilled.'[34] It would seem that he saw what was to happen, not just in terms of his own calling but as something to be undertaken together. Was he, with hindsight, alluding to clouds and silver linings?

> God was preparing both my wife and me for a great change of life, a far more extended field of work than we had before known, and fresh great blessings, which for 20 years she enjoyed with the keenest sense of gratitude tempered by the solemn thoughts which this trial had fixed within her heart.[35]

Nevertheless, his advancement had been secured and there was no doubt that the Queen had been instrumental in bringing it about and directing Lord Palmerston to offer the appointment. 'The story went about that the queen had spoken of the new Bishop as one who, having been tried by such deep sorrow, would be qualified to deal with the troubles which afflicted the Church.' [36]

The challenge of the See of London was something Carlisle had done little to prepare the Taits for, and indeed, Archie once again was going against precedent in that he was the first man for two hundred years to become Bishop of London without any previous episcopal experience. His unsuitability for the post was noted by the *Daily News* which commented: '(he) seems to want calmness, steadiness, consistency, patience and endurance . . . almost as much devoid of pastoral as of Episcopal experience.'[37]

The Taits were surrounded once again by the effects of poverty, as in any large city, but this time it was the metropolis and it had its own particular problems. The immense growth of the capital, its influx of immigrants – dispossessed people from across Europe and fortune-seeking men and women from the impoverished countryside – coming to work in the small industries and service trades of the fast-growing city, meant that the parish structure as it existed in rural England would no longer serve. If the church was to support the new communities of the fast-growing cities, particularly London, then there were opportunities not to be missed, and the Bishop of London was at the forefront, setting up in 1857 the Diocesan Home Mission and himself preaching in ragged schools, in Covent Garden Market and to the gypsies on Shepherd's Bush Green. In addition to the planning and outreach that it was necessary for the church to accomplish, it was also important not to neglect the clergy who were so necessary for its accomplishment.

To assist with this was part of Catharine's role – it was already established that the London clergy and their wives should be welcome at Fulham Palace, but with the special touch of the Bishop's wife and his young family (since the death of their five daughters at Carlisle, two further daughters, Edith and Agnes, had been born), these visits took on a greater charm and spontaneity. There were a thousand London clergy and the palace and its grounds were open to them on very many occasions. The

Bishop's wife had her role, too, in the outreach – not in the establishment of the new churches but in the mission to the population they served. London, as a city, harboured every sort of problem and distress, and it was to address some of these problems that Catharine set up the Ladies' Diocesan Association; it 'came to her one night' and she straightaway set about recruiting 'honourable women not a few'[38] from among the wealthy and the willing with whom her position brought her into contact.

It was indeed her position which was her *entrée* into the society of the highest and lowest in the community. Inevitably her elevated social position brought with it contacts with the rich and powerful, but they were often powerless to enter the other worlds which her situation as a clergy wife allowed her to penetrate. Archie's biographer was clear that she did contribute something extra in the manner in which she carried out her duties:

> Such a woman, under a Bishop, might more effectively gain entrance for Christian visitation and kindly sympathetic influences into some of the workhouses and hospitals in which a shrinking from such assistance had hitherto been manifested by the authorities.[39]

Being the wife of a bishop carried with it extra responsibilities, but it did not exclude the basic social duties and interaction with the poor and the needy that had always been a feature of her life both as a wife and as a daughter. Was she fulfilling knowingly the requirement in the service for the consecration of bishops: 'Will you show yourself gentle, and be merciful for Christ's sake to poor and needy people and to all strangers destitute of health?'[40] Benham continues, in his consideration of her wholehearted assumption of her role as bishop's wife: 'she felt that others might hang back if she, in her prominent position were afraid.'[41] As a mother, she extended this dutiful requirement to her own daughters, so that responding to the needs of those in distress became 'what they did'.

The little girls were taught early to help and care for those around them, and young as they were, regular visits were soon made to the Fulham workhouse. Edith's special duty on these occasions was to read to the old ladies, who in their turn had often to help her out with the long words.[42]

This commitment was so much an underlying part of their lives that it never left them. Craufurd was keen to take holy orders, but first to satisfy his desire to travel abroad and widen his horizons. This done, he began his new life, first of all as chaplain to his father, then curate at Saltwood and finally in his own parish in Notting Hill, but his parochial work still found him visiting the poor and sick, and in some way grateful for the *entrée* an epidemic gave him in overcoming his natural shyness and allowing him to continue to be useful. It is strange that, although he found visiting the sick a fundamental requirement, he had not the ease in accomplishing it that his sisters displayed. On the other hand, for him it was something he did alongside the work he was called to do. For them it *was* in effect the work they were called to do. Their preparation, during their growing years, was for a continuance of a good and holy life and they were brought up, as young women of their station, to continue serving God whether as single women or as wives and mothers.

The education of the girls was at home, though, even with the assistance of governesses, it 'was not so complete as would be received nowadays'.[43] Edith, in her biography written in 1938, chooses to mention this and to express some surprise that their father, particularly, did not seem overly concerned for the education of his daughters. There is here a clear demonstration of the difference in parental expectation. At thirteen Craufurd was sent to Eton and then to Oxford. He was able to fulfil all he sought in terms of travel, apprenticeship as a curate and a clear career path. There seems to have been no consideration of any such path for any of the daughters. It is to be wondered whether, if the 'first' family had survived, any plans would have been made for their continued education, particularly for Catty, the eldest and so much her mother's support, cast even at the age of 10 as pupil teacher in the early education of the other children. That all the women in his household upheld and supported the Archbishop in his work and his increasing infirmity is evident. He records himself that, following the death of his wife, Agnes (Aggie) took on the task of writing his journal.

Catharine's thirst for education was insatiable. She read constantly, widely and improvingly. She encouraged guests to read aloud or share books with her. She and her husband read together and in his later years his daughters read to him. Nor was the nature of their reading limited to 'holy' works. Both Archie and Catharine read the fathers of the English Church and endless works of theology, but they also read a great deal of history, both British and foreign, and quantities of novels. The girls too read from an early age, to each other, to visitors, to their parents and to the old ladies of the workhouse and the hospital. This was reading both for pleasure and for spiritual enrichment. There is no record in any of the biographies of disapproval, but always this constant thirst for knowledge. But to what end? To the end of creating the fully rounded person, the whole woman? Was it indeed part of the 'framing and fashioning' for the lives they would lead and the company they would inevitably keep?

The visitors at Fulham and Lambeth were aware of the warm and welcoming atmosphere of what was so much a family home. Therefore, shared meals and strolls round the gardens would involve conversation and, even when not joining in, listening and absorbing the views and experiences of a wide range of British and overseas clerics and other dignitaries. Archie Tait was an academic and did not abandon this facet of his life when clerical preferment came upon him, for he was involved deeply in university reform as well as in the academic and theological debates which raged throughout his episcopate and primacy. Yet he did not exclude his wife from his deliberations but involved her whenever he was writing a paper or preparing for a debate, valuing always her opinion: 'Sometimes . . . when I was engaged in writing some article or lecture, in which she would take an intense interest and for which she was ever at hand to help me with my reading.'[44]

Strangely, P.T. Marsh's study of Tait's primacy, *The Victorian Church in Decline*, describes what would appear to be a much more 'separate spheres' approach to her involvement: 'Tait did not usually discuss his ecclesiastical dealings with her'[45] – but I think it would have been difficult not to have done so. Inevitably, when seeking refuge at the end of a gruelling day or a succession of meetings, one could understand that to rehearse the day's arguments and decisions would hardly be desirable. There would also have been issues which affected the family in the 'business' that the clergy family did as their daily work – the arrangement of social functions, charity events, campaigns and entertaining – which would be predominately 'managed' by Catharine and which would constitute undoubtedly her 'sphere' but in which her husband might have had an interest. But there was certainly also, in those days of extended visiting and extended families, a great deal of activity in which the Archbishop could and did involve himself, again as an antidote to the pressures of the day.

However, this said, there is much that supports my perception that Catharine was not excluded from ecclesiastical affairs, based on remarks made both in Archie's writing and in that of other biographers, and it was certainly not the perception of his colleagues when they approached her as an intermediary between themselves and her husband. Because of the absence of much of the 'out' correspondence, however, we do not know in what manner she responded to these requests, but we are aware from other sources that she did her best to protect him from intrusion and to limit or distance those requests which might cause him additional anxiety. This does indicate that Catharine was able to operate a filter system, alongside his chaplains and other staff, and that this, which requires discretion, also implies a degree of knowledge, permitting informed decisions about who and what to allow or limit. From all that Archie wrote about his wife, in his correspondence and in her biography, there is a clear indication that he valued her judgement and her intellect. It was certainly the perception of the writer of the Tait entry in the *Dictionary of National Biography*:

> Mrs Tait's force of character and sympathy strengthened every part of her husband's work; her beauty and her social power made his home attractive. She entered into the difficult problems of his work as a bishop, tempering though not deflecting his judgement, while her deep piety, simple tastes, love of literature, and care for the poor, made the home of the prelate akin to that of all classes of his clergy. [46]

It was a relationship of perfect trust, from his confiding of the accounts to her in the early days of their marriage, through the fierce and often acrimonious theological battles of his days in Fulham and Lambeth, to the sharing of sadness and tragic news. He did not concede his wife's ability to compete on equal terms so much as take it for granted, and yet there is the criticism of his daughter Edith that he did not seem to take as much interest in the education of his daughters as she might have expected. Could it have been that his wife was not to him 'women'?

The Fulham incumbency marked a new start in the family life of the Taits, and the changes it involved were probably therapeutic to a family so shell-shocked by the tragedy that had befallen them. If the external life of the Fulham Palace family was concerned with the challenges to the Church of the growth and poverty of the metropolis, and the episcopal life of Archie Tait dominated by issues of ritual and legality, the more domestic domain was ruled by the demands of education and social training. Catharine never had to manage the upbringing of her children entirely on her own. She had always had servants and, in this second family, governesses to assist with their educational progress. That she continued the quest for education on into her own life, that of her husband, her staff, her multitudinous visiting cousins, nieces and nephews and even such house guests as came 'on business', was part of her understanding of life and her total belief in the community of the home. Her obsession with reading was not such that she felt she should withdraw from company but rather that all the company should share good things together. Throughout her life she took on the responsibility for the spiritual and educational nurture of her maids, preparing them for confirmation and for employment in other households, spreading good practice, as well as religious observance and knowledge.

The social aspect of life at Fulham concerned itself much with the duties and pleasures of entertaining and visiting. Entertainment took place on both a grand and a more modest scale. The guest lists and visitors' books for their residences alternate between notes of 'Family 3' or 'Family, 3 Sitwells, 1 Wake' to entries such as that of 15 February 1865, which records 'Catharine Gladstone, Llandaff, Ely, Gloucester, Bangor, Archdeacon of Leicester, Dean of Canterbury, Headmaster of Charterhouse'.[47]

There were also family meals when Archie would join the assembled women and children, and even rare occasions when he and Catharine dined alone: 'Mrs Tait used to tell a story of herself and her husband having once dined alone at Fulham and of the increased appetites so singular a circumstance gave them.'[48] There were days of open house or parties for the London clergy and their wives, garden fetes and celebrations for the old women of the workhouse or the retired governesses, and much grander events to accommodate the British and foreign representatives at the Synod or Lambeth Conference.

The visiting aspect of their lives was that which had been with them always, the need to be involved in the comfort and the relieving of the distress of those about them, in the hospitals, workhouses and the poor courts and alleys of inner London. Wherever they lived, poverty was on their doorstep and Catharine was not able to ignore it. However, just as in Carlisle the enormity of the demand became totally overwhelming, so despite her hard work with the Women's Diocesan Association and her own parish visiting, there was to come a great, but fortunately in this case, less personal demand on all their resources.

Cholera had been a summer visitor to the capital since 1832. By 1854, it had been recognised as being water-borne, but the poor conditions of inner London meant that the prevention of its return was hampered, and in 1866 yet another virulent epidemic gripped the capital. It was recognised that the proportions of this visitation were such that ordinary measures would be insufficient for its containment. The clergy formed bands of workers with lay and professional men and women. A weary Archie Tait was preparing to leave town for his summer vacation and recuperation, but neither he nor Catharine felt they could leave the metropolis in such affliction. There was nothing for it but to join with the clergy and lay workers and involve themselves in caring for the sick. Visiting was an obvious requirement, not only for the sick (many of whom were well past caring how eminent their visitors might be) but also for their relatives and, even more, for the support and encouragement of the workers who struggled to contain this disease and its effects and aftermath. Tait also did what he knew best how to do:

> He preached on the duty of preparing for death, and afterwards gave practical advice on dealing with disease, warning people that it was a mockery to pray to God for relief, if the proper use of health measures was neglected.[49]

He himself described his wife's contribution:

> my dear wife accompanied me regularly in the visits which I made to the infected districts . . . I can see her now standing in one of the large wards of the hospital for

Wapping or St George in the East, quietly soothing the
sufferers . . .[50]

This work became, as her husband described it, 'the crowning labour of
her life'.[51] Her next step, after visiting and learning alongside Archie the
extent and nature of the problems, was to write to the press. thus on 10
August 1866 the following letter appeared in *The Times*:

Sir,

I should feel greatly obliged if you would give publicity to
the following announcement by the insertion of this letter
in your columns. Donations in kind on behalf of the poor
suffering through the present visitation of cholera will
be thankfully received at the House of Charity, 1 Greek
Street, Soho. The articles most desired as likely to be the
most useful are sheets, blankets, old linen, and clothing
of all kinds including black clothes, whether old or new,
tea, arrowroot, sago or wine. Parcels should be addressed
to 'Mrs Tait . . .'[52]

Taking an active role in this campaign was important for Catharine. On the
one hand, it allowed the bishop's household to have a high profile while,
given Archie's physical frailty, permitting her to relieve him of some of
the burden and thus protect him from too great an involvement. But also
it enabled her to engage with other women, not just as she had already
done in her involvement with the clergy wives, or the society ladies of
the Women's Diocesan Association, but with women in leadership and
management roles. She was able to use her position, undoubtedly, but
also her skills of organisation and planning, alongside women of similar
inclination and ability. Such involvement did not pass unnoticed: as was
commented in the press, 'no badge or vainly becoming hood or girdle is
to mark those who enlist with Mrs Tait and Mrs Gladstone.'[53]

It also brought her into working contact with women of the sisterhood
movements. There was significance in this, too, for these groups of
women had found themselves very much courted or shunned by either
end of the religious spectrum of the time. The same article in the *Daily
Telegraph* which so praised the involvement of the Diocesan Women's
Association had also pointed out that the Church of England had not been

in the vanguard of female service in this field: 'We have left it too long to the Church of Rome to fight the beautiful battles of Christianity with Christian Amazons.'[54] In the nursing and caring role of these sisterhoods, any alignment was able to be set aside in the face of the importance of their skills and the people and the churches' need. It was significant, therefore, that the Bishop of London was prepared to ask in all humility: 'God knows we need their help, if they will give it in the way our Church approves.'[55]

A step had been taken towards the recognition of religious sisterhoods. Catharine had a cousin, Harriet Monsall, who was the first mother superior of the Clewer Order and who would have been glad to have encouraged such a recognition after a period of some ostracism and hostility. That Catharine's husband could make moves towards the sisterhoods was not only noticed but attributed to her influence, as an entry in Mann's (1854) background material to the Religious Census commented:

> (ACT) married Catharine Spooner, a woman who was to prove herself a tower of strength to him, as she lovingly fulfilled her wifely duties and kept her own counsel on religious matters, her sympathies being with the Tractarians.[56]

Catharine could visit the sick in the cholera wards alongside her husband or without him. (Had she not been doing this all her life, and was she not already encouraging her children to do likewise in the hospital and workhouse nearby?). She could also identify needs and prepare to meet them by the organisation of collection centres and the deployment of staff to handle and distribute. Catharine was not alone in her concern for the victims of the sickness and particularly the orphans inevitably left behind. Her choice was to set up a home for orphaned girls, while other dedicated and powerful women, notably Eliza Twining, Catherine Gladstone and Catherine Marsh, established convalescent homes and other orphanages. It was an efficient distribution of labour, each concentrating on the area in which she had most interest and expertise. It is recorded that there were many ventures Catharine was drawn to on her arrival in London, but that she determined to pursue only those in which there was some chance of her being able to continue and to make a real contribution. She saw no value in spreading herself thinly, just for the sake of giving her name and little more.[57]

Her daughter Edith records in her biography that she and her sisters, though only small children, were involved in the setting up of the Fulham home and became firm friends with many of the new residents, who became 'almost a part of the Bishop's household',[58] and indeed Catharine's role in the home remained much more than just that of an organiser. She could not be in day-to-day charge but she taught the little girls their hymns and Bible stories and made them welcome as playmates of her own children. Indeed, Edith and Lucy retained their interest and involvement throughout their lives and the orphanage itself moved from Fulham to a property on land owned by the Taits at Broadstairs, so that, once again, it became a neighbouring concern when the family (or rather Archie) was translated to Canterbury. Catharine remained all her life deeply involved, handling financial and property matters as well as having concern for the well-being of the girls and the staff. Staff were employed, but the orphanage was 'her' project and an example of an undertaking begun and seen through. In her biography, Archie attributes her concern thus: 'it cannot be doubted that the ever present thought of her own children, whom she had lost, was an incentive to her care for these destitute little girls.'[59]

The Bishop, visiting the hospital wards during the time of the cholera epidemic, did not go unnoticed in the press. 'He is the most Christian of our bishops,'[60] reported the *Daily Telegraph,* and in the *Church Times:*

> I could not but think what a difference there was between
> this priest of God and the one quoted in your paper of
> Sat. week who, with a bag of camphor about his neck,
> knelt down outside the door of one of the wards, read
> a collect and was out of the place again in five minutes.
> How many too of our bishops are there who would have
> done what the Bishop of London has done, and he too in
> a very imperfect state of health.[61]

This 'very imperfect state of health' was no exaggeration and the additional strain put upon him, together with the impossibility of his being able to take a holiday, meant that, by the time he was able to leave London, he was again gravely ill and was unable to deliver his first 'charge' to the city of London. This was done for him in St Paul's Cathedral and its text was published, outlining his picture of the city as he found it and his plans for its future. But, in addressing the London clergy, he was seen now as one who had, with his wife and family, stood among them in their pain and hardship and for this had paid a heavy price.

Archie Tait had already taken on three elevated positions for which he had had little training and no experience, so it would probably not have come as a surprise when in 1868 he was offered the premier position in the Church of England, that of Archbishop of Canterbury. He was in fact probably better prepared for this post than for any of those he had previously undertaken. He was 57 and Catharine 49. Their 'second family' was growing up to be the support and the credit to their parents they had every reason to expect. Craufurd was at Oxford, but the three daughters, Lucy, Edith and Agnes, who had passed all their lives so far at Fulham, were not so enamoured of the prospect of moving to the gloomy palace on the other side of the Thames. It cannot be, however, that their lives changed all that much. There were tutors and governesses, visitations from relatives, the inevitable visiting and being visited that had been so much a feature of their lives already. But this time the area of their father's concern was much wider. In exchange for the thousand London clergy and their wives and families and city parishes, there was the Church worldwide, with all its bishops and legislation, as well as the pastoral oversight of the enormous diocese of Canterbury. There was the palace, with its extensive park, which could be and indeed was opened up for the use of all sorts and conditions of people, though this did not seem apparent to the leader writer in the *Daily Chronicle* who remarked on the 'magnificent park of 20 acres at Lambeth, to which the poor are not admitted because the Archbishop of Canterbury and his wife require it all for themselves'.[62]

Such is the nature of public misunderstanding, or journalistic misrepresentation, that it was necessary for Randall Davidson, the Archbishop's chaplain, to respond to the paper and remind its readers of the 28 cricket clubs, football teams, rifle clubs, school treats and open days for the sick and aged poor, which occupied those same acres throughout the year. There were other residences, in Canterbury and at Addington, and these were able to provide some of the much-needed retreat and privacy that their public life so often denied them. One of the handbooks for the clergy written while Archie was at Oxford comments that 'Other professions are indeed professions, they are exercised but outwardly . . . But this indulgence . . . is denied the clergyman.'[63]

Gradually, the girls learned to love all their homes, and Archie tried to maintain as much of a family presence as he could, though, as Edith was to remark in her biography, looking back in her old age, 'all the Fulham time is full in my mind of Mother but there is not nearly so much of Father',[64] and once at Lambeth, it was even harder to maintain as much family contact as was desired. Fulham had been a happy home, following the sadness that had caused their being there, and in his end-of-year journal entry Archie reflected on this:

> I have seen the sun of 1868 go down over the Thames as I have watched the last sun of many years back . . . Year has succeeded year and healed our wounds and Craufurd has become a man, and Edith and Agnes have been added to our family and much happiness has by God's mercy been ours in this house.[65]

A month previously, he had noted in his journal his indebtedness to his wife in all he did: 'I thank thee O Lord for the great help I have received from my dear wife. Spare her to me, I beseech thee.'[66] He had also remarked the month before, rejoicing in the possession of their own house at Broadstairs: 'The calm of this seaside retreat is very grateful. We are having a new honeymoon after 25 years of married life,'[67] and, following convalescence there after another bout of illness, 'Now my beloved and I are enjoying the calmness of a Sunday evening together.'[68] These moments were precious to him, the calming and strengthening influence that throughout their life together Catharine had exerted over him. While she was 'spared to him' for ten more years, there was still one more tragedy yet to share.

Throughout many of the crises and major events which determined the course of their life there are gendered differences to the way each was affected – she was the supportive woman in almost every circumstance, yet I do not believe that these influences were as clearly demarcated as one might suppose. While the death of the five daughters was a significant event in both their lives and coloured their attitudes and their relationship thereafter, it was nevertheless Archie's career that changed as a result of it. Similarly, while he was a significant player in the response to the cholera epidemic of 1866, it was this event which gave her a way to mobilise help and engage in what some described as her lifetime's work. Archie's dependence on Catharine never ceased in her lifetime and beyond. Most onerous of all the burdens she was called upon to bear for him were the confidences of friends and doctors when their beloved son Craufurd, who had progressed from his father's chaplaincy to his own parish, was found to be terminally ill. It was felt she could bear the news better than the Archbishop and prepare him for it. They were wrong. Nursing her son towards his death at 29 brought her to the end of her resources and six months later 'all that could die of her was laid to rest'.

Catherine's great strength, not only spiritual but physical, had not gone unnoticed by her husband, who commented in her biography:

> I suppose one secret of her being able to get through so much in the day was her extraordinary bodily strength, which was really greater than falls to the share of most women.[69]

And so it would seem strange that someone so apparently fit should be struck down and die at such a comparatively young age – 59 – from what appeared to be a sudden gastric complaint while on holiday in Scotland following the Lambeth Conference. However, those who had been with her in the preceding weeks and months since the death of Craufurd had been aware of some changes. Help had been sought by Catharine to meet the massive demands of hospitality and entertaining of clerical dignitaries from the 78-year-old Lady Wake and other members of the family 'for neither she nor the Archbishop would shrink from the work that had been so gladly undertaken when all was bright around them.'[70] There are recorded perceptions of many who saw her there, and at other functions, among them the Bishop of Madras: 'Last July Mrs Tait seemed like fruit ripe for the Heavenly Gardener to gather. She was so gentle, loving, devout.'[71] Lady Wake herself describes her sister-in-law: 'Beloved Catharine, her beautiful dark eyes were ever seeming to look beyond, and in the tones of her voice there was a soft echo of sorrow,'[72] and her husband reflected that 'Many noted the heavenly expression of sadness mingled with joy in my dear wife's face.'[73]

Fig. 3.1 Catharine Tait - the engraving used for the frontispiece
of her biography written by her husband after her death

Theirs was not so much a life that was planned: their youthful visions,
as expressed in their correspondence during their engagement, did not
seem to be ambitious and they were both ready to acknowledge that
the path of their life was in God's hands. They had both been 'framed'
within an acknowledged and established structure – the country parish
or the Oxford college – but individually they had grown within and
beyond these structures. Archie entered the arena of academic, religious
and political debate on the one hand, staking out a position that would
inevitably alienate and offend as many as it would please and encourage,
and Catharine was drawn away from a simple evangelical faith towards
'the type of religion of which Keble may be taken as one of the purest and
best exponents' and a 'love for the ceremonial of the English Church . . .
in which her deep inward piety embodied itself'.[74] As husband and wife,
their views on matters of religious form and observance differed, but what
united them was far deeper and stronger than anything that separated
them, such that Catharine remained:

> united to him in the truest fellowship of the soul, while
> still tempering, by the associations of her early Oxford

bias, whatever might otherwise have been harsh in his judgements of the good men from whom on principle he differed.[75]

Framed within such a loving marriage and fashioned by the sorrows, the challenges and the delight in family and in duty, she shone throughout her life:

> a life not less remarkable for its external brightness and prosperity than for the severe afflictions by which it was accompanied. It was a busy, hardworking life made so partly by necessary conditions but still more by her unwearied devotion to good works and to the duties connected with the varied positions which she successively occupied.[76]

However one views the concept of destiny, the rites of their passage were certainly determined by major events: the birth of the Oxford Movement, the sudden death of Arnold of Rugby, Archie Tait's illness, the scarlet fever epidemic in Carlisle, the crisis in the Church of England, with the need for a steady hand to guide it, the cholera epidemic in London – conflict, death or disaster pointing up each time a new challenge. With the growing up of their second family, their circumstances were different from those of their early marriage. Always it was necessary to entertain or be entertained. While this aspect of their life was something that developed in London and continued when Archie moved to Lambeth, there were other things that had to change and develop. He was, as Primate, at the beck and call of not only the prime minister, but also the sovereign, being called in turn to Osborne, Balmoral and Windsor as well as to the committees and synods of the Church. The burden was indeed heavy, but in all these arenas Catharine played her part, at his side at dinner parties, entertaining clergy and politicians, visiting, listening, being the sounding board and the intermediary for matters that might trouble her husband and in which she might be able to share or mediate. Now was the flowering of all her upbringing, for her life was public and at its most exemplary. But if her years of reading and listening assisted her as she sat at table or walked the gardens with the great and the powerful, then her years of care and compassion enabled her to continue to prepare her maids for confirmation, to include the girls of 'her' orphanage in all their family celebrations when in Kent and to continue to visit her old ladies in the workhouse at Lambeth.

In his address to his diocese on her death Archie concludes that:

> my dear wife was my zealous helper and constantly encouraged me in every effort to do my duty amongst you. The daughter of a clergyman and born and brought up in a country parsonage, she knew well the trials and joys of your life. How I shall be able to fulfil my part amongst you hence forward God only knows. [77]

In fact he did survive four more years although 'almost immediately [after Catharine's death] he became an old man'.[78] He was supported lovingly by his three daughters but also by his son-in-law Randall Davison, who became his chaplain. The three girls served and developed in quite different ways. Although Lucy maintained all her life her devotion to the orphanage and its demands, her life was centred around another clergy family, that of the next Archbishop of Canterbury, Edward Benson. It was his wife, and eventually widow, Minnie, whose partner and support she became.

Edith, the middle daughter, was more like her mother in terms of charm and energetic devotion to duty. That she fell in love with her father's chaplain, Randall Davidson, brought with it both joy and sorrow. Their wedding preceded Catharine's death by two weeks, and so the decision whether to accept a parish in Kent or to stay and support the bereft Archbishop was a painful one to make, but duty prevailed and they remained with him at Lambeth for the rest of his life.

On his death, however, they too were bound to move on, andin their case upwards, for Davidson's preferment took him to Windsor as dean, to Winchester as bishop and ultimately back to Lambeth as archbishop. The youngest daughter, Agnes, remained the 'daughter at home' in her father's last years, reading to him and writing his journal but, on his death, she found herself, though beautiful, talented and energetic, nevertheless a spinster without a home, glad of the hospitality of her relations, but without a niche to fill. So she did something unprecedented for women in her family, and enrolled at Lady Margaret Hall in Oxford. She only stayed one year, but it gave her an outlet for the inherited energy and even for what her granddaughter describes as her passion for the stage and her desire to be an actress. With the flowing red-gold hair, the warm colouring and the ample proportions, she appears in the Richmond portrait in the family's possession with arms entwined around her sister Edith, the epitome of the 'liberated' Pre-Raphaelite young women they could never be. Returning from university, she slotted back into the life of the clergy family, marrying John Ellison, one of her father's chaplains. They had one son and then, six weeks after his birth, she died of a wrongly treated blood clot at the age of 29, leaving her baby to be brought up largely by his doting, practical, energetic and unstuffy aunts – the only Tait grandchild.

I think it would be inappropriate to conclude a chronicle of such a positive life on such a sad note. It is, however, important to observe that not all who benefit from such a godly nurturing do grow and flourish as did Catharine Tait. She was blessed, as her husband remarked, with amazingly good health and boundless energy. These are not qualities bestowed equally on the populace, but elements of the circumstances which determine the direction of our lives, no matter what 'framing and fashioning' may have taken place. In considering what were the most significant elements in her character, I would want to isolate four: that she was always seeking knowledge and personal growth, that she was joyfully bound by ties of love and duty which were to her a delight, that she enjoyed a truly loving marriage and family life and that, remembering the bonds that held her to past sorrow, she was always looking with absolute faith to the next world and to the joy of reunion. The memory of the five little girls and their grown-up brother whose passing she had shared with her husband had coloured all of their life together, uniting them in a deep sorrow whose pain was tempered but never eradicated by the prospect of an ultimate reunion. It is not without significance that Archie chose Newman's hymn 'Lead kindly light' for her funeral and it must have been immensely difficult, but one hopes reassuring, to sing the final verse:

So long Thy power hath blest me, sure it still

Will lead me on

O'er moor and fen, o'er crag and torrent, till

The night is gone,

And with the morn those angel faces smile,

Which I have loved long since, and lost awhile.[79]

Acknowledgements

My doctoral supervisors Professor Anne Digby (Oxford Brookes University) and Professor Angela John (University of Greenwich), my employer Professor David Parkin (University of Oxford) and friends, family and colleagues, particularly members of the 19th Century Support Group. In addition special thanks to Mrs Colville, great-granddaughter of Catharine Tait, and to librarians at Lambeth Palace, Fulham Palace and the Bodleian Library, Oxford.

Endnotes

1   from 'The Ordering of Priests', *The Book of Common Prayer.*

2   Benham, William, *Life of Catharine and Craufurd Tait*, 1879, p 3.

3   Richmond, Leigh, *Memoirs of the Rev. Leigh Richmond*, 1828, p 547.

4   ibid, p 548.

5   Tait Papers, Lambeth Palace Library.

6   Benham, *Life of Catharine and Craufurd Tait.*

7   from 'The Pulpit and the Pew' in *The Clerical World* ,1882.

8   letter from Catharine Spooner to Archibald Tait, 1843, Tait papers, Lambeth Palace, vol 102, piece 175.

9   Benham, William, and Randall Davidson, *Life of AC Tait*, 1891, p 206.

10 Wake, Lucy (ed), *Reminiscences of Lady Wake*, 1909, p 202.

11 Tait correspondence, vol 102, piece 216.

12 Tait correspondence, vol 102.

13 ibid.

14 ibid.

15 Review of *Catharine and Craufurd Tait* by Randall Davidson and William Benham in *The Times*, 3 October 1879.

16 Tait correspondence, 1844, piece 134.

17 ibid.

18 ibid.

19 Benham, *Catharine and Craufurd Tait*, p 18.

20 W.B. Whippel, Lower House of Convocation, Westminster, 2 February 1879: Tait papers, vol 99, piece 50.

21 Benham, *Catharine and Craufurd Tait._*

22 ibid, p 396.

23 Wheeler, Michael, *Heaven, Hell and the Victorians*, 1994.

24 Swinton, Georgiana, and Sir Osbert Sitwell, *Two Generations*, 1940.

25 Benham, *Catharine and Craufurd Tait*.

27 The city was in the process of acknowledging its own failings in matters of disease prevention, sanitation and public health, as is evident from a survey published in the city – Rowlinson, Robert, *Report to the General Board of Health, Preliminary Enquiry into the sewage, drainage and supply of water and the sanitary conditions of the inhabitants of Carlisle*, 1850.

28 Benham, *Catharine and Craufurd Tait*, p 256.

29 ibid, p 366.

30 Bickley, A.C., *A Sketch of the Life of A C Tait*, 1883, p 185.

31 Benham, *Catharine and Craufurd Tait*, p 403.

32 Bickley, *A Sketch of the Life of A C Tait*, p 190.

33 Benham, *Catharine and Craufurd* Tait, p 403.

34 ibid, p 186.

35 Benham and Davidson, *Life of AC Tait*, p 56.

36 Review of *Catharine and Craufurd Tait* by Randall Davidson and William Benham in *The Times*, 3 October 1879.

37 *The Daily News*, n.d., 1856 (newspaper cutting in Tait papers).

38 *The Clerical World*, 25 January 1882.

39 Benham and Davidson, *Life of A C Tait*, p 71.

40 *Book of Common Prayer.*   .

41 Benham and Davidson, *Life of A C Tait*, p 73.

42 Davidson, Edith, and Mary Mills, *Edith Davidson of Lambeth*, 1938, p 10.

43 Davidson and Mills, *Edith Davidson of Lambeth*, p 14. Edith was 10 when her father became archbishop, and from then on her education and that of her sisters would have been with governesses.

44 Benham and Davidson, *Life of A C Tait*, p 51.

45 Marsh, P.T., *The Victorian Church in Decline: Archibald Tait and the Church of England 1868–1882*, 1969, p 54.

46 *Dictionary of National Biography.*

47 Visitors' book for Fulham Palace, Tait papers.

48 Bickley, *A Sketch of the Life of A C Tait*, p 77.

49 Peel, M.J., *The London Episcopate of Archibald Campbell Tait,* King's College London PhD, 1989, p 208.

50 Davidson and Mills, *Edith Davidson of Lambeth*, p 11.

51 ibid.

52 *The Times*, 10 August 1866.

53 *Daily Telegraph*, 14 March 1867.

54 ibid.

55 Peel, *The London Episcopate of A 'C Tait*.

56 Mann, *Call to London*, 1854, p 13.

57 Catharine began to go to theology lectures at Queen's College but realised she could not keep up the attendance regularly so she gave it up. See Benham and Davidson, *Life of AC Tait*, p 450.

58 Davidson and Mills, *Edith Davidson of Lambeth*, p 12.

59 Benham, *Catharine and Craufurd Tait*, p 73.

60 *Daily Telegraph*, 25 September 1867.

61 *Church Times*, 25 August 1866.

62 *Daily Chronicle*, 28 September 1878.

63 Wilson Evans, Robert, *The Bishopric of Souls*, 1842, p 199.

64 Davidson and Mills, *Edith Davidson of Lambeth*, p 16.

65 ibid, p 17.

66 Benham, *Catharine and Craufurd Tait*, p 539.

67 ibid, p 535.

68 ibid, p 102.

69 ibid, p 238.

70 Wake, *Reminiscences of Lady Wake*, p 309.

71 Letter from bishop of Madras, 15 February 1879, Tait papers, piece 99-48.

72 Wake, *Reminiscences of Lady Wake*, p 309.

73 Benham and Davidson, *Life of A C Tait*.

74 Review of Davidson and Benham (1879) *Catharine and Craufurd Tait* in *The Times* October 3rd 1879

75 ibid.

76 Review of Davidson and Benham (1879) *Catharine and Craufurd Tait* in *The Times* October 3rd 1879

77 Address to the clergy of the Archdiocese of Canterbury, December 1878.

78 Marsh, *The Victorian Church in Decline*, p x.

79 Newman, John Henry, *Congregational Church Hymnal*, CUEW, 1888, p 333.

CHAPTER 4

Prostitution, Housing and Women's Welfare

Caroline Morrell

Housing was a major problem for single working women in Victorian and Edwardian Britain. It was not one addressed by the mainstream housing reform movement, which concentrated its attention on the housing of working-class families, but it was taken up by a number of women's societies that came together in the period to work for the welfare of vulnerable young women. What I want to look at in this chapter is how those women's organisations defined the problem of women's homelessness, how they responded to it and how this changed over time. In order to explore this I have chosen to examine two organisations in particular, the Girls' Friendly Society (GFS), founded in 1875, and the National Association of Women's Lodging Homes, founded in 1909. Both these organisations were associated with housing for single women, the National Association directly so and the GFS more obliquely, and what I particularly want to focus on is their view of single working women as potential victims of sexual exploitation and the role that the lack of secure housing played in this. I am also interested in the way that these women's groups organised themselves, the vocabulary through which they expressed themselves and whether or not they can be viewed as part of the early women's movement.

It is clear that there was a major housing problem for women in the period, and it was estimated that there were some 80,000 homeless women on the streets of London in the 1880s.[1] It is also clear from contemporary evidence that there was a major problem with prostitution. William Stead, the campaigning journalist, wrote in 1885 of 'a vast horde of London prostitutes, whose numbers no man can compute, but who are probably not much below 50,000'.[2] Fears about prostitution, 'the great social evil', spread right through Victorian and Edwardian society: William Gladstone said that the problem of fallen women was 'the chief burden' of his soul[3] and Mrs Pankhurst said in 1913, 'the problem of prostitution is the greatest evil in the civilised world and perhaps the greatest reason for militancy'.[4] Women's charitable societies saw that prostitution was directly linked to homelessness and unemployment, and in response set up accommodation lodges to house young women, particularly domestic servants, between places.

The way in which most single working-class women found their housing was by going into work which provided accommodation, into service, or into dress or shop work.[5] Living-in meant that, by definition, these women had no homes of their own. If such a worker lost her place, she not only lost her job, she also lost the roof over her head and was left in a very vulnerable position. Large families, overcrowding and poverty meant that working-class girls generally left their parental homes at an early age in order to earn a living and could not easily return to them. Girls who were sent into service from the workhouse or from orphanages were in the worst situation, as they had no home at all to which to return should their situation break down. Women who worked in other occupations either lived at home or found their accommodation in lodgings, and their low wages ensured that this was the poorest sort of housing.[6] The sheer poverty of single working women, whether unmarried, widowed or deserted wives, made them vulnerable to homelessness, and records show that very many were forced to resort to the workhouse.[7] Thousands of women also lived in common lodging houses, shelters, brothels, or literally on the streets.[8] Increasingly, lower middle-class and middle-class women were beginning to enter paid employment and leave home over the period,[9] and they too faced the problem of finding suitable and affordable accommodation.

There was widespread concern about the position of such women, especially young women, and upper and middle-class women organised on a grand scale to meet their needs. Mrs Edith Sellars' report to the International Conference of Women held in Chicago in 1893, *Women's Work for the Welfare of Girls*,[10] provides a useful overview of the range of work in which British women were involved in the late 19th century. The societies she described were divided into two broad categories: those which aimed at preventative work with girls of 'respectable character', and those which aimed at rescue work with girls and young women who were considered 'fallen'. The three largest organisations – the Young Women's Christian Association, set up in 1856, the Metropolitan Association for Befriending Young Servants (1873) and the Girls' Friendly Society (1875) – were concerned with the former group and the accommodation they provided was for young women of 'unblemished character'.

In addition to these major societies, there were also the Ladies Associations for the Care of Friendless Girls, which existed in most towns and aimed to help not only the respectable, but also 'those upon whom the world is somewhat inclined to look askance'.[11] Edith Sellars reported that every religious community ran its own society for helping girls and young women, and that a host of smaller independent homes also existed. There were also hundreds of rescue homes, Magdalene homes for the reclamation of fallen women (named after Mary Magdalene, the prostitute saved by Christ) and penitentiaries where women went to atone for their sins through hard work and prayer. Many of these were managed by committees of men, perhaps in recognition of male responsibility for the plight of these women, but it was usually women, often religious sisters, who undertook the day-to-day running of them. The societies described by Mrs Sellars differed in their particular aims, but this was a major effort by women of the middle and upper classes on behalf of single working women and girls. The largest of these organisations was the Girls' Friendly Society.

The Girls' Friendly Society

The Girls' Friendly Society (GFS) was launched in 1875. It went on to become not only the largest female organisation in Britain, but also a world-wide organisation which by 1914 had branches in twenty-two countries. Although primarily conceived of as a purity organisation, one of its major achievements was the setting up of a comprehensive network of accommodation lodges for single working women. Despite its size and its all-female membership, the GFS has attracted little interest from either housing historians or historians of the women's movement and there is little secondary literature on the Society.[12] However, the Society itself was prolific in the production of literature, and published a number of journals, numerous leaflets and two histories of its own.[13] Some of its early members also left unpublished reminiscences and memoirs.[14]

The idea for the GFS originated with Mrs Mary Townsend (1841–1918). She was married to Frederick Townsend, a wealthy Hampshire landowner and Unionist MP from 1886 to 1892. The couple had no children and Mrs Townsend involved herself in charitable and educational work with her husband's tenants and in church affairs. In 1872 she was asked by the Bishop of Winchester to join an organisation for rescue work in the diocese. She determined instead to start a society to prevent young women from falling in the first place. It was not, Mrs Townsend argued, that there was not a need for rescue work, but that there were already many agencies working in this field. 'England is full of homes for the depraved', she said, and what was needed was a society 'whose aim should be to set before the maidens of England the beauty of a blameless life'.[15]

In 1874 she called together a meeting with three other women to discuss her idea: Mrs Tait, the wife of the Archbishop of Canterbury, Mrs Browne, the wife of the Bishop of Winchester, and Mrs Jane Nassau Senior, the founder of the Metropolitan Association for Befriending Young Servants. One man was present, the Rev T. Fosbery, a friend of Mrs Townsend. The meeting was held at Lambeth Palace and this setting, together with the status of the women attending, was to set the tone for the Society: one that was organised by ladies of a high social standing and set within the structure of the Anglican Church. Mrs Townsend's vision was of a national society in which ladies in every parish would befriend young girls working away from home. She was motivated by her concern over what she saw as the forlorn and friendless plight of many young working girls, especially that of domestic servants. She said:

> Ah! If we only knew how many poor girls are lost, how
> many lives are wasted, not for want of money or expensive

organisations, but just for the want of a 'a little love', a few kind words, a smile of interest to show that they are cared for. If only the moment a girl went out into the world she could be furnished with a letter to another friend who would care for her well-being.[16]

She set about setting up just such a system, consisting of ladies, known as Associates, who would take a kindly interest in a number of young working girls – the Members – in their parishes and see to it that if they moved, they would be passed on to the care of another Associate in their new parish. It was very much a class-based system, with ladies of the servant-keeping classes acting as the Associates and poor working girls as the Members, but both Members and Associates were enjoined to work in the spirit of friendship and of 'banded womanhood', so there were also strong elements of female solidarity in the GFS.

Following the Lambeth Palace meeting, work began immediately on organising the new Society. A national office was set up in London and in 1875 a Central Council was elected. By 1882 each diocese had its own council, which in turn elected delegates to the Central Council. Mrs Townsend became the first President of the Society and the Archbishop of Canterbury its first patron. Work began on drawing up the constitution and rules of the Society in 1876 and these were approved at a meeting in 1880. The fact that it took four years to draw up and approve the constitution reflects the difficulties the ladies of the GFS experienced in organising themselves from a group of like-minded friends into a formal body. Agnes Money, one of the early members, wrote feelingly of the problems they faced in learning how to run committees and contrasted their ineptitude with the ease with which men ran their organisations.[17] However, they did succeed and the GFS took pride in the fact that it was a society of women capable of operating in the public world of committees and accountability. In 1892 the *Associates' Journal* wrote that the GFS Central Council was 'certainly the largest assembly of women exercising so much power'.[18]

Fig. 4.1 'The historic five' reproduced by kind permission of GFS Platform

The GFS was an immediate success. A sister society was started in Scotland in 1875, followed in 1877 by one in Ireland, and in the same year the society's first overseas branch was launched in Lowell, Massachusetts. In 1880 Queen Victoria, almost invariably referred to in GFS literature as 'our dear Queen', became patron and an Honorary Associate. In 1884, ten years after its inception, the Society numbered over 100,000 women in England and Wales, and Mrs Townsend described it as the largest society of women ever formed.[19] Membership reached its peak in 1913 with 197,493 Members and 39,926 Associates,[20] and in 1914 there were also 81,374 Candidates[21] (the junior category of membership added in 1877 for girls aged between eight and twelve), thus making a total of over 300,000 girls and women who belonged to the GFS just before the First World War. The scale of the Society's work can be judged from the Associates' List for 1892, which lists 56 accommodation lodges in England and Wales, 87 employment registries, 222 clubs and recreation rooms, 61 Homes of Rest, and arrangements for meeting members at 159 railway stations.[22] The overseas work of the Society expanded until it became a world-wide organisation, and in 1905 it was said that 'a GFS member may now travel from Paris to Odessa, or from Biarritz to St Petersburg and be safe in the care of the GFS all the way'.[23]

By any standards this was a large and successful organisation. Part of the Society's success can be explained by the way it was organised through the Anglican Church. Structured as it was through parish and diocese branches, it had access to communities the length and breadth of the country, and potential Members and Associates could be easily identified and recruited through the activities of the local church. The Society also had immediate attractions for both groups of women. For the Members, often isolated servant girls, it offered companionship and activities, and over and above this, very tangible benefits in the shape of premiums for good service, savings schemes and the Society's network of accommodation lodges and employment registries. For the upper-class women who made up the Associates, it provided a meaningful role in the public world which could be comfortably accommodated within the accepted structure of church and neighbourhood activities. As the work of Prochaska shows,[24] women were becoming involved in great numbers in philanthropic work in this period and the GFS Associates were part of this movement. At the same time, the widespread concern about prostitution and social purity provided a moral imperative to become involved in work to uphold family values and to protect young women. It could be merely a pastime, 'poor peopling' as Florence Nightingale called it, but for those who became involved in the regional and national running of the Society, it meant considerable responsibility and, importantly, work with, and for, other women.

However, the Society was not, as Brian Harrison points out in his article 'For Church, Queen and Family',[25] a feminist organisation in any self-conscious sense of the word. Although some of its most prominent members were supporters of women's suffrage,[26] the Society expressed no interest at an organisational level in the issue of the vote and in 1919 it refused an invitation to an Anglican thanksgiving service for the enfranchisement of women. Some of the Associates displayed distinctly anti-feminist sentiments. Charlotte Yonge, the novelist, who was one of the first Associates, said, without apparent irony, 'I have no hesitation in declaring my full belief in the inferiority of woman, nor that she has brought it on herself.'[27] In line with much of the debate over women's role at the time, the GFS was more concerned with women's duties than with women's rights. It advocated duty and service to all its members, Associate and Member alike, and certainly did not encourage thoughts of independence, or of women's rights, among its working-class membership.

The major constituency of the Society was domestic servants, the largest group of young women working away from home, but from the start it also recruited women from other occupations. In 1877 it said, 'we are very anxious to make it known that our Society admits all working girls, those in shops, factories etc (as well as those at home and in service)'.[28] By 1906 domestic servants made up 49 per cent of the total employed membership of the Society,[29] 19 per cent worked in mills, factories and laundries, 19 per cent in business (shops and offices) and 10 per cent in the professions[30] (mainly teaching and nursing), which broadly reflects national occupational figures at the time. Problems were encountered in bonding this diverse group of women together. In 1884 an Associate commented that 'business girls should be addressed as "young ladies", not as "young women": nor would they think of joining the GFS if told to do so for their own good.'[31]

The Society provided a great number of benefits for its Members and the welfare system it created was a comprehensive and far-reaching one. In addition to its employment registries and accommodation lodges, the Society set up Homes of Rest (for members exhausted by work), holiday homes, nursing homes, a hospice for women with incurable diseases, a home for epileptic members, almshouses for impoverished Members and Associates and a needlework scheme to provide employment for invalid members.[32] The Industrial Training Department also provided occupational guidance and training for Members in a variety of jobs.[33] The annual subscription members paid for these benefits was sixpence; Associates paid 2s 6d per annum. All this was in place by the end of the century, before the Liberal government's social reforms of the Edwardian period (which made some provision for insured workers, but very little for women), and must have made life considerably more secure for working-class members of the GFS.

The main aim of the Society, however, was to preserve young women's sexual purity. Mrs Townsend said, 'the Society owes its origin firstly to the fearfully prevalent and increasing sin of impurity, secondly to the conviction that "prevention is better than cure".'[34] It did not intend to be a rescue society, but to protect women from 'falling' in the first place, and safe accommodation was seen as one way of achieving that end. The GFS painted a lurid picture of the dangers of big cities for girls, especially those who were new to them:

> A country girl comes into a large town in search of work, if she is alone and inexperienced, those who know the state of large towns will shudder to think of the perils that surround her . . .[35]

It is difficult to know how accurate was this picture of the dangers of the streets for young women. Something of a moral panic had been created in the late Victorian period by the publication of pamphlets such as Andrew Mearns's *Bitter Cry of Outcast London* (1883) and William Stead's *Maiden Tribute to Modern Babylon* (1885), and there were widespread fears about both child prostitution and the existence of an organised white-slave trade that preyed on young women. Historians such as Judith Walkowitz discount the existence of such a traffic on a large scale and see prostitution as an economic choice, an occupation that women moved into and out of rather than a trade which preyed upon innocent women.[36] There were enough contemporary accounts of girls being lured into prostitution, however, to make one suspect that it had some basis in truth[37] (and recent revelations about the widespread traffic in girls in Europe confirms the suspicion that this was more than a moral panic). The provision of safe accommodation in the city was seen by the GFS as a priority in safeguarding young women from such a fate.

A G.F.S. CATECHISM.

MOTTO :—'Bear ye one another's burbens.'

1. What is the G. F. S. ?

   A great Society, spread nearly all over the world; many thousands of women and girls belong to it; Members and Associates.

2. What is the chief *use* of the G. F. S. ?

   To raise the standard of *Purity* among all classes of women.

3. Is it a Society for Servants chiefly?

   Certainly not; every girl and every young woman should join it who can do so according to the rules, for every one can influence others for good.

4. What is the work in the Society of those called *Working Associates* ?

   To admit Members, to pray for them, to watch over them, to help and strengthen them, and to be their friend, wherever they go.

5. Ought *Mothers* to wish their daughters to belong to the Society?

   Yes; for the better and purer the daughter is, the more dutiful and useful will she be.

6. Ought *Employers* to wish their assistants to belong to the Society?

   Yes; for modest, self-respectful maidens are the most likely to be valuable and faithful.

7. Why do Associates pay 2s. 6d., and Members 1s. a-year to the Society?

   Because we are bound to bear 'one another's burdens,' and after the necessary expenses of printing and suchlike are paid, the rest of the money is spent in providing 'Homes of Rest,' and 'Lodges' in towns, and helps in sickness and distress for those Members who need such.

8. Should a girl say, 'I have well-to-do parents, and a good home and kind friends, and good health; I do not want any of these helps, nor yet premiums for service nor bonus on savings, so what good will the G. F. S. do me?'

   No girl should say this, but each should feel it an *honour* to belong to this great Society, and each should say :—
   'I want to *give* and not to *get.*
   'It is more blessed to give than to receive.'

9. What can girls give ?

   Love, sympathy, and a good example.
   'Love is the fulfilling of Christ's law;' and
   'None of us liveth to himself.'

10. Why does not every English maiden ask to be enrolled?

    Some do not know about the Society;
    Some (selfishly) do not want to think of or care for others;
    Some do not see the importance and help such an Association may be for promoting purity;
    But for those who *do* know about it and care for these things, any other objections will easily be overcome.

11. Where should Members be enrolled?

    If possible, in their own *home Branch,* to which they would always belong, and from which they would be commended on leaving home.

12. What should be the signs by which G. F. S. Members should be known?

    Happy and modest *looks.*
    Respectful and retiring *manners.*
    Gentle and soft *voices.*
    Neat and quiet *dress.*

'BLESSED ARE THE PURE IN HEART.'

A. M. D.

Fig. 4.2 'GFS Catechism' from Friendly Leaves, 1884, reproduced by kind permission of GFS Platform

The first headquarters of the GFS were set up in an existing servants' home for 'little maids of all work' in Brixton. Miss Hawkesley, who began the home, wrote of her concern over these girls, 'their helplessness when, as too often happened, they were out of a place, the dangers to which they were exposed as they went on their errands late at night'.[38] And some of these girls were very young. Mrs Townsend wrote that in London alone there were 10,000 maids of all work between the ages of ten to fifteen, an age, she said, 'when our girls are mostly safe in the shelter of happy homes'.[39] From this first venture, a network of accommodation lodges was set up throughout the country. In its first year of operation the Society opened five lodges in London and two others in the country towns of Shipston-on-Stour and Weymouth. The work expanded rapidly after this, and between 1875 and 1914, 81 lodges were opened in England and Wales.[40] Some of these were fairly short-lived and some had several changes of address, but on the whole it was a record of sustained development which resulted in a national network of accommodation lodges for women. Every Member was issued with a guide containing a list of respectable lodgings and homes to which she could apply for 'friendly shelter and help'.

At the start the lodges were aimed at domestic servants between places, but as the Society began to take in young women employed in other occupations, it extended its housing mission accordingly. In 1879 Holborn Lodge in Red Lion Square, London, was opened by William Gladstone to provide rooms for London business girls. This was a significant step as it meant that women could live in the lodges on a permanent basis rather than as a stop-gap between places. It also signalled a recognition on the part of the GFS that new areas of work were opening up for women in the city, and that these workers faced great difficulty in finding affordable and respectable lodgings.

For the first thirty years the lodges were run on a local basis, some, it appears, less successfully than others, and in 1905 a central committee was set up to enquire into the financial safety of the Society's lodges, homes of rest and training homes. Miss Millicent Hotchkin took up the post of Central Head of the Lodges Department in the following year and set about regulating its affairs. She recommended amalgamating the Departments of Lodges and Homes of Rest into one and bringing them under the central control of the Society. There was resistance to this from some of the local Associates, who liked to be able 'to choose their own homes for their girls',[41] but Miss Hotchkin won the argument and in 1908 a committee was appointed to manage a central fund for lodges and homes of rest. A campaign was launched to raise a sum of £20,000 to improve existing lodges and to open new ones. This target was reached in 1910 and a grand ceremony was held in the Queen's Hall, London, where the moneys collected were presented to the Princess of Wales. By 1913 the GFS was running 64 lodges in Great Britain – 10 in London, 45 in England and Wales, four in Scotland and five in Ireland – offering 1,133 beds in total.[42]

There is little information in the GFS's national records on how individual lodges were run, but the records of the Oxford branch give a fuller picture of a local lodge in action. It was opened in 1891 and provided four beds as temporary places for commended Members (from another branch); a lady superintendent was appointed and six women stayed in the lodge in the first year. By 1897 the lodge had moved to larger premises with 19 beds, and 123 women stayed there in that year. The boarders in 1897 were described as young girls being trained for service, and servants staying for short periods while waiting for places. Several girls had been taken in late at night because, through missing a train or some other emergency, they had been left stranded in Oxford. The lodge also operated an employment registry and from 1908 a scheme for meeting young women arriving at the station. Members 'in need of a change of air' could also be sent to the Diocesan Home of Rest in Reading.[43]

The GFS went from strength to strength up to the First World War, and in 1914 its hostels came into their own for war work. Initially, those in the south took in women returning from jobs on the Continent and subsequently they were used to house munitions workers, land-workers and women in the WAAC and WRNS. They returned to GFS use after the war, but as membership of the GFS declined, the number of hostels decreased until by the beginning of the 21st century there were only 12. A decision was taken in 2003–4 to disengage from accommodation work and to focus upon youth work, and the Society now has only one house left, which accommodates young mothers and babies. The name of the Society has been changed to GFS Platform and although a much smaller organisation than in its glory days in the late nineteenth and early twentieth century, it still runs a number of projects round the country for girls and young women and is active in 23 other countries.[44]

The GFS was a very successful body. It quickly grew to become the largest women's organisation in Britain, expanded overseas and provided a comprehensive range of welfare provisions for girls and young women. In this sense it can be seen as very much a female 'friendly society', but it never lost sight of its original intention, 'the maintenance of a virtuous British maidenhood,' and these provisions were part of its armoury against sin. The Society made no social or economic analysis of the position of its young members and did not question the fact that girls needed substitute homes and 'mothering' precisely because they had to leave their own homes and mothers at a young age in order to earn a living. Neither did it offer any challenge to the gender inequalities involved. Young women were to be strengthened against temptation to sin by both material and spiritual means, and unscrupulous white slavers were to be outwitted, but the question of the power relations between men and women – which allowed sexual exploitation to occur – was not addressed.

Both the language and the ideology of the GFS seem alien to us now, but I do not think that its good intent can be faulted. It was working for women's good in a very practical way: to lose one's character or to become pregnant out of wedlock spelt ruin to women of any social class and especially to poor women. The GFS, by making provision for women when they were unemployed and potentially homeless, and by its many mechanisms to instil an ideal of virtue in its members, must have helped very many young women to avoid such a disaster. There were, of course, large numbers of women who did not fall within the remit of the GFS – older women, discharged servants, casually employed and itinerant women, and women who did not, or would not, conform to the ideal of 'virtuous maidenhood' – and these were excluded from the provision made by the more respectable women's societies. The second organisation I have chosen to look at is one that aimed to help all homeless women, regardless of character: the National Association for Women's Lodging-Homes.

National Association for Women's Lodging Homes

The National Association for Women's Lodging-Homes was set up in 1909 with the primary aim of campaigning for the provision of a national system of municipal lodging houses for women. It was a very different body from the GFS, but it too was a women's organisation set up by middle and upper-class women in order to help their poorer sisters and it shared many of its concerns. It was only in existence for six years but in its short life it succeeded in establishing a formidable and effective organisation. Little has been written about the National Association, however, in either the context of housing reform or women's history.[45] Its history can be traced from the reports, pamphlets and conference proceeding it published, and from the writings of its founder, Mary Higgs, on women's homelessness. She wrote prolifically, passionately and forcefully on behalf of her cause and it is her writings which form the main body of literature of the

Association. Mary Higgs was an extraordinary woman. Born in 1854, she was one of the first five Girton students and the first woman to be awarded the Natural Sciences *tripos*.[46] An expert on homelessness and self-styled 'viatrix' (female wayfarer), she was also a scientist, a teacher, a journalist, a noted biblical scholar and an advocate of the causes of temperance, pacifism, housing reform, the garden city movement and mother and child welfare. She was also a suffragist and a member of the Oldham Society for Women's Suffrage, and was active in the National Union of Women Workers[47] at a local, national and international level. There are no biographies of Mary Higgs, apart from a short memoir published privately by her daughter.[48] Famous in her lifetime as 'Mother Mary, friend of the down-and-outs',[49] she is almost totally forgotten today.

Fig. 4.3 Picture of Mary Higgs, reproduced by kind permission of Oldham Public Library

In 1879 she married Thomas Kilpin Higgs, a Congregationalist minister, and the couple had three children. In 1891 her husband moved to a ministry in Oldham and Mary joined the ladies' committee of the Oldham workhouse. It was here that her interest in women's homelessness began. 'When she visited the casual and maternity wards,' wrote her daughter, 'the dire need and danger of a destitute woman tramping the roads became startlingly clear.'[50] In response she set up a small home for destitute women and there, she said, she was able to study their lives first-hand. Her interest became a serious one and she began a systematic study of the Poor Law and its dealing with vagrancy, visited a number of remedial agencies, both in Britain and abroad, and interrogated a number of social experts. Finally, at the age of 50, she took the bold step of going out on the road herself in the guise of a female tramp in order to experience the life of a homeless woman at first hand. In the summer of 1903, together with an anonymous female friend, she undertook a five-day tour of towns in West Yorkshire, staying in common lodging houses, the casual wards of workhouses and charitable shelters. 'Exploration', she said, 'was the method of science,'[51] and she 'resolved to make a first-hand exploration, by that method of personal experiment, which is the nearest road to accurate knowledge, of the conditions under which destitute women were placed who sought the shelter of the common lodging house or the workhouse'.[52]

Despite her scientific approach to the question of homelessness, Mary Higgs wrote in the most emotive terms about the plight of homeless women and her account of her expedition gives a very vivid picture of their lives. Mary and her companion set off on their journey on a Monday with two shillings and sixpence in their pockets, suitably disguised:

> We dressed very shabbily, but were respectable and clean. We wore shawls and carried hats, which we used if desirable, according to whether we had sunshine or rain, or wished to look more or less respectable. We carried soap, a towel, a change of stockings, and a few other small articles, wrapped in an old shawl. My boots were in holes, and my companion wore a grey tweed well-worn suit. My hat was a certificate for any tramp ward, and my shawl was ragged though clean. We had one umbrella between us.[53]

Mary discovered, as she had expected, that lodging houses were dirty and overcrowded, with little division of the sexes, that casual wards operated too harsh and punitive a regime for most women to choose to stay in them and that charitable shelters, while better run, were too few and far between. Most important of all, provision for women was totally inadequate and that which did exist promoted immorality. What was needed, she urged, was a system of municipal lodging houses for women on a scale to match those provided for men. 'It is not enough to receive women into the workhouse,' she said. 'In every town there is needed some safe place for a working woman to sleep and some provision of employment to stand between a struggling woman and vice.'[54]

The story of her expedition was published by the Women Guardians and Local Government Association in a pamphlet entitled *Five Days and Nights as a Tramp among Tramps.* It had a wide circulation and Mary was gaining a reputation as an expert on vagrancy. In 1904 she was called as a witness, the only female witness, before the Departmental Committee on Vagrancy. Between 1903 and 1906 she undertook five further undercover investigations into provision for homeless women in the North and in London. She wrote about her expeditions in the press and in pamphlets, and in 1906 brought out a collection of her articles on homelessness entitled *Glimpses into the Abyss.*[55]

A number of themes emerge from Mary Higgs's writings: her analysis of the causes which forced women into homelessness, their pitiful plight once reduced to this way of life and the pressure upon them to resort to prostitution in order to survive. At the forefront of her argument was the point that homelessness was caused by structural factors: unemployment, poverty and housing scarcity. She also pointed out that the preponderance of single women in the population, added to by widowhood and desertion, left a large vulnerable group of women 'who would easily fall prey to wrong conditions'.[56] 'If a woman "cannot get work",' she asked, 'where is she to go? What is she to do?'[57] Importantly, she made the point that women's homelessness was often disguised by prostitution. 'The harlot is the female tramp,' she said, 'driven by hard social conditions to primitive freedom of sexual relationship.'[58] In her willingness to name prostitution rather than vaguely allude to it, Mary was more direct than the GFS. However, she too shared their concerns about the unprotected state of young single women and the dangers that existed for them in the cities. She referred more than once to the existence of an organised trade in young women, 'a spider's web' that enmeshed young friendless girls into prostitution.[59] She was also concerned by the plight of the older women she met in her travels: 'widows, separated wives, old age pension women', she commented, 'drift miserably from daughter to daughter, or lodging to lodging, unwanted, whereas all they want is a self-respecting place to live, other than the workhouse.'[60]

Fig. 4.4 Exterior of a common lodging house

She recognised that homelessness was the inevitable result of women's disadvantaged economic position and that the need could not be met by voluntary effort alone. Importantly, she talked in terms of rights, saying, 'the national recognition of the right of the individual to employment and subsistence seems to me to be the remedy for the harlot and the tramp.'[61] Her solution was the provision of municipal lodging houses for women on the same scale as they were provided for men. The 'way-out', she said (in a reference to William Booth's *In Darkest England and the Way-out*), 'is to provide in every town, under charge of the municipality, well-regulated, sanitary and sufficient accommodation. Especially for women, municipal lodging houses are a necessity.'[62]

Mary clearly had strong feminist views. She pointed out that women often constituted the majority of the population of a city and had 'a right to settle problems affecting their own sex'.[63] She also called upon more fortunate women to come forward and help their poorer sisters, saying, 'surely it belongs to womanhood to befriend womanhood'.[64] She talked of 'universal sisterhood',[65] but went further than the ladies of the GFS in showing real anger at male exploitation of women. 'Those intimately acquainted with the white slave traffic', she wrote, 'can bear witness to the fact that it does not proceed from the struggle of women for self support, so much as the struggle of men to make women support them.'[66]

In 1907 Mary was elected as a member of the British Institute for Social Service[67] and it was under the auspices of this organisation that she was to form the National Association for Women's Lodging-Homes. In 1909, at Mary's request, the Institute called together a conference to consider 'the urgency of the need for providing more and better accommodation for women than is afforded by common lodging houses and casual wards'.[68] Mary Higgs was among the speakers at the conference and its outcome was the formation of the National Association. The four objectives of the Association were declared to be: to link together all organisations and individuals interested in running hostels for women and girls; to collect and disseminate information on the existing accommodation; to promote legislation for the better running of common lodging houses; and to encourage local committees to affiliate with the parent Association.[69]

None of the lack of confidence shown by the ladies of the GFS in the 1870s, seems to have been present in this organisation. It quickly constituted itself with a General Council and Northern and Southern Committees and Mary Higgs became Secretary of the Northern Committee. In 1910 the Duchess of Marlborough was elected as President. Twenty-two organisations were represented on the Council, including the National Union of Women Workers, the Salvation Army, the Church Army, the Women's Industrial Council, the YWCA and the Society of Friends. The Association was predominantly, but not exclusively, a female organisation, and of the 40 people who made up its first Council, 12 were men, mostly clergymen.

One of the first acts of the Association was to set out its case in a full-length book, *Where Shall She Live? The Homelessness of the Woman Worker,* published in 1910.[70] The first half of the book was written by Edward Hayward, the honorary organising secretary of the Association, and provided a systematic analysis of the major female occupations and the types of housing associated with them, showing how low wages and the living-in system left women vulnerable to homelessness. The second half was written by Mary and dealt with the consequences of women's precarious economic situation, particularly their vulnerability to prostitution. The following year the Association began its lobbying activities and in February 1911 sent a deputation to the Housing Committee of London County Council drawing attention to the pressing need for lodging house accommodation for women in London. They were met with 'a cordial reception' and the Housing Committee subsequently appointed a sub-committee 'to enquire into the whole question of the provision by the municipality of suitable accommodation for women'.[71] This seemed promising, but in the event the LCC never went further than this and no women's hostels were opened by them.

The Corporation of London was sympathetic to their aims and in May 1911 a National Association conference was held in the Guildhall under the joint presidency of the Duchess of Marlborough and the Lord Mayor of London. Some 500 delegates attended the conference from all over the country and over 58 organisations were represented, including the GFS. Twelve papers were read at the conference and three resolutions passed. These called for municipal authorities to tighten up their inspection of common lodging houses and for women's lodging houses to be inspected by women; for respectable, cheap women's lodging houses to be provided by municipal authorities, philanthropic societies and private building enterprise; and for the National Association to draw up schemes which the LCC and the Corporation of the City of London might put into effect.[72] A great deal of anger was expressed at the conference that while men were well catered for by the municipalities women were not. A delegate from Liverpool spoke of the ample lodging-house provision that existed for men in the city and how three women's deputations to the city council asking for a lodging house for women had been turned down on grounds of cost. 'Perhaps,' she said, 'when we get a few more City Mothers in the Council something worthy of the city may be done to help in the uplifting of the homeless and the inarticulate section of the womanhood in the busy cities!'[73]

The conference was a major event and the spread of organisations represented shows the degree of interest which was being taken in the question of women's housing. The whole question of housing and homelessness was high on the national agenda. From the 1880s, when economic depression had made homelessness more than usually visible on the streets of London, the Salvation Army and Church Army had been active in pioneering new methods of rehabilitating the homeless and destitute; in 1898 the Women's National Housing Council had been founded; in 1906 the Departmental Committee on Vagrancy had reported; and the Royal Commission on the Poor Laws, which reported in 1909, had spent much of its time discussing the problems of destitution and vagrancy and the inefficacy of the existing system to deal with them.

Following the 1911 conference, the National Association concentrated on collecting information for a national directory of women's hostels and on lobbying and campaigning activities. In 1912 Mary Higgs produced a pamphlet, *How to start a women's lodging house*,[74] which laid down guidelines on how to lobby local authorities to make provision for women. At the time the National Association was formed in 1909, only Glasgow had a municipal lodging house for women. Built in 1878, it had 248 beds at threepence and fourpence a night. According to Mary Higgs it was well run and well used, and she cited it as an example of how a lodging house for women could be successfully run without making a financial loss. In 1910, Manchester opened the second municipal lodging house for women, Ashton House, with 220 beds. This was named in honour of Margaret Ashton, the Manchester councillor who was the main force behind it and also a member of the National Association.

The Association was primarily a campaigning and coordinating body, but a number of hostels were opened under its auspices. In 1913 the Association opened Mary Curzon House in central London, described as a model lodging house.[75] This had accommodation for 54 residents and was funded by the Duchess of Marlborough. New hostels were also started at Tunbridge Wells and Brighton, following joint meetings held by the National Association and local branches of the National Union of Women Workers.[76] It was much more successful in the voluntary sector than the statutory one, and indeed made little headway in persuading local authorities to open hostels for women. In 1913 it was reported that 'after repeated efforts on the part of the National Association, the Bristol Municipality had resolved to equip a Women's Municipal Lodging House', but that Sheffield, Hull and Liverpool have not yet yielded to the desires of repeated deputations.[77] The reluctance of local authorities to provide lodging houses for women appeared to be based on fears that they would be under-used and hence financially unviable, and also that they might attract prostitutes. Much of the Association's literature was aimed at refuting these fears, giving examples of how lodging houses could be run efficiently and well, but despite sympathetic responses from some municipalities, few were prepared to take the risk.

Where the Association was more successful was in coordinating the efforts of the many individual groups working in the field of women's housing and in disseminating information. It encouraged existing women's lodges to affiliate to it and by 1915 it had built up a network of 46 affiliated lodges, including some run by the Girls' Friendly Society. Its annual reports contained brief reports from all these hostels and news on developments in the field. In 1913 it published its directory, which covered the whole of the United Kingdom and listed 420 lodges and hostels for women.[78] Hostels were classified according to the type of woman for whom they were intended, and information was given on the size of the hostel, charges, opening hours and age limits. This was a major piece of work and provides a comprehensive picture of the extent of women's voluntary efforts in housing in the pre-war period.

An effective national organisation had been put in place in a comparatively short period of time, and if war had not broken out in 1914, the Association might well have succeeded in its aims of having the housing needs of women recognised at a statutory level. War meant that women's hostels were put to different uses, and many were taken over by the government as hostels for munitions workers. Mary Higgs's daughter wrote that as the hostels passed into public management, 'her work as secretary was finished and she concentrated on local needs'.[79] The last report of the Association appeared in 1915.

The outbreak of war marked the end of a concerted period of attention on women's housing, and the demands of the war economy ensured that women were employed and provided with housing. Afterwards their needs were again relegated to second place, behind those of returning servicemen. Mrs Cecil Chesterton, who worked with Mary Higgs in the National Association, repeated her experiment of posing as a homeless woman in London in the 1920s and her experiences and findings were very similar to those of Mary Higgs 20 years before.[80] After the war Mary Higgs turned again to the issue of homelessness, but from now on she concentrated primarily on the needs of boys and young men rather than women, taking a special interest in the Borstal movement. She gave evidence before two more departmental committees, on Casual Ward Reform in 1924 and on the Relief of the Casual Poor in 1929–30. In 1937 she was awarded the OBE in recognition of her work for Oldham. She died the same year at the age of 83 and her death was reported in the national press. The *Manchester Guardian* headlined its article: 'Mrs Mary Higgs – Death of a Great Social Reformer'.[81]

In its six years of existence the National Association succeeded in holding a major national conference, drawing together an extensive and diverse network of interested societies and individuals, and in publishing a book, several pamphlets and a comprehensive national directory of women's housing provision. It was also instrumental in opening a number of women's hostels, and if war had not intervened, may have succeeded in persuading more municipalities to open lodging houses for women. What is most significant about the National Association is that it went further than other organisations in focusing on the housing needs of single women and that it succeeded in placing the issue on the national agenda. Significantly, it was also a campaigning body, and here it went further than previous women's welfare societies in acting in an overtly political way – women were lobbying here and making demands. Possibly this reflects a growing mood of militancy among women and there is evidence of real anger, rather than sorrow, at the exploitation of women.

The national association also aimed its efforts at all women in need rather than differentiating between the deserving and undeserving poor. This is a considerable change in the way that women's housing needs were viewed, and must in part reflect the shift in thinking from the moral to the economic causes of poverty. It also coincided with an important moment in the women's movement when the high-profile activities of the suffragette movement placed the question of women's rights high on the agenda.

Conclusions

The GFS and the National Association were two very different organisations and meaningful comparison between them is difficult. The GFS dwarfed the National Association in terms of size; it was a membership organisation and, importantly, a religious organisation set within the structure of the Anglican Church and insisting upon a virtuous character among its members. Housing, while an important element of its work, was only a part of it. The National Association was a much smaller organisation; it was a campaigning body; it was secular; and housing for women was its priority. Importantly, it worked for all women in need, including those who would have been considered to be leading abandoned lives. The ladies of the GFS attempted no structural understanding of the social and economic position of the women for whom they worked, while at the core of the Association's case were the facts and figures of homelessness and its connections with unemployment and poverty.

However, there were also strong parallels between the work of these two groups. While the National Association, with its campaigning orientation and emphasis on women's rights, at first glance seems very different from the more conservative GFS, underlying both organisations was the same concern with women's sexual vulnerability and their need for protection. Vocabulary, rhetoric and ideology may have differed between the two, but for both there was a conflation of women's housing needs with their sexuality. Concern about women's homelessness was inextricably connected with anxiety about prostitution, with the result that there was no concession that single women should be able to live independently. Indeed, the campaign of the National Association and the provision of the

GFS were both largely aimed at keeping young women out of independent lodgings and under supervision.

Both groups were concerned with the moral supervision of the women with whom they worked and they both involved middle and upper-class women working for the benefit of working-class women. This was typical of other voluntary and charitable groups of the time and raises questions about the tensions between social welfare and social control and the complex relationship between class and gender. Undoubtedly, elements of social control were there. However, genuine concern for women's welfare seems to have been the major motivating factor. The ladies of the GFS were concerned with the loneliness and vulnerability of young women far from home; Mary Higgs demonstrated the extent of her commitment to the outcasts of society by undertaking personal journeys into the abyss. These women were not working to provide housing for themselves, and altruism was there in great measure. We do not have the perspective of the working-class women who were the objects of their activities, of course, but one can only suppose that to have a roof over their head and an interest taken in them must have been preferable to being on the streets. Safe and affordable lodging-house accommodation made life in the city much more tenable for women.

Both the GFS and the National Association were clearly women's movements, but what do they exemplify in terms of *the* women's movement? The National Association was an overtly feminist organisation that asserted women's rights in housing, protested at their differential treatment and acted politically. The GFS came from a very different tradition of women's organisation: it did not perceive itself as feminist and it embraced values which in many ways seem antithetical to women's emancipation. Yet it talked of sisterhood and was conscious of itself as a women's movement, and its claim to be the largest women's organisation of Victorian and Edwardian Britain must make it significant in women's history. The work the GFS did for women, its pride in being an all-female society and its enormous success can all be seen as very concrete contributions to raising the profile and status of women. As Brian Harrison points out: 'women's emancipation should not be seen solely in terms of feminist history: the GFS's contribution lay rather in expanding women's self-respect, and in pioneering new opportunities for careers and usefulness.'[82]

It is not only aims that constitute a feminist approach. Process is perhaps as important a measure, and identification with women and particular ways of working together also marked the women's movement of the time. As a number of writers have commented, women's societies and groupings provided a supportive environment in which women could develop their skills and confidence.[83] The associates of the GFS were for the most part ladies who came from the tradition of benevolent parish work, but participation in such a large society enabled those who chose it to exercise impressive skills of organisation and management. Involvement in the National Association entailed women campaigning, lobbying, challenging local authorities and very much acting upon the public stage. The women of both groups achieved their own agency through their work and this was a crucial part of the movement from the private to the public for women.

Finally, it is salutary to reflect upon both the scale of the work in which these women were involved and their comparative absence from the historical record. The GFS provided a national and international network of accommodation for single women, the national association did pioneering work in exposing the problem of women's homelessness – and they were just a part of a huge movement of women's voluntary organisations. The extent of women's activities in housing was truly impressive and yet this part of women's history has largely been forgotten. Certain sorts of histories are prioritised over others and women's work in housing and welfare does not generally capture interest, but the lives of Mary Townsend and Mary Higgs and the organisations they led deserve celebration.

Acknowledgements

I wish to thank the staff at the Girls' Friendly Society and Oldham Public Library for kindly giving me acces to their archives and allowing me to reproduce illustrations and also to acknowledge the Bodleian Library, University of Oxford for allowing me to reproduce illustrations from their collection, Soc.24725 d.58, 0.281, Per 24785 e 35 (1884/1917, p.35

Endnotes

1. See: Hendessi, Mandana, *4 in 10: Report on young women who become homeless as a result of sexual abuse,* CHAR, 1992, p 1.

2. Stead, William, *The Maiden Tribute to Modern Babylon,* reprinted from the *Pall Mall Gazette,* 1885, p 2.

3. Quoted in Walkowitz, Judith, *Prostitution and Victorian Society: Women, Class and the State,* Cambridge University Press, 1980, p 32.

4. Mrs Pankhurst in *Suffragette,* 13 June 1913, quoted in Rosen, Andrew, *Rise up Women: the Militant Campaign of the Women's Social and Political Union,* Routledge & Kegan Paul, 1974, p 208.

5. In 1911, for example, these three trades employed 57 per cent of all occupied females over 10 years of age; *Census of England and Wales, 1911,* PP1913, Cd7018, lxxviii, 321, p 159.

6. See Butler, Josephine (ed), *Women's work and women's culture,* Macmillan & Co, 1869, and Zimmern, Dorothy M, 'The wages of women in industry', National conference on the prevention of destitution, PS King & Sons, 1912.

7. The 1861 Census recorded 63,042 female occupants of the workhouse in England and Wales; *Census of England and Wales, 1861,* PP 1863, 3221, LIII Part 1, 265, p 66. By 1911 this had risen to 103,544 females; *Census of England and Wales, 1911,* PP 1914-16, CD 7929 lxxxl, 385, p 72.

8. See the *Report of the Departmental Committee on Vagrancy,* 1906, CD 2852, ciii, I.

9. The percentage of commercial and business clerks who were female, for example, rose from 0.5 per cent in 1861 to 24 per cent in 1911; *Census of England and Wales, 1911*, PP1914-16, Cd 8491, xxxv, 483, p 16.

10. Sellars, Edith, 'Women's Work for the Welfare of Girls', in Baroness Burdett-Coutts (ed), *Women's Mission: a series of congress papers on the philanthropic work of women by eminent writers*, Sampson Low, Marston & Co, 1893, p 278.

11. The Ladies Associations had been set up in the 1880s following the national tour made by Ellice Hopkins, the famous social purity worker, and by the 1890s there were 120 such Associations; Sellars, op cit, p 42.

12. It is a male historian, Brian Harrison, who has written one of the few articles on the Girls' Friendly Society, setting it in the context of both the Anglican and Conservative revival of late Victorian Britain; 'For Church, Queen and Family', in *Past and Present*, no 61, November 1963, pp 107–38. Work is being done on the GFS archive at the Women's Library under the auspices of the Vera Douie Fellowship in order to develop a website considering the idea of 'protection' in women and girls' welfare.

13. See Money, Agnes, *The History of the Girls' Friendly Society*, 1897 (revised in 1905 and 1913) and Heath-Stubbs, Mary, *Friendship's Highway: being the story of the Girls' Friendly Society, 1875–1925*, GFS, 1926.

14. Townsend, M.E., *Memories of a life*, n.d.; Townsend, Frederick and Mary, *Sketches and Impressions*, 1901; Mrs Townsend, *Some friends of the past*, 1913; Townsend, Kathleen M., *Some memories of Mrs Townsend*, 1923.

15. Townsend, M.E., *An appeal to the mistresses of elementary schools from the Girls' Friendly Society*, Hatchards, 1882, p 7.

16. Townsend, M.E., in *Addresses delivered on the aims and objectives of the Girls' Friendly Society*, Hatchards, 1884.

17. Money, *History of the Girls' Friendly Society*, 1905, pp 15–16.

18. Harrison, op cit, p 122.

19. Townsend, M.E., in *Addresses delivered on the aims and objectives of the Girls' Friendly Society*, Hatchards, 1884.

20. Harrison, op cit, p 109.

21. ibid.

22. ibid, pp 111–12.

23. Money, op cit, p 57.

24. Prochaska, Frank, *Women and Philanthropy in 19th century England*, Oxford University Press, 1980.

25. Harrison, op cit, p 120.

26. Two of the leading members of the central council of the GFS, Lady Knightley of Fawsley and Lady Selborne, daughter of Lord Salisbury, were supporters of women's suffrage and together set up the Conservative and Unionist Women's Franchise League.

27. Harrison, op cit, p 121.

28. *The Girls' Friendly Society*, pamphlet reprinted from *The Monthly Packet*, 1877, p 3.

29. Harrison, op cit, p 117.

30. ibid, p 120.

31. ibid.

32. See Heath-Stubbs, op cit, chapter VI.

33. The Department for Domestic Economy and Industrial Training was established in 1881 and issued a series of career guides for young women entitled *Work, and how to do it,* that covered 'national and

private teaching, sick nursing, needlework, cooking, housework, nursing children, work in shops and factories, dress-making, telegraphy, clerks' work and art work etc'; Mercier, Anne, untitled pamphlet, Hatchards, 1885, p 2.

34. Townsend, M.E., *An Appeal to the School Mistresses of Elementary Schools*, Hatchards, 1882, p 6.

35. GFS pamphlet, *The Need for the Girls' Friendly Society*, n.d., p 5.

36. See Walkowitz, op cit.

37. See, for example, Blocklehurst, Revd Theodore, 'The Economics of Hell', reprinted from *the Spectator*, 24 December 1912, in *The White Slave Traffic*, n.d., and Mrs Mackirdy and M.N. Wallis, *The White Slave Market*, 1912.

38. Heath-Stubbs, op cit, p 43.

39. Townsend, M.E., untitled, undated pamphlet (GFS Archive, 4/12).

40. Figures derived from Heath-Stubbs, op cit, and from Minutes of the GFS Lodgings Committees.

41. *Minutes of the Committee concerning the proposed amalgamation of Lodges and Homes of Rest into one Department*, 3 December 1907 (GFS Archive 1/37).

42. *The Revised Handbook of Lodging Homes for Women and Girls*, National Association of Lodging Houses for Women, 1913.

43. Information derived from annual reports of the Oxford branch of the Girls' Friendly Society, 1891–1908.

44. *GFS Platform, Annual Report, 2005*.

45. The work of the National Association for Women's Lodging Homes is briefly discussed in Watson, S., and H. Austerberry, *Housing and Homelessness: a feminist perspective*, Routledge & Kegan Paul, 1986,

and an extract from Mary Higgs's essay 'Three nights in women's lodging houses' is included in Peter Keating's collection of writings about the life of the poor, *Into Unknown England 1866-1913: Selections from the social explorers*, Fontana, 1976.

46. Girton College Register describes Mary Higgs as 'a mystic, social reformer, poet, authoress, lecturer and preacher' (GCR 1869–1946).

47. The National Union of Women Workers was started in 1895 by Miss Emily Janes to bring together local unions of women workers active in social affairs. It was inspired by the work of Ellice Hopkins with 'friendless girls' but covered a much wider field of social work and reform. In 1918 it became the National Council of Women.

48. Higgs, Mary, *The life of Mary Higgs of Oldham*, a memoir written by her daughter, printed for private circulation by Clare, Son & Co Ltd, n.d.

49. See obituaries of Mary Higgs in the *Daily Despatch* and *Daily Herald*, 20 March 1937.

50. Higgs, *The life of Mary Higgs of Oldham*, p 11.

51. Higgs, Mary, *Glimpses into the Abyss*, P S King & Sons, 1906, Preface, p vii.

52. Higgs, Mary, 'Five days and five nights as a tramp among tramps', in *Glimpses into the Abyss*, p 87.

53. ibid, p 88.

54. ibid, Appendix VIII, 'Common Lodging-houses versus Shelters', p 326.

55. Higgs, Mary 'Common Lodging-House Life' in Glimpses into the Abyss, P.S. King and Sons, 1906.

56. Mary, Higgs, 'Common Lodging-House Life', in *Glimpses into the Abyss*, p 248.

57. Higgs, Mary, 'Three nights in women's lodging houses', in *Glimpses into the Abyss*, p 211.

58. ibid, p 214.

59. ibid, p 211.

60. Higgs, Mary, and Hayward, Edward, *Where shall she live? The homelessness of the woman worker*, P S King & Sons, 1910, pp 128–9.

61. Higgs, *Glimpses into the Abyss,* op. cit., p.214.

62. ibid, p 326.

63. Higgs and Hayward, op cit, p 155.

64. Higgs, *Glimpses into the Abyss*, op cit, p 323.

65. ibid, p 322.

66. Higgs and Hayward, op cit, p 118.

67. The British Institute for Social Service was set up in 1904 as an umbrella body to coordinate organizations working in the field of social reform and social work. It published a monthly journal called *Progress* to which Mary Higgs contributed a number of articles.

68. *British Institute for Social Service, Annual Report*, 1909, p 9.

69. Ibid.

70. Higgs and Hayward, op cit.

71. *Report on the Proceedings of the National Conference on Lodging House Accommodation for women*, 17 May 1911, p 4.

72. ibid, pp 5–6.

73. ibid, p 35.

74. Higgs, Mary, *How to start a women's lodging house*, National Association of Lodging Homes for Women, P S King & Sons Ltd, London, 1912.

75. *British Institute for Social Service Annual Report, 1913*, p 5.

76. *National Association of Lodging Homes for Women, Report for the Year 1913*, p 5.

77. *National Association of Lodging Homes for Women, Report for the Year 1913*, p 12.

78. *Handbook of lodging homes for women and girls*, National Association of Lodging Homes for Women, 1913.

79. Higgs, *Mary Higgs of Oldham*, p 26.

80. Chesterton, Mrs Cecil, *In Darkest London*, Stanley Paul & Co, 1926.

81. *Manchester Guardian*, 20 March 1937.

82. Harrison, op cit, p 120.

83 See, for example, Andrews, Maggie, *The Acceptable Face of Feminism: the Women's Institute as a Social Movement*, Lawrence & Wishart, 1997; Kelly, Joan, 'The doubled vision of feminist theory', in Newton, J., Ryan, M., and J. Walkowitz (eds), *Sex and Class in Women's History*, Routledge & Kegan Paul, 1983, p 262.

Section Two: Women in the Professions

The chapters in this section share a surprising number of commonalities as well as perhaps less surprising contrasts. Both reflect on the lives of women who may be seen as pioneers in establishing their respective professions and, in doing so, faced a succession of struggles both in the private and public spheres. In the more public aspects of their lives, these struggles encompassed financial worries that threatened their careers, the problems of establishing their professional status and credentials in forging their place in their sphere of work. In addition the pressures of overwork familiar to subsequent generations of women who have appeared to be attempting 'superwoman' status in order to prove themselves as professionals, was a heavy burden. Both groups of women had to learn to cope with the loneliness of working with a considerable degree of autonomy and responsibility, needing to establish and maintain professional standards of practice and to face challenges to their judgement in a male-dominated professional arena. It was inevitable, then, that these stresses and strains should permeate into their private lives, particularly as both groups of women lived within the communities in which they worked. The pressures of their workload and type of work occasionally compromised their health as well as quite considerably impinging on their social lives – unlike the philanthropists, to the professional women marriage represented the end of their careers. And they were in the main 'wedded to the job', making marriage in the future even more unlikely. Furthermore, as well as having demanding roles, this first generation of professionals incorporated within their job descriptions a sum of jobs which would nowadays be allotted to several individuals; the Principals, for example, acted also more-or-less as Estates Bursar, Finance Bursar, Development Director and Housekeeper, whilst the nurses were sometimes a combination of nurse, midwife, school nurse, health visitor and assistant to the GP for minor-surgical cases.

Nevertheless there are stark contrasts between the women principals of Oxford colleges and district nurses working 'in the field' in industrial Lancashire. Not least of these must be their respective family, social and educational backgrounds. For example, where *one* inspirational role model for the university principals would have been educated male family members from the upper classes, the nature of the (largely 'domestic') caring and nurturing role carried out by district nurses, implies that their sole influences would have been other women, whilst backgrounds varied but they were largely drawn from the middle to lower classes. This set the latter at a distinct disadvantage when faced with the demands of a male-dominated medical profession and a lay employing committee of 'Ladies'.

Methodologically, chapter five takes a small-scale case study of local history to illustrate and examine some of the fundamental hurdles faced by the district nurse during the first half of the twentieth century, asking how and why their professional status changed. Chapter six, also a local study, explores the inconsistencies and pressures of Oxford women principals from the last quarter of the nineteenth century through the first quarter of the twentieth.

CHAPTER 5

Festina Lente: Oxford Women Principals 1879-1925

Anne Keene

When the first Oxford women's colleges were founded, London University, where the status of female higher education was already fairly advanced, was on the verge of admitting its first women graduates.[1] Women at Oxford, although students at the university from 1879 onwards, were not granted degrees until 1920, and their peers at Cambridge had to wait until 1948 to become full graduates. There were therefore considerable differences between English universities in the timeline of women's higher education.

Key to the success of women's colleges in Oxford were their principals, and a number of difficulties consistently dogged these women in the late nineteenth and early twentieth century. These were problems commonly faced by other professional women of the period and affected the Oxford principals to varying degrees. The challenges which these women had to face became subtle pressures, gradually wearing down the strength of those they affected, and many of these problems appear to have been contributory factors in precipitating the leaves of absence and illnesses which characterized the tenures of nine out of 14 of the Oxford principals between 1879 and 1925.[2]

Madeleine Shaw Lefevre (1879–1888) wrote to Somerville Council in February 1885, expressing her wish to retire as soon as a successor could be appointed. She was in fact persuaded to withdraw her resignation and accepted, instead, a substantial leave of absence between June 1885 and Easter 1886.[3] One reason for her wishing to resign at this point appears to have been a desire to be with her sisters, prompted by the death of her mother the previous year,[4] although comments which she made when newly appointed to the post of principal may provide a clue to additional factors involved. She wrote that the job at Somerville would be 'a useful work though full of small cares and difficulties and I hate the idea of living alone – I mean without any of my own people and with no-one to consult.'[5]

Miss Lefevre was initially appointed for one year only and, as she wrote in the same letter, 'on my own terms, namely – to reside during the terms and to be free to go home during the vacations,'[6] which would seem to indicate a measure of ambivalence on her part right from the start. Only a year after her appointment there is an unexplained reference in the Somerville Council Minutes to 'Miss Shaw Lefevre's unavoidable absence for the first fortnight of term,'[7] a period which appears not to have been clearly defined, as it was suggested at the next meeting of Council that she should return 'if possible' by 8 November.[8]

Miss Lefevre's successor, Agnes Maitland (1889–1906), died while still in office. In her last months she appears to have suffered from a serious illness and, although the illness is not anywhere named, it may well have been cancer, as it seems to have overtaken her quite swiftly and to have been extremely painful.[9] This was not her only significant illness, as, 10 years previously, it had been recorded in the Somerville Council Minutes of March 1896 that the principal was 'in need of rest and change' and, in the opinion of Council, 'it is not necessary that she should reside during the whole of the ensuing Summer Term.'[10] Moreover, Miss Maitland, 'on account of illness', was granted leave during the Michaelmas term of 1897, when Miss Lefevre was appointed acting principal. The need for rest and change in this case would indicate that the illness referred to was different from the fatal illness from which Miss Maitland suffered in 1905–6, 'change' suggesting particularly that the principal needed relief from the cares of her post.

Emily Penrose (1907–26) eventually retired from office in 1926 on the advice of her doctors, clearly suffering from overwork, as testified to by the comments of some of her friends at the time of her resignation. Ethel Hurlbatt, principal of Royal Victoria College for Women, Montreal, wrote to her, 'No-one at your age should lead the driven life',[11] and Grace Hadow, fellow of the college, commented that 'we could not be selfish enough to keep you in defiance of doctor's orders'.[12] In an article in the *Oxford Magazine* following the announcement of Miss Penrose's resignation, the comment was made: 'It can occasion no wonder . . . that her wholehearted devotion of time and strength to the college over which she has presided with such distinction . . . has left its mark upon her health.'[13]

Henrietta Jex-Blake (1909–21), exhausted at the end of her time at Lady Margaret Hall, was, according to her obituary, greatly weighed down by the war years,[14] and the worry of the influenza epidemic of 1918 also took its toll on the principal. 'Her health had suffered, and she felt it keenly that she was not able always to commend to the Council the course of action of whose rightness she was convinced . . . In 1921 she tendered her resignation.'[15] Christine Burrows (St Hilda's, 1910–19; Oxford Home Students, 1921–8) had three leaves of absence during her total of 35 years of work at the women's colleges, firstly in 1902 while vice-principal of St Hilda's College, again in 1910, immediately before taking up office as principal of the college, and thirdly in 1927, while she was principal of the Oxford Home Students. In addition, in 1924 she expressed her wish to resign, four years before she eventually ceased to be principal, but was dissuaded from this course of action by Bertha Johnson, former principal of the Society of Home Students.

In 1901–2, Lilian Counsell was appointed temporarily as vice-principal of St Hilda's on account of Miss Burrows's illness. No details exist as to the nature of this illness, but it must have been lengthy, as it was not until Trinity term of 1903 that she returned from America, welcomed by a firework display at the college. One comment[16] suggests that she had returned from a period of recuperation: 'We are glad to hear that she has had an enjoyable time, and that she feels the benefit of her change.'[17] At the time of being appointed to the principalship of St Hilda's in 1910, Miss Burrows was in Vermont, convalescing from illness and overwork.[18] She therefore began her term of office in a rather unpropitious fashion. Letters which she wrote during her period abroad in 1910 suggest that her illness was of nervous origin as, on commenting that she was sleeping better, Christine added, 'there is a doctor who gives electricity, but I don't want to get over-stimulated.' One week later she referred to her 'ebb times' and to the 'nerve-strain', which all around her said took two to three years to 'get over'.[19] Miss Burrows stayed away from Oxford longer than she had planned, returning just in time for the beginning of Michaelmas term 1910 to take up her new appointment. However, during her work as principal of St Hilda's, she seems to have enjoyed good health, resigning in order to look after her mother and not for any health reasons of her own.

Christine Burrows accepted the post of principal of the Society of Home Students in February 1921, intriguingly 'with reservation of right to resign'.[20] It is clear from a letter written by Bertha Johnson to Ruth Butler, vice-principal of the Society, in 1924 that, three years later, Christine Burrows wished to avail herself of that right. Mrs Johnson comments that Miss Burrows 'does find the work very incessant'[21] and for various other reasons had expressed her desire to resign at the end of her five-year appointment. It seems that Mrs Johnson, together with Ruth Butler and Annie Rogers, managed to persuade Miss Burrows to change her mind by advising her on means of lessening her workload and by attempting to alleviate her financial worries for the college.

Nevertheless, just over two years later Christine Burrows was again ill and spent part of the Michaelmas term of 1927 in a nursing home in West Ilsey. When she handed in her resignation, in February 1928, she wrote to Ruth Butler that:

> while my strength is perhaps enough for ordinary life and a little over, it is growingly not enough for even the measure of alertness, ability and readiness for all things I should like to bring to this . . . I can serve the Society best by leaving it before great harm is done . . . A monitor within (not only on physical grounds) bids me stop.[22]

Eleanor Jourdain (1915–24) died in office in the throes of the now famous St Hugh's Row.[23] It is of course merely conjecture whether the strain of the turmoil between some of the college tutors and herself actually contributed to her early demise, but it is a theory worth considering and one which has been hinted at:

> there is good reason to suppose that the Treasurer's communication was the occasion of the heart attack from which she died on 6 April 1924.[24]

Miss Winifred Moberly (St Hilda's College, 1919–28) was another principal who suffered from failing health. By Hilary term 1924, Julia de Lacy Mann, who in fact became the next head of college, was standing in for Miss Moberly, who was ill and away from St Hilda's. The principal was away again in Hilary and Trinity terms 1925. As the college history records:

> Over the next three years Miss Mann was often replacing the Principal until, in March 1928, the Council accepted that Miss Moberly would never again be physically or mentally fit. Miss Moberly's appointment was terminated on March 31st and she died, less than a week later, on April 6th.[25]

It is noteworthy, too, that Barbara Gwyer, appointed in 1924 as Principal of St Hugh's, was, according to *The Fritillary* of Hilary Term 1926, 'obliged by illness to be away the greater part of the term'.[26]

Illness among nineteenth-century women educationists was not an exclusively Oxford phenomenon. Emily Davies, founder of Girton College, Cambridge, and its fourth mistress (1872–5), suffered what appeared to have been a nervous breakdown in 1876 and withdrew from her many activities for several months. Constance Maynard, founding mistress of Westfield College in London, was the victim of overwork, as telling phrases from her biography reveal that 'the strain of overwork and anxiety told upon Constance', and reference is made later in the book to her stable family background which helped her 'to weather the stresses of work at Westfield'.[27] The comment has been made elsewhere that, in addition to administrative and teaching duties, many early headmistresses had to deal with domestic problems, ranging from leaking roofs and faulty drains to epidemics. Playing several professional roles simultaneously, they therefore overtaxed their health and had to resign or take sick leave.[28]

As so many of the principals of women's colleges at Oxford appear to have suffered from illness, stress or a reluctance to continue in the job, it is worth examining the problems and pressures encountered by these leaders.

Opposition to the higher education of women

A major problem, and one encountered by all women wishing to undertake university-level studies in the 1870s, was that of opposition to the actual concept of women being equipped, either physically or mentally, to cope with the demands of academic work. This opposition was, on the one hand, given substance by the widely publicized arguments of Edward Clarke, Henry Maudsley and John Thorburn,[29] and, on the other hand, was experienced by Oxford women students and their mentors through the attitudes and reactions of those with whom they came into contact. In 1874, Maudsley wrote:

> Before sanctioning the proposal to subject women to a system of mental training which has been framed and adapted for men . . . it is needful to consider whether this can be done without serious injury to her health and strength . . . It will have to be considered whether women can scorn delights, and live laborious days of intellectual exercise and production, without injury to their functions as the conceivers, mothers, and nurses of children.[30]

These views had therefore been thoroughly aired by the time women's colleges emerged in Oxford in 1879.[31] Indeed, Emily Davies, nurturing her recent foundation of Girton College (1869), was greatly dismayed by the article, writing to her friend Barbara Bodichon in April 1874, 'Why could he not have waited until Girton was on its feet? . . . Girton is ruined,'[32] and promptly composing, with Dr Elizabeth Garrett Anderson, a spirited and well-argued reply, which was published in the *Fortnightly Review* the following month.[33]

The early principals in Oxford must surely have been aware of the impact of Maudsley's views. Here was an insidious but persistent problem with which these women had to contend right from the outset. Lord Aberdare, speaking at a meeting of friends and supporters of Somerville Hall in Trinity Term 1881, indicated, in the presence of Madeleine Shaw Lefevre, that this issue was one which could not be ignored but which would eventually be overcome:

> when fathers and mothers all over the country saw young ladies returning home from these institutions greatly improved in their knowledge, and without having lost their freshness of character or anything they wished them to retain, then . . . would they be able to control and vanquish the amount of prejudice which undoubtedly still existed on this subject.[34]

The case against women students as argued on medical grounds often gave rise to, or backed up, 'gut-feeling' opposition which was not always voiced but which was nevertheless tangible. This came sometimes from parents, from male members of the university, from other women who were unsympathetic to the cause of women's higher education[35] and from local residents, as testified by a comment in a letter written to Christine Burrows in 1911, shortly after she had sent down a student who had ignored the chaperonage rules: 'It only shows us more clearly than ever that we wish there were no women students in Oxford.'[36]

The querying of the right of women actually to be students was therefore a fundamental challenge to the early principals and a potential obstacle to the acquisition of new students. Viewed through the arguments described above, the principals may be perceived as leaders of a revolutionary group of women, and leaders who stood, as it were, in the first line of defence, and needed to be resolutely sure of their commitment to women's higher education.

Attacks on the ability of women to undertake mental work of a strenuous nature were also potential attacks on the principals themselves. What were to be the effects on their female physiques of the challenging posts which they were undertaking? The principals must surely have recognized that, in addition to their students, they themselves were also guinea pigs who could prove or disprove the theories which were rife.[37]

Professional tension

Friction, at several levels, was ever a potential source of difficulty for the principals. They were constantly striving to maintain relationships between themselves and a number of factions, namely with their sister principals, women tutors, college councils, the AEW, Oxford University and the students.[38] Tension inevitably arose in some of these spheres and there was an unspoken onus on women principals to act as pivotal peacemakers and even as go-betweens in the interests of progress for women.

A series of interpersonal problems emerged during the first few decades of women's colleges. Although the pattern of relationships between the principals themselves appears generally to have been one of cooperation, there was a noticeable coolness between Bertha Johnson and Agnes Maitland in 1891 in the course of a power struggle between the AEW and the women's halls.[39] The problem which led to these events was the desire of some women tutors, mainly at Somerville College, to liaise directly with students without involving the AEW in tuition arrangements. This move was supported by Agnes Maitland, who was very ambitious for the development of Somerville and for the development of a tutorial system within the college. Mrs Johnson, as secretary of the AEW, did not recognize that there was a problem with the current system, believing that a centralized structure for the organization of students' work had been, and always would be, the best way forward. That Bertha Johnson was angry with the principal of Somerville can be in no doubt in the light of the apologetic letter written from Miss Maitland to Mrs Johnson in October 1891.[40] Acrimony was not limited to these two women. A series of letters in St Anne's archive written between February 1891 and January 1893 indicate the strong feelings of members both of the AEW and of the other women's colleges.[41] The politics at work were on the verge of becoming antagonistic at times. A member of the AEW commented in 1892: 'Very likely Somerville Hall does not want to secede; but what it does want is to use L.M.H. to force the hand of the Association in its own direction, to get its own way and this we ought not to allow.'[42] Charlotte Green, member of Somerville College Council, bemoaning the 'bad manners' of her Somerville colleagues after an AEW meeting of 1893, wrote to Bertha Johnson: 'Differences of opinion we may all have – but we need not show claws and teeth.'[43] [There was a danger of Agnes Maitland being marginalized, Annie Moberly and Elizabeth Wordsworth, while wishing for more freedom, yet being less antagonistic towards Bertha Johnson in the dispute.[44]] The dispute, had it not been resolved, could have damaged the reputation of academic women at Oxford, showing them in a most unfavourable light and suggesting that they could not work together successfully.

As has been noted, friction between Eleanor Jourdain and tutors at St Hugh's College led to the notorious St Hugh's Row of 1923–4, when the principal found herself at odds with Cecilia Ady, a gifted and ambitious tutor of the college. Eleanor was also grappling with the demands of a group of women tutors who desired a greater share in the government of the college. The main stumbling blocks to a resolution of these problems appear to have been autocratic government on the part of Miss Jourdain, combined with a lack of recognition of the professional needs of her college staff.[45] In Henrietta Jex-Blake's case, the difficulty in her relationship with college tutors seems to have been more one of a lack of common ground between her and them. Helena Deneke, tutor in German at Lady Margaret Hall 1913–38, wrote about Miss Jex-Blake and the tutors at the hall:

> Miss Jex-Blake kept in the background . . . she left to E.C. Lodge what was outside her competence, dealings with students on the intellectual side and with the Delegacy . . . We hardly ever met her as a body: she was, I think, a little afraid of us . . . She felt herself at a disadvantage and measured herself in true humility, conscious that she had not been through a University course.[46]

The suggested inferiority complex felt by Henrietta Jex-Blake may well have been shared by the other early principals, none of whom had academic qualifications. Female tutors, on the other hand, were products of the first generation of university education for women and therefore were of a different professional species.

One of the leading lights in the advancement of women's higher education in Oxford appears to have been a frequent cause of friction on a personal level. Annie Rogers, honorary secretary of the AEW 1894–1920 and tutor for the AEW 1878–1920, was also on the councils of the Society of Home

Students and St Hugh's and was on many committees related to Oxford women students. Although others with whom the principals worked may have had difficult personalities, Miss Rogers merits classification as a source of friction by virtue of her stature in the women's education movement and also because of the considerable length of her influence on it. Her strident personality and campaigning spirit made her an immovable force in Oxford circles, but also irritated many colleagues and even impeded good relations on occasions. Her behaviour was one of the factors which prompted Christine Burrows to wish to resign in 1924. On this matter Bertha Johnson wrote to Ruth Butler that 'I feel certain that nothing can alter that position: it was quite hopeless in my day . . . always made any move of mine half as difficult again,'[47] and further commenting that Christine 'has told her [Annie Rogers] plainly that the constant letters are doing us harm.'[48] This comment may well have been prompted by a letter from A.W. Pickard-Cambridge to Miss Burrows in 1924, in which he wrote:

> She deluges me (and probably others) with letters & [sic] requests for interviews, and my own strong feeling is (1) that she is the worst possible advocate & does her cause great harm (2) that in any case it would be much better if any statement, or reply to Council, came formally from you, and not in the shape of informal communication from Miss Rogers.[49]

Other comments on Miss Rogers indicate both the significance of her position in Oxford and her difficult nature. Elizabeth Wordsworth wrote to her sister-in-law Esther in June 1879 that 'I had a long talk with Miss Rogers in the morning: it will go hard if she and I do not make friends,'[50] a remark which suggests that Elizabeth Wordsworth was dubious about her new acquaintance. Gemma Bailey, a student at Lady Margaret Hall, made the astute comment in her diary that Miss Rogers 'is so omniscient and bossing and thinks she is the only person in the world who knows anything and loves to run everyone'.[51]

Relationships between principals and students were also sometimes problematic.[52] This seems to have been exacerbated in the case of Somerville by the existence of students from a more catholic range of backgrounds than those at the other colleges:

> The first Somerville students, like their successors, differed to a marked degree from the daughters of clerical homes at Lady Margaret Hall. Being unrestricted by a denominational foundation, they belonged to no special creed, class, race, or social section, and brought to Oxford a variety rather than a type.[53]

Miss Shaw Lefevre evidently found some of the students difficult to work with. Her sister Rachael wrote in November 1880 that Madeleine was 'not satisfied with the new life' and that 'they are sending a younger and inferior class of girls, who give her a great deal of trouble'.[54]

The students' descriptions of their principals frequently supply clues to the subtle pressures applied to these women through the medium of their young charges. The letters of Ina Brooksbank to her family in 1917–20 suggest that she was less than enamoured with the principal of St Hugh's. With reference to a piece of news about which Miss Jourdain couldn't possibly have been informed, she comments, 'I think she ought to have known seeing that she's got second sight about which we are hearing very weird stories at present,'[55] a snide reference to the Versailles experience of Eleanor Jourdain and Annie Moberly.[56] On being late for chapel Ina records that she wasn't sorry because 'Miss Jourdain reads something about something for ½ [sic] an hour, & [sic] you can't possibly be interested'.[57]

Vera Brittain, who came to Oxford as a student in 1915, described Emily Penrose, third principal of Somerville College, as 'the scholarly and intimidating Principal of Somerville' and also as 'just like a tiger-cat'.[58] While Christine Burrows was principal of the Oxford Home Students, students were also clearly questioning various matters, and the principals' minutes books of 1910–25 indicate that students were continually making requests for mixed societies and for greater freedom generally.[59]

For some female students, the unparalleled freedoms offered by their new way of life must have cast their principals in the role of gaolers. The principals had the unenviable task of placating the observers of the new colleges, students' parents and also the students themselves, who, as future advocates of women's colleges, needed to leave Oxford with favourable impressions of the college environment.

Demanding nature of the work

A common problem faced by nineteenth-century principals was that of overwork, caused by the unreasonable demands of their positions. Their jobs were overloaded because these demands had not been clearly defined, because of a lack of finance or because of a combination of the two. In the biography of Constance Maynard, first mistress of Westfield College, the comment is made that 'the Council expected Constance to be lecturer, secretary, housekeeper, as well as principal'.[60] Indeed, Ralph Frances Gray, her friend and classics tutor at Westfield, said to her, 'Don't you see you are doing the work of three women?'[61] – a comment which could well have been made to any of the Oxford principals,[62] who concurrently carried out a multitude of roles in the manner of Constance Maynard. To the job specification quoted above could be added responsibility for finances, pastoral care of students and ambassadorial role on behalf of the college. The job was undoubtedly more intensive during term time, but even vacations entailed ongoing responsibility,[63] preparation for the next term or academic year and, frequently, holidays spent in the company of colleagues.

Two letters written by Elizabeth Wordsworth, each describing a typical day in her life, accurately illustrate the full timetable to which principals were subjected.[64] During these two days she liaised with students, attended a frustrating committee meeting, received a series of people socially, dealt with administrative details of the college, went to an evening concert with friends (which she didn't enjoy because she was overtired), attended evening prayers, tutored a student in Greek, was tutored in algebra, did some translation work for Professor Nettleship and rose, after having gone to bed, to check the gas. The unexpected nature of many of these demands must have been stressful for principals. People would call unannounced, students would come to the principals with their problems or household crises would occur, all at any time of the day or evening. Once again, the situation can be compared to that of a mother, always on call. The cry of Frances Buss, founding headmistress of North London Collegiate School, comes to mind: 'I have never known leisure.'[65]

This situation was exacerbated by the fact that, with the exception of Mrs Johnson, all of the principals were living on site and therefore, unless they went out, were continually on call, an arrangement which made these single women truly 'wedded to the job'. Indeed, Miss Wordsworth commented that when she dined at Keble, it was 'a positive rest to me to dine out at that sort of party where one need only listen, for here of course with the girls I have rather to keep things going'.[66] The stress of these all-demanding posts at the early women's colleges must have been enormous, and it is not surprising to read in one of Elizabeth Wordsworth's letters, written as early as November 1879, a memo to herself that she 'must take longer walks and not work so Hard'.[67] Although, in time, principals delegated duties to a certain extent, the principalship of an Oxford women's college was still very taxing in the early years of the twentieth century. Even in 1920 Henrietta Jex-Blake had no regular secretarial assistance at Lady Margaret Hall[68] and, according to Helena Deneke, wrote all letters in her own hand.

Why was work pressure on principals so great, and why was it not reduced? Initially, principals were seen as little more than gracious lady hostesses presiding over a small group of genteel female students who were hoping to improve their minds at a leisurely pace. In the 1880s, neither the founders nor the early principals envisaged the emergence of the women's halls into full-blown colleges. The task was therefore not recognized as such a great one as it turned out to be, and plans were not made for substantial secretarial, administrative or pastoral help, the need for which grew imperceptibly as the colleges gradually expanded.

In addition, some principals, such as Elizabeth Wordsworth and Annie Moberly, saw their work almost as a vocation and were so dedicated to it that they did not seriously question its demands. Bertha Johnson was equally devoted to her position, predicting that when she retired someone would offer to continue her work for no financial reward. If the early principals were cast in the image of quasi-mothers bringing up much-loved daughters, then, in the time-honoured mould of sacrificial motherhood, they were unlikely to wish to shirk the demands of this role.

There was also an undoubted sense of adventure involved in being responsible for the first women students at Oxford and an awareness that the role of principal was gradually evolving as developments in that field progressed. The excitement of a new venture is captured in a letter written by Christine Burrows to her mother shortly after Esther Burrows had agreed to be principal of St Hilda's: 'Well darling – and so it's done. I hope we shan't regret it but it <u>seems</u> all right. I think you will feel more settled now things are so far decided. We shall have to work hard next Long shan't we?'[69]

The challenge of a role which was totally new and which was even arousing a certain degree of opposition in the town may have given extra energy and determination to these women so that in the early days they did not actively demand extra help. The fact that more support was not actually given was largely due to lack of funds. Neither extra secretarial nor administrative help was supplied, because money was short. Treasurers were appointed on an honorary basis and vice-principals, when they were appointed, were usually busy tutors who fitted in extra tasks to help the principals when they could.

The quasi-ambassadorial role which was an inherent aspect of the work of principal also contributed to the pressure on these women. In a letter written to her sister Dora in December 1880, Elizabeth Wordsworth comments: 'One feels like a walking advertisement . . . one of those sandwich men one sees in London Streets.'[70] The women's colleges were like a very public experiment which many watched with relish in the hope that it would be unsuccessful. Every action of their inhabitants was noticed and the principals must have been aware that they were on show every time they appeared in public. One aspect of their role was to market the college, in the knowledge that the circles in which they mixed outside their colleges contained parents, aunts and uncles and acquaintances of possible future students. In January 1890, for example, Charles Dodgson asked Elizabeth Wordsworth if she would meet his brother Wilfred who 'has a host of daughters . . . wishes to get some information about Ladies' colleges'.[71] To refuse such a request would have been tantamount to failing to carry out the role of principal as it was then defined.

Another problem, shared equally with other pioneering women in the worlds of education, medicine or politics, was the lack of role models from whom to seek guidance. Although the principals did derive inspiration from a variety of sources, there was a dearth of women principals to whom to look. Annie Clough had already encountered this problem at Newnham, Cambridge, in relating to her students, finding that 'her authority over them was not defined either by tradition or by any constitution'.[72] Where were the principals to find their inspiration and direction? Apart from a handful of other principals at Cambridge and London, there was no one. Even looking to the existing principals for advice was not always considered to be the best path. Shortly before becoming principal of Somerville, Madeleine Shaw Lefevre visited Annie Clough, who urged her colleague not to follow Newnham as if it were perfect. Miss Clough was anxious that Somerville should act with caution, for, as Miss Lefevre commented, 'there is no doubt that any false step on our part would have reacted on Cambridge and would have prejudiced the cause which she had so safely pioneered'.[73]

What other choices were open to the newly appointed principals? Should they model themselves on male heads of house, on their projected female version of this, on the small number of colleagues or on positions in their former lives? Were they to look to the college councils for guidance? This variety of options available, coupled with a dearth of clear guidance, led to a diversity of styles of leadership, with related problems and anxieties.

Family demands

Many emerging professional women of the nineteenth century had to contend with the competing demands of family and work. As elderly relatives became ill and needed care, women found themselves looking after parents, in traditional mode as unmarried daughters, while holding down a more than full-time job at the same time. Some principals also felt a responsibility towards unmarried sisters after the death of their parents.[74] These family demands inevitably led to tension and jeopardized the health of the women themselves. This pressure was a trend seen in the lives of other principals during the late nineteenth century and early twentieth century. While Annie Clough was in charge of her pioneering school in Ambleside, she was at the same time caring for her mother, a dual task which was inevitably very stressful for her: 'Her mother's long illness . . . was exceedingly distressing to her, and must latterly have been a great strain upon her health.'[75] Such a situation also raised the question of priorities and must have created a situation of divided loyalties: 'It is clear that as long as Mrs. Clough lived, her health and comfort were, as it were, a first charge upon Miss Clough's attention, to which her other interests and occupations were subordinated.'[76]

Annie Clough's situation mirrored that of many women in responsible positions at this time, most of whom had neither the emotional nor the financial support of a husband. Furthermore, unless their families were enlightened enthusiasts of the causes which their daughters had espoused, there might be little understanding of the demands of their new work. Equally, many with whom the principals worked, such as male colleagues and female students, may not have recognized this pressure as such, believing that other members of the principals' families would occupy themselves with caring for sick relatives.

In Oxford, a number of the women principals were coping with family demands on their time in tandem with the work for their colleges. Both of Elizabeth Wordsworth's parents were ill during her principalship of Lady Margaret Hall and although she had siblings who were able to take care of her mother and father, she felt their illnesses keenly. In the autumn of 1884, her mother, who was seriously ill, was very much on her mind: 'Elizabeth Wordsworth found herself in an unhappy predicament, longing to be with her parents but knowing that duty demanded she should stay in Oxford.'[77]

Christine Burrows, who resigned from her post as principal of St Hilda's College because of her mother's failing health, wrote of a conflict which closely resembled that of Annie Clough and Elizabeth Wordsworth, commenting of her mother that she was 'beginning to need my continued presence to make her life a natural and a happy one. The demands of the Hall are too imperative to admit of the two being compatible in my case.'[78]

How did the principals deal with these conflicting demands on their time and energy? Elizabeth Wordsworth, Henrietta Jex-Blake and Madeleine Shaw Lefevre kept in close touch with their families during term time and gave physical help and support during vacations, an approach which brought with it a danger of overwork. Miss Jex-Blake 'had long spent the vacations in caring for her mother and rarely took a real holiday'.[79] Miss Lefevre was concerned for her mother up to her death in 1883 and thereafter seems to have been conscious of a responsibility towards her three unmarried sisters, none of whom was employed outside the home.

Eleanor Jourdain chose to move her mother, ailing younger sister and a nurse to Oxford in 1919, having 'detested her obligatory half-yearly visits to Broadwindsor, Dorset'.[80] With her mother and sister living at 24 St Margaret's Road, Jourdain presumably felt that she could better cope with both college work and family concerns. Christine Burrows's solution to the problem of her mother's increasing frailty was, in 1919, to resign from her post as principal of St Hilda's, in order to be able to reside at home with her mother and to give her more care and attention. She was able, in 1921, to take on the principalship of the Society of Home Students because it was a non-resident post. Yet the responsibility of her mother, whose only daughter she was, clearly concerned her. Bertha Johnson, writing to Ruth Butler concerning Miss Burrows's possible resignation in 1924, commented that Christine 'wonders whether she <u>ought</u> to be so much occupied, on acct. [sic] of her Mother'.[81] Bertha Johnson's reply to this was that the young life with which Miss Burrows's job brought her mother into contact could only be a good thing, and also that it would be 'a big let-down' for both mother and daughter if Christine were just doing a little coaching.[82] Mrs Johnson probably also recognized the value of Mrs Burrows to the Society of Home Students, as described in the following appreciation of mother and daughter which appears in a history of the society: 'The Merton Street house in which Miss Burrows and her mother entertained students so warmly and so gracefully became an important element in the life of the Society.'[83]

A number of the Oxford women principals were therefore involved in family matters which their male counterparts would traditionally have delegated to female members of their families. Whereas men were able to create space between their public and private spheres,[84] women's family life unavoidably encroached upon their work. Care for their elderly, ill or dependent families was a considerable extra work load for the principals and represented a source of pressure for them.

Financial constraints

A worry common to all of the Oxford women principals was that of money. The cause of this anxiety was succinctly summed up by Emily Penrose in notes which she wrote on membership of Somerville College. She first of all pointed out the unique financial position of the women's colleges in Oxford. Although all modern universities were entitled to government grants in their first two years of existence,[85] new colleges at Oxford did not qualify for these, as both Oxford and Cambridge were excluded from the grants because of ancient university endowments. Miss Penrose commented: 'So we who have neither grants nor endowments are dependent on careful financing and the help of friends.'[86]

Principals were therefore constantly aware of the twin needs to economize and to attract new financial resources for their colleges. Madeleine Shaw Lefevre saw the lack of money as a definite drawback, referring to her anxiety over funds 'which hampered us in many ways and made strict economy necessary'.[87] Indeed, parsimony was a feature of the women's colleges throughout the period considered. There are many references to the varying degrees of lack of comfort. The students at St Hugh's suffered especially, living in spartan conditions from the outset because of the greater shortage of money than at the other colleges. Helena Deneke referred to the meagre supplies of furniture in her room at the college[88] and Joan Evans commented that the rooms were 'deplorably furnished'.[89] Conditions at the other colleges do not seem to have been much better. In the early days at Lady Margaret Hall, Bertha Johnson, who advised Elizabeth Wordsworth at the outset, famously declared, 'I *never* buy any lard, and never allow cooking butter; any butter that is wanted the cook has to contrive out of odds and ends.'[90] John Buchan described the poor conditions at Lady Margaret Hall in the early days: 'All the chimneys smoked, every room had a collection of draughts, and the best it could do for a chapel was the ground-floor pantry.'[91] Bertha Johnson too made economies at the Society of Home Students, accepting no remuneration and carrying out all society work at her home, thereby forgoing the need for an office and incurring minimal expenses. At the foundation of the colleges, furniture and other gifts were therefore gratefully received, as were gifts of books and money in subsequent years.[92]

How did the principals cope with financial problems? They dealt with them firstly by their practice, described above, of economizing, and secondly by encouraging, or by participating in, fundraising. In addition, as mentioned above, they were recipients of gifts from friends of women's education, of whom two were foundresses, namely Elizabeth Wordsworth herself, who gave money inherited from her father to found St Hugh's, and Dorothea Beale, who from 1893, when she founded St Hilda's, was financially responsible for the college, giving £50,000 in total during her connection with the college. Miss Beale's philosophy prevented St Hilda's from being involved in fundraising in the early days; she preferred to give money herself, gather the financial support of a few friends or count on revenue from the annual summer schools, other conferences or visitors, to whom St Hilda's would regularly let out its buildings. One of the principles on which she ran the college was that money earned in this way, together with students' fees, was expected to cover all expenses. She commented to a friend in 1894: 'I am sure it is good to have to pay one's way. I believe our Universities would do better work if they had nothing.'[93]

From the foundation of the women's colleges in Oxford, fundraising was, however, an exercise recognized by some as necessary to their survival. Annie Moberly was aware of the need to make strategic contacts, as noted by a senior student: 'Indeed, Miss Moberly has suggested to us that the limitations of St Hugh's Chapel would form a suitable topic of conversation with any millionaires we may happen to know';[94] and a prominent benefactor of the college, Clara Mordan, also praised Miss Moberly's 'gift of inducing people to make loans'.[95] In her account of the founding of Somerville, Madeleine Shaw Lefevre applauded the members of Council, whom she describes as 'indefatigable'[96] in their exertions to make the start of the college a success. They not only gave money themselves, but also held meetings in Reading, Birmingham and London, forming fundraising committees in these cities. Friends of Lady Margaret Hall also worked to raise money for the college. An appeal fund for a complex of new buildings was opened in 1893, accompanied by a leaflet incorporating a letter from the principal, appealing for contributions. As very little money was forthcoming as a result of this appeal, building work eventually went ahead financed by loans from friends and the principal herself, who contributed £1,000. A few years earlier, in 1889, when the college had initially been in need of extra accommodation, Elizabeth Wordsworth had also made a personal contribution, buying a house herself and leasing it to the college. The same tactic was to be employed by Eleanor Jourdain in 1919, when St Hugh's, already short of money, needed more buildings for accommodation. The principal of the college bought 4 St Margaret's Road and let it to St Hugh's.

Once it was established, Somerville College was in the fortunate position of being the recipient of two benefactions. The gymnasium, completed in

1890, was built thanks to a gift of money from Miss Forster, an old friend of Miss Lefevre, and the Eleanor Smith Cottage, now known as the Hostel, was largely built with money bequeathed by Miss Smith, who had been involved in the work for women's higher education since the 1860s. Miss Smith's legacy was augmented by donations from Professor Dicey, whose wife was a member of Council (1888–1904), Eleanor Powell, a Somerville tutor, and Madeleine Shaw Lefevre. In 1898–9 Agnes Maitland set up a library fund at Somerville College to provide much-needed accommodation for the rapidly increasing number of books at the college.

> The construction of the Library was Miss Maitland's cherished idea, and she threw herself wholeheartedly into the task of raising the sum necessary for its accomplishment. Mainly through her initiative a library fund was started, and so successful was the appeal that, at the Gaudy in 1901, she was able to announce that only £50 was wanting to complete the £2,000.[97]

The zeal of Agnes Maitland was matched by Emily Penrose's enthusiasm when she lent her support to a scheme instituted by Margery Fry and others, by which old students and friends of the college were invited to take up debenture shares. This appeal for a loan at small interest was in aid of the proposed new building, which was eventually to be Maitland Hall. It was completed in 1913 at a cost of £17,000, which had been borne entirely by old students, their friends and the friends of the college.

Help from the government was forthcoming in the early 1920s as a result of a recommendation by the Asquith Commission (1919–22) that the women's colleges at Oxford receive a grant of £4,000 a year from the University Grant Committee. This proved to be a cause of friction for Lady Margaret Hall and the Society of Home Students. Both Henrietta Jex-Blake and the chairman of Lady Margaret Hall Council, Joseph Wells, warden of Wadham College, expressed their reluctance to be exposed to government control of this kind. Jex-Blake wrote to Bertha Johnson in 1919:

> I entirely agree with the Warden of Wadham that we do not want Government money – I think it would be a fatal blow to our future. There would certainly be interference with a Church College of a very drastic kind. This may

come from the Government side later on in any case – but I do hope we shall not take any steps to bring it on ourselves.[98]

When the money was granted, the Society of Home Students was not included and Bertha Johnson commented in a letter to Ruth Butler in 1924 that 'I still think it must have been a mistake that the Univ. [sic] gave all the £4,000 a year to four of the Societies and left the fifth out altogether'.[99]

An 'Appeal for the Women's Colleges in Oxford' was set up in 1921 by the five women's societies, to raise endowments for staff salaries, for advanced studies and research and for the development of libraries and buildings.[100] The stated aim of the appeal was to raise £185,000.[101] However, in spite of royal support and lavish and dedicated fundraising events,[102] including balls under aristocratic patronage in the Hyde Park Hotel and a Mansion House meeting addressed by the Archbishop of York, the result of the Appeal was disappointing, having raised only £20,000 by the time it closed in 1925.

Apart from Esther and Christine Burrows, the financial problems faced by the women principals were exclusively of a professional nature. These other principals had private incomes, either emanating from their families, as was the case with Elizabeth Wordsworth and Madeleine Shaw Lefevre, or from previous earnings, like Eleanor Jourdain, who had worked as a headmistress and who owned a flat in Paris, or Agnes Maitland, who had worked in various capacities before becoming principal of Somerville. The Burrowses had the additional burden of personal financial worries, compounded by the fact that Dorothea Beale did not pay them an adequate salary. By 1904 Mrs Burrows was only paid £100 per annum,[103] plus a variable bonus, an amount well below what would currently have been paid to the head of a girls' school. Esther Burrows was compelled to raise the matter with the founder of St Hilda's on several occasions in order to ensure a reasonable income for both her and her daughter, who worked as a tutor and, from 1896 onwards, as vice-principal of the college, in both cases in an unremunerated capacity. In later years matters clearly did not improve for the Burrowses and their financial difficulties must have been public knowledge, as a former student of the Society of Home Students wrote to Ruth Butler in 1929 that 'I do hope Miss Burrows has enough to live on. It is a harrowing thought.'[104]

Solutions

How did the principals react to the pressures which were a feature of their posts? One outcome of the stress suffered by these women was that which has already been discussed: illness of various kinds. This was a natural bodily reaction, over which they had very little control. More proactive responses included escape in the form of recreational activities or of relaxation with family and friends, conscious acceptance of the current state of affairs and, where it was appropriate, action to improve a given situation.

Involvement in other interests offered refreshment to the principals in various ways. Elizabeth Wordsworth ran weekly Bible classes for her students which, far from being an extra burden to her, provided an outlet for her deep understanding of Scripture. She also gave regular addresses in chapel on Sunday evening and her love of writing kept her much occupied. She composed poems, novels, plays and newspaper articles, being throughout her life a frequent contributor to the *Guardian*. Walking was also a source of relaxation to her. Annie Moberly also derived a large degree of fulfilment from the delivery of her Sunday evening Bible talks, which her students found most inspiring, and from the academic study to which she devoted herself daily, studying the first 15 centuries of the Christian era and making notes for *Five Visions of the Revelation*. In addition, she involved herself enthusiastically in the St Hugh's music groups.

In fact, music was an outlet enjoyed by several of the principals. Henrietta Jex-Blake was an accomplished violinist[105] and Eleanor Jourdain and Bertha Johnson both derived much pleasure from playing the piano. Madeleine Shaw Lefevre had a passion for gardening, recalled by the comment of a former student, who referred to 'her love of gardening' and conjured up a typical picture of the Principal:

> My next [recollection] brings a vision of her in the garden,
> her dachs at her heels, prodding with a small garden fork
> round the tubers of the irises which grew in profusion
> where now the library buildings stand. She catches sight
> of me and beckons me to her to say: 'You know, my dear,
> to do well irises should be moved every three years.'[10]

Emily Penrose had a number of interests, including climbing, skating, painting, embroidery and acting,[107] all of which she indulged in her spare time.

Agnes Maitland had involvements outside Somerville which claimed her attention but could hardly be described as recreational. Amongst other activities, she investigated conditions in girls' schools for the British Association for the Advancement of Science, organized a deputation in 1904 to the Board of Education to plead for more women schools inspectors and represented the AEW for many years at the annual conference of the National Union of Women Workers. She was also on the committee of the University Women's Club. On her leisure pursuits there is no information, which may suggest that she enjoyed work and found it a refreshment in itself.

Apart from recreational activities, the principals relaxed in vacations with their families, whether with a husband and two children, like Bertha Johnson, parents and siblings, who were very dear to Elizabeth Wordsworth, Madeleine Shaw Lefevre, Henrietta Jex-Blake and Charlotte Moberly, nieces and nephews, in the case of Emily Penrose, or with mainly one family member, as with the Burrowses, who seemed to delight in each other's company. The principals also enjoyed travel, holidays abroad being a feature of their much-needed escape from problems and pressures.

One strategy employed by these women to counteract the problems they encountered was patient acceptance of existing conditions. Far from being disillusionment, this was a form of maintaining their long-term goals on the back burner, until conditions became more propitious. Allied to a tactic of caution, which meant that the principals were able to defuse tensions, this enabled them to sustain a precarious balance between conflicting issues and thus to maintain the status quo. It was this wise acceptance of the current state of affairs which guided Emily Penrose, when asked by Somerville students for a revision of chaperonage rules, to reply, 'Wait; this is not the time; wait.'[108] In another, totally different situation, Bertha Johnson accepted that Annie Rogers would not alter her irritating ways of working and so ceased to try to change her.

On the other hand, the principals also acted, at the right time, to deal with their difficulties, so that Miss Jourdain moved her mother nearer to her in order to be able to care for her while carrying out the role of principal, Miss Wordsworth lent personal money to her college to enable it to expand and Miss Maitland ensured that Somerville Hall took on the name of Somerville College when she became convinced that the question of status was involved. To Annie Moberly can be attributed her gift of inducing people to make loans, which prompted friends of hers to give money to St Hugh's College, and which was so praised by Clara Mordan,[109] one of the college's chief benefactors.

Conclusion

There is no doubt that the role of principal of an Oxford women's college was a lonely one. The pressures and problems chronicled in this chapter can only have exacerbated the isolation of this role, captured so vividly by Vera Brittain in her description of Emily Penrose as 'a lonely Olympian, secure in the legend of her purpose, her omnipotence and her inhumanity. Who knew what Spartan ideal of justice, endurance and self-sacrifice had inspired the ruthless impartiality of that splendid isolation?'[110]

As colleges grew larger, the social space between principals and their students widened. The paradox of the principal's role was that although she could appear austere, she was inwardly prey to a large degree of insecurity, the inherent outcome of being a pioneer and of treading unknown territory. The loneliness of their position was a factor over which the principals had very little control, as they were indisputably pioneers in the true sense of the word and could be described as those who 'initiate or originate, go before, lead or conduct other persons'[111] – those other persons inevitably looking to the pioneers for guidance.

The overall challenge for the principals was to be at least the equals of men in competence and efficiency, supermen in effect, and also to retain the traditional gendered role of carer in their private lives, acting all in all as superwomen. As has been shown, the difficulties encountered by the Oxford women principals of 1879–1925 were not unique to their situation, but were experienced by other women principals and by headmistresses of the period. However, as female leaders in a male world who were living apart from their families and in effect residing in the workplace, the nature of the principals' lives as compared with those of most single women within their social grouping was unusual. Most of their problems – lack of role models, financial strictures on a large scale, coping with a combination of work and family demands and a surfeit of work-related pressures – were atypical of women of their social peer group, and these women's departure from the normal lifestyle experienced by other women meant that any support which was available to them was all the more welcome. Looking at these problems, it would seem that the difficulties experienced by the Oxford women principals bore many similarities to those faced by professional women of the late twentieth century who find themselves in positions of authority within traditional male contexts. Some of the common problems experienced by the token woman manager in the workplace[112] are exactly the difficulties which were faced by the Oxford women principals. Although the women principals were not token appointments, a half-hearted attempt to attain equality for women at work, they do fall into this category numerically.[113] Among the disadvantages encountered by token women are 'increased performance pressure', 'visibility', 'isolation and lack of female role models' and 'exclusion from male groups',[114] all of which were experienced by the principals.

Just like women of the 1990s, the principals may well have carried a burden of guilt for having neglected, to some degree, the private duties for the public ones. The stress caused by these conflicts was worse for early professional women since, mainly without the support of a husband, and cut off from their families for long periods of time, they were facing pressures alone. Those means of support which were available to them were therefore vital.

Acknowledgements

Warm thanks go to Oxford Librarians and Archivists who made their libraries and archival material freely available – Pauline Adams at Somerville College, Elizabeth Boardman and Maria Crogan at St. Hilda's College, Debbie Quare at St. Hugh's College, David Smith at St. Anne's College and Roberta Staples and Julie Courtney at Lady Margaret Hall; this material formed the major part of my primary sources. I am also grateful to the staff of the Bodleian Library.

I am appreciative of interviews given to me by those involved in women's higher education in Oxford, notably the late Marjorie Reeves, and the late Rachel Trickett. In addition, I am grateful to Major John Penrose and Mrs. Anne Milner who granted me access to their private papers.

APPENDIX 1

EXTRACT FROM LETTER: ELIZABETH WORDSWORTH TO HER SISTER-IN-LAW SUSAN (SUSIE), 2 NOVEMBER, 1879

My enclosure which may be burnt will shew the way we go on. Take yesterday afternoon as a sample. First a call from Mr. A. Butler to speak about a winter lawn tennis ground. Then before he was gone Mr. Strachan D.[115] – who talked and laughed for ten minutes till I told him I expected a visit from Miss Marsh – "What the Miss Marsh of all Miss Marshes?" said he – and bolted instantly (she is Miss Anstruther's aunt). Then off to my committee. Stopped on the doorstep by Miss Chevalier – who wants a situation as governess – can you find her one? £80, but would take 60. Asked her to tea some day. Caught again by Mr. Coxe and Cha (who looks very well). Walked a little way back with them. ¼ hour late for committee, find them in the midst of a long discussion about land and leases – don't take in half of it. Then plunge into smoky chimney which is <u>our</u> grievance – Principal of Jesus draws pattern of cowl and sub-committee is formed. Tussle (as usual between W. of Keble, who flushes a good deal, and Mrs. A. J. Johnson who is extremely self-possessed) about a sentence in new Report about our Ch. Of England principles. Eventually settle to have no report at all. Home again, and find Miss Shaw Stuart having tea – Miss Marsh with her niece. Interview with her which lasts till dressing time. Louisa Rivaz and Mrs. Moss rolled into one; with an amount of vitality that one would gladly have half of – in this instance the half wd. be decidedly more than the whole. No sooner do I get off to my room, than enter Miss Bradby – "Please may I be excused coming to dinner, I feel so faint!" Sofa, Cranford, and poached egg. Must take longer walks and not work so hard. Rush down to dinner – meat disgracefully underdone. Freeman put out, and Ann Winch in my very bad books.

Hurry off to concert in Town Hall, with Miss Cobbe, Jones, and Ward. Noisy undergraduates, glare of gas nearly blinding – delightful singing of

Miss Robertson's, and almost everything encored. Fly not forthcoming – no gentleman – bother with flyman – and so ends one day of my life.[116]

EXTRACT FROM LETTER: ELIZABETH WORDSWORTH TO HER SISTER DORA, 2 DECEMBER 1880

One feels like a walking advertisement – one of those sandwich men one sees in London streets. I will just tell you a day – yesterday – as a specimen. 9 to 10. Girls reading Political Economy. 10. Mean to go to church. Miss Jones comes in with a grievance because two of the others want to practise singing and disturb her reading. Pacify her as well as I can and get to church in the middle of liturgy. Then to Northgate. Doctors come and I go. 11.30. Talk with the other party about these unlucky singing lessons. 12. 3 girls come to read "Much Ado about Nothing." (rather appropriate!) 1. Lunch. Write to Warden of Keble to ask him to come and address them on Friday, as I think everybody is getting rather demoralized. 2.30. go with Mrs. Price for drive up Headington Hill with her daughter Mrs. Mozley whom Papa and Mamma met at Leeds. Call on Mrs. Markby. About 6 other callers. Noise enough for a railway station. Stay there the best part of an hour. Wonder how any woman ever <u>can</u> have an "afternoon" at home. Make another call. Drive back. Pick up Mary Smith – take her to 5 o'c. tea at the Harpers (Principal of Jesus) who simply overpower us with kindness. 6. get back – do Greek with Edith Argles and Elsie Johnson. 7. Dinner. 8. Have a tremendous talk with Ellie Magee about Work versus Society. She takes it very nicely. Quarter to 9. Prayers. 9.30. Miss Lee comes to coach me in Algebra. We try to understand how a minus becomes a plus when you are doing subtraction. I shall have to get Edward to coach me some day. Do a bit of translation for Mr. Nettleship. Make a final attempt to get Evelyn Anstruther out of Edith Pearson's room and so to bed. Panic about gas in passage. Jump out of bed to see if it is all right . Eventually to sleep. The only thing that really tried me in that day was the afternoon call. That was <u>perfect misery</u>. The voices hurt one's head so. I do think these "afternoons" are the greatest mistake.[117]

Endnotes:

1   The decision to admit women to degrees of the University of London was taken in 1878 and the four women who graduated from the university in 1880 were the first to do so.

2   Another factor to be considered is that of age: all of the principals were going through the menopause during their period of office.

3   *Somerville College Archive*, Minutes of Somerville Council, 7 May 1885. This leave of absence was eventually extended to one academic year. See Minutes of Council, 18 February 1886.

4   See Willson, F.M.G., *A Strong Supporting Cast*, Athlone Press, 1993, p 302. Miss Lefevre spent six months of her leave of absence with her sister Rachael who, with her husband Arthur Hamilton-Gordon, later Baron Stanmore, was living in Ceylon.

5   *Private collection of Mr. and Mrs. J. W. O. Elliot*, Elliot MSS, Madeleine to Jane, 5 May 1879, as cited in Willson, *A Strong Supporting Cast*, p 300.6 Elliot MSS, Madeleine to Jane, 5 May 1879, as cited in Willson, *A Strong Supporting Cast*, p 300. This agreement also represented an act of deference on the part of Council, who had originally planned to appoint a principal who would reside in Hall continually during eight weeks of the long vacation. See Minutes of Somerville Council, 20 March 1879.7 Minutes of Somerville Council, 13 October 1880.8 Minutes of Somerville Council, 19 October 1880.

9   Elizabeth Wordsworth wrote to her niece Ruth in February 1906: 'They are all very sad at Somerville. Miss Maitland had to go to town for another operation – but the doctors say she cannot have anything done . . . I don't suppose she will ever come back for the few months that may presumably still be granted her here. They hope they may do something to alleviate the pain.' *Lady Margaret Hall Archive*, Elizabeth Wordsworth to Ruth Wordsworth, Correspondence of Elizabeth Wordsworth 1898–1917, 22 February 1906.

10 Minutes of Somerville Council, 16 March 1896.

11 *Somerville College Archive*, Emily Penrose File, Ethel Hurlbatt to Emily Penrose, undated. 12 *Somerville College Archive*, Emily Penrose File, Grace Hadow to Emily Penrose, 30 November 1925.

13 'Notes and News' in *The Oxford Magazine*, 4 February 1926, pp 250–1.

14 'The strain of these years told heavily on Miss Jex-Blake.' Obituary of Henrietta Jex-Blake, *The Times*, 22 May 1953.

15 Obituary, *The Times*, 22 May 1953.

16 *The Fritillary*, first published in 1894, was the joint magazine of the women's colleges.

17 College news in *The Fritillary*, June 1903.

18 It is perplexing that the St Hilda's College Council should have appointed as principal someone who was so clearly unwell. Did they feel that the appointment of Christine Burrows made financial sense, as Miss Burrows would not expect a rise in the principal's salary and her mother would continue to be involved with the college, giving unpaid assistance.

19 *Collection of Mrs Anne Milner*, Letters from Christine Burrows to Esther Burrows, 20 and 27 June 1910.

20 *St Anne's College Archive*, Women Students' Collection, W8 8/4, Acceptance letter of Christine Burrows, 4 February 1921.

21 *Bodleian Library*, Uncatalogued collection, Family correspondence and personal papers of Misses O.H.E. and R.F. Butler 1885–1940, Bertha Johnson to Ruth Butler, 17 December 1924.

22 *Bodleian Library*, Uncatalogued collection, Family correspondence and personal papers of Misses O.H.E. and R.F. Butler 1885–1940, Christine Burrows to Ruth Butler, 9 February 1928.

23 See Keene, Anne, *The Role of an Oxford Women's Principal 1879–1925*, doctoral thesis, Oxford Brookes University, 1998, Chapter 2, pp 35–7, or Griffin, *St Hugh's*, p 48 ff., for further details of the St Hugh's Row.

24 Trickett, 'The Row', in Griffin, *St Hugh's*, p 60.

25 Rayner, Margaret, *The Centenary History of St Hilda's College*, Lindsay Ross Publishing Ltd, 1979, p 62.

26 College news in *The Fritillary*, March 1926.27 Firth, Catherine B., *Constance Louisa Maynard, Mistress of Westfield College*, George Allen & Unwin, 1949, pp 199 and 206.

28 Kamm, Josephine, *Indicative Past: A Hundred Years of the Girls' Public Day School Trust*, George Allen & Unwin, 1971, p 68.

29 *Sex in Education*, by Dr Edward Clarke, was published in America in 1873. Although this book, which questioned the effects of education upon women's 'female apparatus', succeeded in having 17 printings, 'His attack reinforced the determination of educators to make the college woman a healthy specimen, conspicuous for her vigor in mind and body' and the excitement over his warnings subsided quite swiftly. See Solomon, Barbara, *In the Company of Educated Women*, Yale University Press, 1985, p 56. Dr Henry Maudsley, Professor of Medical Jurisprudence at University College, London, wrote the famous article in *Fortnightly Review* quoted below. John Thorburn, Professor of Obstetrics at Owens College, Manchester, was also prominent in the attack on women's suitability for intensive mental work and in 1884 wrote *Female Education from a Physiological Point of View*. 30 Maudsley, Henry, 'Sex and Mind in Education' in *Fortnightly Review*, April 1874

31 These attacks did not cease with publications in the 1870s. In 1896 Alfred Marshall, who had been teaching women at Cambridge, wrote a pamphlet *On Cambridge Degrees for Women*, in which he claimed that women had lower intellectual potential than men.

32 *Girton College Archive*, Bodichon Papers, Emily Davies to Barbara Bodichon, April 1874, as cited in Bennett, Daphne, *Emily Davies and the Liberation of Women*, Andre Deutsch, 1990, p 157.

33 Anderson, Elizabeth, 'Sex and Mind in Education: A Reply' in *Fortnightly Review*, May 1874.

34 'Somerville Hall. Address by Lord Aberdare' in *Oxford Chronicle*, 4 June 1881.

35 This prejudice extended to women who came from identical backgrounds to those of the principals. Charlotte Yonge, popular author of the late nineteenth century and a close friend of Elizabeth Wordsworth, was not convinced of the wisdom of colleges for women. See Battiscombe, Georgina, *Reluctant Pioneer*, Constable, 1978, pp 70–1.

36 Rayner, *The Centenary History*, p 37.37 In 1887 a committee from the women's colleges in Oxford and Cambridge carried out a study of the health of women students as compared with their non-student sisters. The result – Sidgwick, Eleanor, *Health Statistics of Women Students at Cambridge and Oxford and their Sisters*, Cambridge, 1890 – indicated that 'as large a proportion of women students enjoyed good health after going through college as had enjoyed it before'. See McWilliams-Tullberg, R, *Women at Cambridge: A Men's University, Though of a Mixed Type*, London, 1975, p 103. This report was an encouragement to women students and to the principals.

38 The AEW was the Association for the Higher Education of Women, a body set up in 1879 to promote women's higher education in Oxford. The relationship of the principals with these bodies is documented in Chapter 6, *Internal and External Politics*.

39 Although not full colleges at this stage, Somerville and the others were frequently called 'college', but often went by their more correct nomenclature of 'hall'. See earlier reference to this struggle, Keene, Anne, 'The Role of', Chapter 2, pp 8–9, and the extract from a letter from Agnes Maitland to Bertha Johnson which indicates that there had been friction between the two women.

40 *St Anne's College Archive*, Johnson Collection, J 3/1, Letter from Agnes Maitland to Bertha Johnson, 29 October 1891. The Somerville principal was clearly anxious to smooth over any trouble which had occurred and finished her letter by voicing her high opinion of the secretary of the AEW: 'I will . . . ask you to believe that no one can be more conscious than I am of all you have done for the education of women in Oxford and that even though we may differ in details and methods, our aim is really the same.'

41 See *St Anne's College Archive*, Johnson Collection, J 3/1.

42 *St Anne's College Archive*, Johnson Collection, J 3/1, CMJ to Bertha Johnson, 16 November 1892.43 *St Anne's College Archive*, Johnson Collection, J 3/1,Charlotte Green to Bertha Johnson, 1893, no month or day.

44 Annie Moberly wrote to Bertha Johnson in 1893 that 'I believe that St Hugh's, at any rate, could have worked the present arrangements with very good effect for itself . . . . The ideal of course is that the Secretary and Principals should be personal friends in full communication with one another.' Undated notes in Bertha Johnson's handwriting indicate that there had been no friction between her and Lady Margaret Hall. She wrote of the college that 'It has *not* been the object of the Hall authority to glorify the Hall at the expense of the Association.' *St Anne's College Archive*, Johnson Collection, J 3/1, Charlotte Moberly to Bertha Johnson, 1893. Notes of Bertha Johnson, undated.

45 A similarly bitter dispute arose between Emily Davies, when she was mistress of Girton College, and Louisa Lumsden, one of the college tutors. After a number of acrimonious disagreements regarding the running of the college, Louisa Lumsden resigned in 1874, soon after (in 1877) becoming the first headmistress of St Leonard's School in Scotland. See Bowerman, Elsie, *Stands There a School*, Wycombe Abbey School Seniors, 1965, p 25.

46 *Lady Margaret Hall Archive*, Deneke Memoirs, Deneke, Helena, 'What I Remember III', pp 145–6.

47 *Bodleian Library*, Family correspondence and personal papers of Misses O. H. E. and R. F. Butler 1885–1940, Bertha Johnson to Ruth Butler, 17 December 1924.

48 *Bodleian Library*, Family correspondence and personal papers of Misses O. H. E. and R. F. Butler 1885–1940, Bertha Johnson to Ruth Butler, 17 December 1924.49 *St Anne's College Archive*, Home Students Collection, H 51/9, A.W. Pickard-Cambridge to Christine Burrows, undated (during 1924–25).

50 *Lady Margaret Hall Archive*, Correspondence of Elizabeth Wordsworth 1879–97, Elizabeth Wordsworth to Esther Wordsworth, 11 June 1879.51 *Lady Margaret Hall Archive*, Bailey, Gemma, *Diaries and Letters*, diary extract, 29 March 1906, privately printed by Mary Bailey.

52 These problems were echoes of the difficulties which Emily Davies had with some of her early students. See McWilliams-Tullberg, *Women at Cambridge: A Men's University, Though of a Mixed Type*, p 66.

53 Brittain, Vera, *The Women at Oxford*, Harrap, 1961, p 83.

54 *British Library*, Add MSS 49225. Rachael to AHG, 23 November 1880, as cited in Willson, *A Strong Supporting Cast*, p 304. Also see Chapter 7, p 5, for evidence of difficulties which Madeleine Shaw Lefevre was experiencing with Somerville students.

55 *St Hugh's College Archive*, Ina Brooksbank to her mother, October 1917.

56 See Keene, Anne, 'The Role of', Chapter 1, p 30.

57 *St Hugh's College Archive*, Ina Brooksbank to her mother, 18 November 1917.

58 Brittain, Vera, *Testament of Youth*, Fontana, 1933, p 65.

59 *Bodleian Library*, Papers relating to the education of women at Oxford University, 1910–79, Dep. c. 688, Dep. c. 689, Dep. c. 690, Dep. c. 694, Dep. d. 759, dep. d. 763, Dep. d. 765, Dep. d. 766, Dep. d. 767.

60 Firth, *Constance Louisa Maynard*, p 189.

61 Firth, *Constance Louisa Maynard*, p 201.

62 The comment was made in Annie Moberly's obituary that 'It was no easy task which she had undertaken, for she had to combine in the own person the offices of Vice-Principal, Bursar, and Secretary as well as that of Principal'. Edith Wardale, 'Obituary of C. A. E. Moberly' in *St Hugh's College Chronicle*, 1937–38.63 At St Hilda's, Esther and Christine Burrows were often involved in the organization of the summer schools which were based at the college. The vacations of Eleanor Jourdain have been described as 'overcast . . . by endless College correspondence'. Evans, *Prelude and Fugue*, p 100.

64 See Appendix 1.

65 Strachey, Ray, *The Cause*, G. Bell and Sons, 1928, p 126.66 *Lady Margaret Hall Archive*, Correspondence of Elizabeth Wordsworth 1879–97, Elizabeth Wordsworth to Dora Leeke, 2 December 1880.

67 *Lady Margaret Hall Archive*, Correspondence of Elizabeth Wordsworth 1879–97, Elizabeth Wordsworth to Esther Susan (Susie) Wordsworth, 2 November 1879.

68 Eleanor Lodge, vice-principal of Lady Margaret Hall 1906–21, wrote of Henrietta Jex-Blake that she 'was her own Secretary . . . and must have spent many arduous hours over the ever-increasing business of letter-writing'. Lodge, Eleanor, *Terms and Vacations*, Oxford University Press, 1938, p 107. At Somerville College, however, the principal had some secretarial assistance from 1887 onwards. See *Somerville College Archive*, Minutes of Council, 8 March 1887.

69 *Collection of Mrs Anne Milner*, Christine Burrows to Esther Burrows, 27 November 1892.

70 *Lady Margaret Hall Archive*, Correspondence of Elizabeth Wordsworth 1879–97, Elizabeth Wordsworth to Dora Leeke, 2 December 1880.71 *Lady Margaret Hall Archive*, Dodgson and Wordsworth correspondence, Charles Dodgson to Elizabeth Wordsworth, 30 January 1890.

72 Clough, Blanche Athena, *A Memoir of Anne Jemima Clough*, Edward Arnold, 1897, p 195.73 *Somerville College Archive*, Shaw Lefevre, Madeleine, *Personal Recollections*, undated.

74 When her unmarried sisters moved in with their brother to look after his now motherless children, and as a consequence the home which Annie Moberly had shared with her sisters was broken up, Miss Moberly wrote in confessional mode to Bertha Johnson that the move 'may have the good effect of throwing me more completely into the work and life at Oxford, which I know did not always come first to me before'. *St Anne's College Archive*, Johnson Collection, J8, Annie Moberly to Bertha Johnson, undated.

75 Clough, p 95.

76 Clough, p 86.77 Battiscombe, *Reluctant Pioneer*, p 111.

78 *St Hilda's College Archive*, Burrows, Christine, 'President's Letter' in *St Hilda's Hall, Oxford. Chronicle of the Old Students' Association*, January 1919.

79 'In Memoriam. Henrietta Jex-Blake 1862–1953' in *The Brown Book. Lady Margaret Hall Chronicle*, December 1953.

80 Spurling, Hilary, *Secrets of a Woman's Heart*, Hodder and Stoughton, 1984, p 96.81 *Bodleian Library*, Family correspondence and personal papers of Misses O.H.E. and R.F. Butler 1885–1940, Bertha Johnson to Ruth Butler, 17 December 1924.

82 *Bodleian Library*, Family correspondence and personal papers of Misses O.H.E. and R.F. Butler 1885–1940, Bertha Johnson to Ruth Butler, 17 December 1924.

83 Reeves, Marjorie, *St Anne's College, Oxford*, p 14.84 See Burstyn, Joan, *Victorian Education and the Ideal of Womanhood*, Croom Helm, 1980, pp 19–20, for further discussion of these spheres.

85 By 1904 the government grant available to all universities, excluding Oxford and Cambridge, amounted to £54,000 in total. See Armytage,

W. H. G., *Civic universities: aspects of a British tradition*, London, 1955.86 *Somerville College Archive*, Penrose, Emily, *Qualification for Membership*, undated.

87 *Somerville College Archive*, Shaw Lefevre, Madeleine, *Personal Recollections*.

88 Deneke, 'What I Remember III', p 146.

89 Evans, *Prelude and Fugue*, p 69.

90 Battiscombe, *Reluctant Pioneer*, p 73.

91 Buchan, John, 'The Dream and the Fact' in *The Heritage*, no 1, Trinity Term, 1921.

92 The gift book at Somerville College 'reveals that almost all the familiar objects from the pictures and the furniture to the very shrubs in the garden, are gifts of Somerville's friends'. Byrne, Muriel St Clair, and Mansfield, Catherine Hope, *Somerville College 1879–1921*, Oxford University Press, 1921, p 29.

93 Raikes, E., *Dorothea Beale of Cheltenham*, Constable, 1908, p 388, as cited in Rayner, *The Centenary History*, p 21.

94 Letter from Senior Student in *St Hugh's Club News*, January 1899.

95 Kemp, 'The Early History', p 46.

96 *Somerville College Archive*, Shaw Lefevre, Madeleine, 'For those that come after' in *Account of the Founding of Somerville*.

97 Byrne and Mansfield, *Somerville College 1879–1921*, p 25.

98 *St Anne's College Archive*, Johnson Collection, J 8/5, Henrietta Jex-Blake to Bertha Johnson, 15 August 1919.

99 *Bodleian Library*, Family correspondence and personal papers of Misses O. H. E. and R. F. Butler, Bertha Johnson to Ruth Butler, 17 December 1924.

100 *Bodleian Library*, Papers of the Association for the Higher Education of Women, Loose Papers Ms. Top. Oxon. c. 817, 117–18, 'Appeal for the Women's Colleges in Oxford.'

101 John Buchan, however, who wrote a long supportive article in the appeal newspaper, suggested that £100,000 would clear the existing debt that had been incurred by four of the colleges and 'endowment funds of £80,000 for each of the four would ease them of their worst anxieties and unfetter their hands for their new tasks', thereby hinting at an ideal target of £420,000! See Buchan, 'The Dream'.

102 In addition to those events mentioned in the text, these also comprised 'approaches to foundations and city companies, to American women's colleges and former Rhodes scholars, to women golfers and to girls' schools . . . a bridge drive . . . lectures, concerts, jumble sales and the like put on by women dons in their spare time.' See Howarth, Janet, 'Women' in Harrison, Brian (ed), *The History of the University of Oxford. Volume 8: The Twentieth Century*, 1994, p 360.

103 £100 was the starting salary of the principals of Lady Margaret Hall and of Somerville College in 1879. By 1895 the principal of Somerville was paid £250 and by 1906 she received £400. When, in 1921, the Society of Home Students eventually paid a salary to its principal, the amount agreed was £600.104 *St. Anne's College Archive*, Home Students Collection, H 51/9, Katharine Wallis to Ruth Butler, undated.

105 Henrietta Jex-Blake used regularly to play the violin with friends. 'She found opportunity to play her beloved violin and, in this, was in touch with Mary Venables, with Paul Benecke and Alice Price and, in her student days, Evelyn Kirkaldy would provide a cello.' Deneke, 'What I Remember III', p 145.

106 Farnell, *A Somervillian*, p 9.

107 Vera Farnell describes Emily Penrose as an accomplished amateur actress and refers to some of her more colourful roles. See Farnell, *A Somervillian*, p 35.108 Farnell, *A Somervillian*, p 44.

109 Griffin, *St Hugh's*, p 46.

110 Brittain, *Testament*, p 501.

111 *The Concise Oxford Dictionary*, Oxford University Press, 1990.

112 Davidson, Marilyn J., and Cooper, Cary L., *Shattering the Glass Ceiling: The Woman Manager*, Paul Chapman Publishing, 1992, pp 83–6.

113 Davidson and Cooper define token women managers as being less than 15 per cent of the workforce. Davidson and Cooper, *Shattering the Glass Ceiling*, p 83.

114 Davidson and Cooper, *Shattering the Glass Ceiling*, pp 83–6.

115 Mr Strachan Davidson, Master of Balliol College 1907–16, in 1879 Senior Dean and Fellow of the college.

116 *Lady Margaret Hall Archive*, Elizabeth Wordsworth File, Correspondence of Elizabeth Wordsworth 1879–97, Elizabeth Wordsworth to Susan Wordsworth, 2 November 1879.

117 *Lady Margaret Hall Archive*, Elizabeth Wordsworth File, Correspondence of Elizabeth Wordsworth 1879–97, Elizabeth Wordsworth to Dora Leeke, 2 December 1880.

CHAPTER 6

Town Nurse and Country Nurse: viewing an early
twentieth century district nursing landscape.

Helen Sweet

Introduction

This chapter will look at the changing experience of women practising
as district nurses during the twentieth century. It will focus on a micro-
scale within the contexts of regionalisation and culture. A small-scale
study allows detailed consideration of regional, local and personal
diversities whilst testing and extending the generalized findings relating
to professionalisation, working conditions, changing status and role of
the district nurse emerging from a wider study.[1] District nursing was
essentially a *local* service run by *local* volunteers and later by the *local*
authorities. This application of community history[2] to the study of
community nursing is of dual importance within a study of the history
of women. Firstly, it is valuable in demonstrating the immediacy of the
effect of locality and local issues on the daily life and work of a group of
professional women in terms of changing social conditions, conditions
of service and pressures of work. Secondly, it is also helpful in exposing
some of the underlying tensions of employment relationships between the
nurses and the lay district nursing committee that employed them.

It is difficult to define the role of a district nurse, as it was continually evolving throughout the late nineteenth and most of the twentieth centuries. When the term was first used, in the mid-nineteenth century, it referred mainly to those women who provided care for a section of the community generally known as the 'sick poor'. The principle behind this was to care for the poor in their own homes as far as possible rather than removing them to hospital unnecessarily. These nurses worked within clearly geographically defined 'districts'; however, the role adopted by them continually changed to encompass patients from the working, middle and even upper classes. At the same time the role moved from being predominantly focused upon sanitary and moral reform within the homes of the poor, to the hands-on nursing care of a wide range of medical and surgical conditions. In some (mostly rural) areas the nurse would also be required to practice midwifery, and possibly to carry out the duties of a health visitor and/or school nurse. Added to this, developments in hospital medicine and surgery resulted in a steady increase in the numbers of elderly, chronically sick or terminally ill patients being discharged into the community, requiring a great deal of arduous and time-consuming nursing care and at times becoming the mainstay of her daily duties.[3] As the type and range of care needing to be provided changed, so did the training and organisational requirements of the district nursing associations for which they worked.

Until the NHS Act (1946) came into force in 1948, district nursing was organised through a voluntary system of local associations, many of which were affiliated to the Queen's Nursing Institute (henceforth referred to as QNI) and adhered to its standards of practice and system of supervision. From its institution in 1889 the QNI remained the dominant force in district nursing in Britain until it ceased training district nurses in 1970. The local associations were run by a lay committee which raised the funds to employ the nurse(s) and to provide suitable accommodation, and to whom, as we shall see from this study, the nurse was accountable on a day-to-day basis. Throughout this period the salary of the district nurse generally compared unfavourably with salaries offered elsewhere, whilst the work was seen more as a vocation than a normal job, being physically and emotionally demanding. As the nurses lived within the community which they served, their hours could be very unpredictable, with very little official time off duty, and often included being called out in the evenings or at night. Yet there was also a professional status and a degree of public respect and prestige accorded to the district nurse which is impossible to quantify, but which undoubtedly existed.[4]

District nursing in Lancashire

There are differences in the cultural backgrounds of the communities amongst whom the nurses I have studied lived and worked. Apart from the obvious differences of language or dialect, their defining characteristics were particularly elusive, but were often attributed in oral histories with health professionals who worked in the region, to a particularly strong 'sense of community' or to parochial attitudes towards 'outsiders', although the intimate relationship established through the practice of district nursing seemed to lessen this. In addition, the nursing experience differed in some of the industrial areas, such as South Wales, Yorkshire, Lancashire and the Midlands, because of associated industrial injuries or diseases. For example, respiratory diseases and hand or limb injuries would have been common in the mining communities or textile-manufacturing areas, and similar industrial injuries in glass-manufacturing or pottery-making areas, whereas the district nurse working in rural Dorset or East Anglia would have different problems to contend with.

However, the cultural backgrounds of the people living in Lancashire produced quite a distinctive range of lifestyles and societies. Elizabeth Roberts[5] notes the diversity of Lancashire's economic base, from the heavy industries of Barrow and Liverpool to the textile towns of Preston and Bolton and the broader spread of Lancaster's mixed economy. Lancashire's County Association had at least 100 QNI-affiliated district nursing associations by 1939 together with Manchester, Liverpool, Lancaster, Preston, Blackburn, Blackpool and Burnley, which were all allocated QNI 'county borough' status. Lancashire's district nursing service was extremely proud of its contribution towards the founding of district nursing by trained nurses, and it may have been this sense of tradition that made the service seem more ready to pioneer new developments in this field. Amongst these were the QNI William Rathbone Staff College in Liverpool, which ran refresher courses for district nurses, courses in community health administration and ward management and courses for 'overseas nurses'.[6] Lancashire was also the first county to train students on their own districts whilst they attended lecture centres at either Manchester or

Liverpool. A report referring to this innovative experiment noted: 'there are a few district nurse/midwife/health visitors in the north, about sixty district nurse/midwives in the other rural areas, and general district nurses in the more urban and industrial areas'. [7] Apart from superintendents, there were 420 district nurses working in the county in 1958 – a fall of 16.5 per cent since the 1930s. Lancashire had a larger population than the whole of South Wales in 1931, yet only 1 per cent of that population was considered to be 'un-nursed' at that time, compared with 68 per cent of the Welsh population. Even so, it was felt by the Lancashire authorities that 184 more nurses were needed to cope adequately with the heavy workload.

In Liverpool there was a QNI training centre and nurses' home which was very proud of its long tradition, and which served a culturally diverse population, as the city was a major port and centre for trade and commerce. It was the experience of care provided by a trained private nurse, Mrs Mary Robinson, in the home of William Rathbone after his wife died of consumption in 1859 that provided the inspiration for Rathbone's philanthropic establishment of district nurse training and provision for the sick poor of Liverpool. In 1862 Rathbone established a training school and home for nurses attached to the Liverpool Royal Infirmary, and founded the Liverpool Queen Victoria District Nursing Association. These provided trained nurses for the infirmary, some private nurses and district nurses for the poor, who were supervised by a 'Lady Superintendent' and worked as 'mission nurses' – that is, they were recruited from the poor areas and, once trained, returned to work in these areas with which they were familiar to spread the sanitary gospel by example. Stocks describes a confrontation between north and south and between several members of the Rathbone family. Although Liverpool eventually agreed to accept the Queen's Institute system of training and examination in 1909, Stocks maintained that resentment lingered between the 'emissaries from an arrogant metropolis' and the 'older organisation which felt that it required no outsider from the south to tell it how to manage its own business'.

A study conducted in 1938 by the Pilgrim Trust described Liverpool as 'a port with a past of great prosperity but now suffering from prolonged depression', [8] which included heavy and long-term unemployment. Queen's nursing probationers were drawn from across the north of England and

North Wales, and could be placed for one year after training wherever they were most needed. A nurse who worked in St Helen's described her training, which was divided between St Helen's and Liverpool with some time spent in rural Oxenholme:

> And we went there for a week's experience . . . And they taught us, they took us round. And, of course, they were health visitor trained as well . . . But they didn't have as many patients, that's what struck me. They didn't have as many patients as we did, because it was a more rural area. [Prompt: Yes. They'd be covering a larger mileage, presumably?] Mmm, mmm. Much bigger. We went to the farms, and they would do, like, general nursing care, and the health visiting . . . weighing babies and . . . (Prompt: Were they doing midwifery as well?) Yes, yes. There were all three. They were . . . triple duty, I can remember her weighing the babies and that, when I was there. Yes, very pleasant.[9]

It is not therefore intended that this case study of one District Nursing Association (henceforth referred to as DNA) in one county (Lancashire) should represent a 'typical' district nursing association, as each was to some extent unique. However, there are many elements and experiences that seem to have been shared by other associations, whilst other aspects may provide a more regional flavour. In addition, there are valuable insights contained within committee minutes and the district nurses' and Queen's Institute inspectors' reports, which shed light on the delicate relationship between the voluntary lay administrators of this particular nursing association and its nursing staff.

Bacup – nursing amid the 'dark satanic mills'

Fig. 6.1. Back-to-back housing in Bacup, 1898

The records of the Borough of Bacup District Nursing Society were deposited with the Royal College of Nursing archives in spring 2002 and provide a uniquely comprehensive record of the organisation and of the work of the district nurses who practised there from 1915 to 1939, with some insight into its subsequent role as a 'Comforts Guild' following the NHS Act (1946), from which point the employment of district nurses was taken under the umbrella of the Health Service.[10] The material relating to Bacup's DNA consisted of annual reports and accounts for, and listings of, 'comforts' supplied by Bacup District Nursing Association Comforts Guild after 1948, together with monthly reports of the nurses' work, assorted press cuttings, stationery, pre-printed forms and receipts and minutes of meetings of the Borough of Bacup Sick Nursing Society spread between 1915 and 1948.

Fig. 6.2 Map of Bacup (From O.S. Map c 1890)

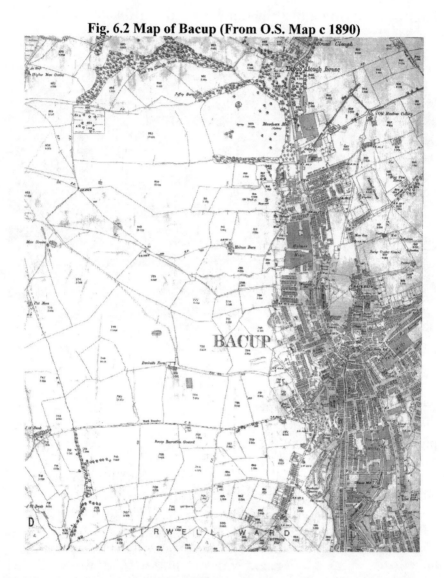

Bacup is a relatively small industrial town, with Stackstead as a similar, close but generally wealthier neighbour. They are situated approximately halfway between Burnley and Rochdale (now served by the East Lancashire Health Authority). The nearest large town is Rawtenstall, seven miles west from Bacup. The town's main industries throughout the period I'm looking at here were textiles and footwear manufacture, with a small percentage of the population involved in coal mining, quarrying and sheep farming.

The population in 1851 was about 7,000 whilst by 1902 it had risen to about 25,000.[11] The 1891 census statistics showed that most people were living in terraced 'back to back', one-up one-down houses. The majority of these houses had a living room and kitchen-scullery and quite often a cellar, with either one or two bedrooms plus an attic. This would have provided accommodation for a family of about six but often considerably more. In 1895 there were 255 cellar dwellings in Bacup, 152 of which were occupied by families and 103 were empty.[12] By 1974 the population had fallen back to 14,990,[13] a reflection of the fact that the Lancashire cotton industry had effectively peaked in 1914 – at which point Bacup had 25 textile firms in operation – and was in decline throughout the period of this case study.

The area has been described even recently as predominantly 'poor' as well as being in some ways rather insular – 'outsiders', according to a medical historian who knew this area well,[14] are easily recognized as such, partly because the inhabitants have retained a distinct dialect (unlike much of the rest of Lancashire where this has been lost). Bowden's excellent *Book of Bacup*[15] provides some vivid insights into the lives of the townspeople and the health and welfare problems encountered by the nurses on a daily basis – for example:

> A typical Bacup house in the early 20th century comprised a living room/kitchen lit by a single incandescent gas mantle. All cooking was done on the coal fire or in the adjoining oven, and the kettle would often be permanently bubbling away ready for whatever meal or task was due. There was no bathroom — even in 1951 60% of Bacup's houses had no fixed bathroom; there was usually just a cold water tap downstairs over a shallow stone sink under the window.[16]

District nursing bedridden patients in conditions such as these would have been particularly difficult and time-consuming, thus emphasising the difference between hospital and community nursing. Problems such as incontinence would have been much harder to deal with where washing and sanitary facilities were so limited, as would the observation of aseptic technique for performing dressings, for example, and advice on sanitation and diet may well have been given in the knowledge that in practical terms it was unrealistic.

When Bacup received its Charter of Incorporation in 1882 the Bacup Hospital Charities Fund was set up: collections were made throughout the wider community through events called 'Hospital Saturday' and 'Hospital Sunday' and from the working-class community by collections in the mills, factories and churches. The money raised was then sent as a grant to various hospitals, such as Rochdale Infirmary, Manchester Royal Infirmary, Southport Convalescent Home, the Devonshire Hospital in Buxton and Sourhall Isolation Hospital, as well as providing donations to the Bacup Sick Nursing Association. Consequently any patient from Bacup needing treatment or care could either be sent to one of these hospitals and receive treatment or could have the attention of one of the nurses provided through the Sick Nursing Association.[17]

An example of this in 1915 concerned a young girl suffering from St Vitus' dance (Sydenham chorea) whose family was very poor. She needed admission to the convalescent home in Southport, but as this was filled with military war casualties it was decided that nursing care and extra nourishment be provided by the District Nursing Association.

Relationships between the 'Ladies' Committee' of Bacup's district nursing association and its district nurses

I will now look briefly at the foundation and administration of the society. The Borough of Bacup District Nursing Association was founded, as were many others, in 1897, at the time of the Queen's Diamond Jubilee, and a considerable local fundraising effort resulted in the purchase in 1906 of a house at 33 Dale Street, a fairly central and mainly residential location of terraced housing. The house itself would have had a front room and back room with a little scullery-type kitchen, and upstairs front and back bedrooms and probably a toilet in the backyard. It was not therefore in the 'back-to-back' class of dwelling found in the poorer, overcrowded areas closer to the mills, such as Underbank opposite to Holmes Mill. But neither was it a conventional 'nurses' home' as would have been found in larger towns.

The economic foundation of the society was therefore largely dependent on charitable collections and the proceeds of fundraising events, such as concerts and productions by the local amateur dramatic society. However, there were sizeable monetary gifts from time to time, reflecting the philanthropic support of local dignitaries[18] as well as the key role played by the Bacup Hospitals Charities Committee. In addition, the society's minutes for September 1930 gave notification that the Public Assistance Committee of Lancashire County Council 'have decided to make a grant of £10.10.0 towards funds' of the association for 1931, raised to £16 the following year. This was slightly later than most local authorities in England and Wales, many of which began to contribute towards the public health aspect of district nursing from 1928.

Nothing appears to have survived relating to the work of the first nurse(s) appointed, until it is recorded that Nurse Dixon and Nurse Awre practised there from 1915 to 1920. From January 1915, a detailed monthly record of their work and that of their successors survives, giving numbers of cases nursed and visits made, often incorporating details of outcomes and particular problems encountered – these will be considered later in this chapter. Nevertheless, it is probable from contemporary accounts that in a routine day the nurses would have encountered patients suffering from tuberculosis, epilepsy, respiratory diseases including pneumonia, congestive cardiac failure, blindness, paralysis and terminal illnesses.

The first minuted account of the district nursing society available[19] refers to a meeting held on 16 January 1924 which notes that the previous minutes had been read and signed, but these have apparently not survived. The nurses' reports for the previous month were read, as was done at every subsequent meeting (although there is no record of any direct comment on or discussion of these), and agreement was reached to order a waterbed and pillow 'for the use of patients' to be paid for out of the society's funds; this tradition of providing equipment and 'comforts' for patients continued until long after the NHS Act. However, the main discussion at this and subsequent meetings focused on fundraising activities (Dramatic Society's play, 'Alexandra Day', the 'Christmas Doll Draw', etc) and on co-opting new committee members – a process arrived at by general consensus on this and future occasions.

The annual reports show that Bacup is typical of most district nursing associations throughout the inter-war years in having a committee consisting mostly of the wives of notable figures such as town councillors. For example, in 1944 the president and vice president were respectively Mrs Ireland, a JP and the mayor's wife, and Lady Maden, also a JP and wife of the previous mayor; Mrs J.P. Brown was wife to Dr Brown, a GP and one of the doctors connected with the local (Fernhill) military hospital. In addition, there are two other ladies on the list who are justices of the peace! This was quite typical of other associations I have looked at, and it must have made things very difficult for the nurses, who generally came from upper working-class or lower middle-class backgrounds, at a time when class meant much more in terms of social position and deference.

In employing QNs, the society committed itself to operating on the understanding that nursing care would be provided to the 'sick poor' without charge. However, others apparently availed themselves of this service from quite early on, and by 1915 it was felt necessary to request a financial contribution from these patients. A form of 'provident system' was eventually introduced in 1926 under the local hospital fund scheme[20] and the 'Penny A Week' subscription system was adopted, but throughout the inter-war period the borough hospital committee was responsible for a large portion of the society's income-giving grants, which annually totalled £300 or more.[21] However, in July 1938 it was noted in a QNI inspector's report read before the committee that a provident scheme had still not been fully adopted, and a more strongly worded recommendation was lodged in 1939 stating that a provident scheme should urgently be adopted 'so that everyone needing nursing care should be able to avail themselves of this service'.[22]

The ties with the hospital fund scheme effectively reduced the society's allegiance to the QNI, and the communication with the Queen's Institute over Queen Alexandra's memorial[23] exemplifies this. Regret was expressed that 'owing to the state of trade in the town, it would not be possible for the committee to undertake any collecting'; two years earlier, it had been decided that the Alexandra Day collection[24] could no longer be supported by the society 'owing to the express wish of the New Borough Hospital Committee with whom we have now to work and on whom we are now dependent for our funds'. As with many other urban district nursing societies, cooperation in payment through work-based contributory schemes was also solicited from local employers: for example, a letter was sent in 1937 to the 'Shoe and Slipper Operatives Union Insurance Society at Bacup re. payment for nursing services to their members',[25] and I am assured that some local employers did cooperate in this way as well as providing generous donations to the society from time to time.[26]

In May 1928 it is recorded that a county nursing association was to be formed for Lancashire to which the Bacup society might wish to affiliate. As presented in the minutes, the advantages of such an association would lie in its providing:

1. A means of regular, frequent and common council.

2. Immediate consultation with County Superintendent.

3. Supply of permanent staff.

4. Expert professional advice for staff in difficult or emergency matters.

5. Increase of revenue from statutory grants which are now largely unapplied for [sic].

6. In general, the non-assessable strength and status to be derived from association and the benefits accruing from unity.

The advantages to the bestowed:

1. Concerned for the un-nursed areas, and participation in a County effort intimately affecting the homes and the well-being of the people of Lancashire.

2. Co-operation with adjacent associations to mutually arrange nursing boundaries so that not one household is unprovided for.

3. Experience gained in health development and participation in all the Maternal Health Movements proceeding on every hand.

After some discussion it was decided to join, and at a subsequent meeting it was revealed that, of the 134 nursing associations at work within the county of Lancashire, 110 had also decided to affiliate. It should be noted that this decision – and many others affecting the membership of largely working-class subscribers or contributors – was taken by the committee, which as we have seen generally comprised the wives of the employing and professional classes of Bacup, with no referral to the subscribers. This was standard practice with most district nursing association committees at this time.[27]

Nurses Dixon and Awre ran the neighbouring districts of Bacup and Stackstead jointly from 1915 to 1920, being replaced by Nurses Hamilton and Neary, who left in 1925 to become health visitors in Manchester – quite a common cause of resignation in many district nursing associations nationwide, and an apparently natural step in professional development rather than a permanent move across to health visiting. Nurses Morgan and Bonham, both previously working in Huddersfield, replaced them. Interestingly, it was only felt necessary for the executive of the committee to interview one of the nurses, as they were friends; the two stayed until 1938, when their joint resignation occurred under something of a cloud. Several nurses were appointed during the war years, but Nurses Cummings and John stayed at least twenty-one years, from 1944 to 1965. This pattern of staff turnover was fairly average, although many nursing associations had a more rapid movement of nursing staff responding to local and regional variables.

Nurses' pay and conditions of service

At the January 1924 meeting referred to earlier it was noted that 'the Todmorden Corporation were willing to grant free bus passes to the two nurses'.[28] As this area is extremely hilly – treacherously so in winter conditions – this would have represented a considerable relief to the nurses, who according to the society's minutes travelled either by bicycle or public transport (bus or tram), with no other form of motorized transport until a car was bought in 1942. Two years later a similar comment relating to the recognition of district nursing locally noted that any nursing requirements could 'now be bought at Messrs. Boots Ltd. by the nurse with a professional discount of 10% for cash'.[29] It does not clarify whether the nurse would have to pay from her own purse and then be reimbursed, but this would seem likely.

Another aspect of the committee's work each year was making the arrangements for a holiday relief nurse. The same nurse (Nurse Hoyle) was appointed through the secretary for several successive years, and was paid £2 per week, with the nurses being obliged to take their whole month's annual leave at one time, according to dates largely dictated by the committee. Later on a correspondence was entered into between the QNI and the committee agreeing to a suitable temporary appointment, but not until 1936 was it decided that the nurse should interview and brief the relief nurse herself, and advise the committee as to her professional suitability. Also at that January meeting in 1924, a proposed pension scheme for the nurses was discussed, resulting in a decision recorded a year later to abide by the recommendations from the QNI that £3 was to be paid per nurse by each association to give a pension of £20 per nurse after 21 years' service or at the age of 55. To put this into context, in March 1930 a discussion about the proposed increases in QNs' salaries led eventually to agreement to provide an increase in the commencing salary to £70 per annum, rising by £5 annually to £80, 'and where midwifery is practised to £90' (a new scale came into force in 1937, by which time both nurses were on the maximum salary of £100 a year and at which point the QNI Long Service Fund also became active).

In 1931 a meeting of the county nursing association was held to explain the proposed superannuation scheme to local organisers; it was then discussed and the decision made to join the scheme. It was also the role of the county association to advise on the purchase of new equipment: for example, a sterilizer was recommended by the county adviser and its purchase was approved following the meeting. This seems a fairly minor piece of apparatus now, and has been superseded by pre-packaged disposables, but at the time it would have made a considerable change to the daily round for the district nurses and their patients. It is perhaps significant that, as was the case in most other district nursing associations, the nurses did not attend these committee meetings, and there is no evidence to suggest that their views were represented. If this was the situation, it seems unlikely that they could have exerted much influence on the outcome of such discussions, despite the effect these and similar items would have had on their daily work. This situation did change slightly towards the end of the 1930s and during wartime: for example, on several occasions in 1939 one of the nurses was invited into the committee meeting to discuss the inspection and availability of appliances supplied to patients by the association. After reporting in 1940 that their cases had become 'quite inadequate for carrying all the appliances which they needed in order to perform their duties successfully', one of the nurses was invited to demonstrate the problem, resulting in a decision to purchase two new 'regulation' bags.

Other pressures exerted by the committee on the nurses were sometimes a result of national policy: for example, a letter from the Ministry of Health with regard to an application made by the committee for a midwifery grant was read at the September 1924 meeting. It stated:

> it is regretted that on the basis already adopted for assessing such grants to Nursing Associations working in Urban Districts in England, no grant is this year payable to the Bacup District Nursing Society.

Nevertheless, the report of the Queen's Institute inspector had noted that year that whilst there were currently no midwifery cases on the books at the date of her visit, 'this branch of the work appeared to be progressing well – the patients seen were being attended with care and skill'. Immediately after this a large amount of equipment was purchased 'for the nurses bag', listed as '1 Pelvimeter, 3 forceps, 3 probes, 2 pairs scissors, 3 clinical thermometers, 1 bath thermometer, 1 pair balances, 1 spatula, 1 kidney tray, 2 nail brushes, plus lint, gauze, cord dressing and ligature' – this seems highly likely to be intended to support a move towards increased midwifery practice. By 1927 the annual report notes that midwifery fees had risen to £104 17s 6d – representing more than two-thirds of the total income (£144 13s 6d) from fees and subscriptions – and that cases had risen from 45 recorded in 1924 to 59 in 1927. However, a special meeting was held just two years later, in 1929, 'to consider discontinuing the midwifery side of the work as there are now 5 midwives in the town and the work has also been taken up by the poor law authority at "Monlands" where a new block has recently been opened'. It was therefore decided to discontinue this aspect of the work apart from emergency cases – there is no record of any formal discussion having taken place to consult the nurses on this decision.

Work and workloads - how 'busy' were the district nurses?

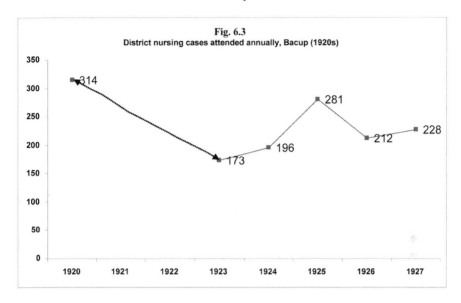

Fig. 6.3
District nursing cases attended annually, Bacup (1920s)

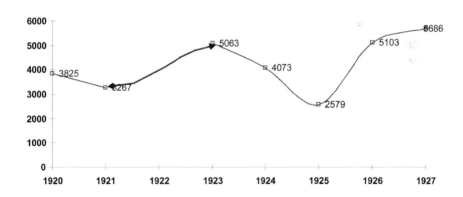

Fig. 6.4

District Nurse's annual total visits, Bacup (1920s)

At the January 1925 meeting, 'A discussion took place on the increasing work of the nurses and it was suggested that local help be obtained when necessary as in the case of illness of either nurse or rush of work'. It can be seen from figures 3 and 4 that although the total number of visits over the year actually decreased, and a steady fall in numbers of visits can be seen from a high point reached in 1923, nevertheless there was a significant rise in the number of cases that year, and by 1926 the numbers of visits had again risen sharply. Furthermore, monthly records (see figure 5) kept by the nurses show that they would have felt severely pressured by 'rush of work', with January to April appearing consistently heavy when compared with the summer months of July and August. In comparison with the national scale, the nurses at Bacup were consistently attending more cases: for example, in 1925 they attended 281 cases compared with a national average of 153.

Fig. 6.5 Bacup district cases nursed on monthly basis (5 yearly, 1915-1940)

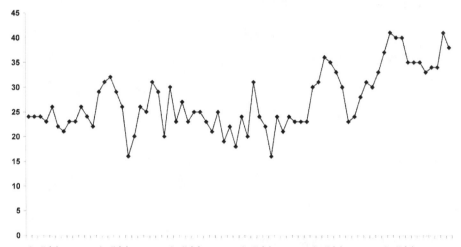

Ten years later, the heavy workload became a cause for concern to the Queen's Institute inspector, whose report in January 1937 was noted in the committee's minutes: 'the size of the population and amount of work to be undertaken indicate the need for an additional nurse.' However, this does not appear to have been addressed at the meeting, and there are no records in later minutes to suggest that the committee discussed the issue. In addition, there are suggestions throughout the records that the committee was not fully aware of its nurses' daily routine. Yet in 1941 the nurses made a request to the committee that they might be allowed to sleep out on their half-day holidays, and this request was referred to the county superintendent. The verdict was that they could only take the half-day each week and one weekend per month 'except in unusual circumstances', and so had to be back in the home that night. This supports the idea that, throughout the inter-war years, district nurses possessed considerable professional autonomy in their work, yet lacked independence from the 'Committee of Ladies' in other ways.

References to the actual work carried out by the nurses are comparatively rare throughout the 28 years of reports and minutes studied. However, the monthly reports in 1915 and 1916 record school inspections for the second half of the year, and these are quite revealing, as well as confirming that at this point school nursing was included in their work. The report of June 1915 notes that the cases being treated included ringworm, sore and dirty eyes and conjunctivitis, discharging ears, 'sore and filthy heads', 'verminous bodies', sores on face '(due to dirt and neglect)'. The number of children receiving attention in June was 290: this included 176 seen at the clinic and a further 96 who received home visits – no details are given for the remaining 12 children. Although the numbers seen in clinic during the winter months are rather smaller (the November and December clinic attendances were down to 71 and 119 respectively), the number of home visits rose substantially (to 66 and 78 over the same months). It is likely, therefore, that the nurses saw their role as including an educational remit, visiting the homes to advise mothers on bodily hygiene, diet and child-care.

Nevertheless, the mainstay of their work at this time was evidently domiciliary nursing. The deaths of patients recorded by the nurses that year have been collated and are shown in the graph, with cancers, tuberculosis and 'senile decay' making up a high proportion of the terminal care nursing provided – a total of 43 that year.

In 1920 their replacements, Nurses Dodds and Clarke, no longer recorded school visits, but causes of patients' death on the district were still recorded, with a subtle change in nomenclature: Cancer of Liver (3), Cerebral Tumour (1), Sarcoma of Breast (1), other Cancers (2), Phthisis (Tuberculosis) (2), Pernicious Anaemia (1), Cardiac and/or Brights Disease (5), Cerebral Haemorrhage (4), Senile Decay (6), Abscesses of head (1), 'Double Pneumonia' (1), Injuries caused by accident (1), Pleurisy (1). The total number is 29 – almost a third less than in 1915. Of the total cases for the year, 31 were surgical and 72 medical, with 11 operations. The notes suggest this is a big drop in numbers compared with 1919 – which may be a reference to the Spanish flu epidemic – but the general trend in all these areas was clearly towards an increase in workload.

From 1923, midwifery fees were recorded – and by 1925[30] midwifery seems to have become well established by the new nurse-midwives. Also, there were fewer deaths, although the prime causes – carcinoma, cardiac failure, senile decay, phthisis and pneumonia – remained unchanged. Interestingly, there was one death due to malaria, and one patient died post-operatively; unfortunately, no details were given for either of these. It is nevertheless clear from the yearly statistics that a steady increase in workload included a rise from assisting at just 11 surgical operations in 1920 to 21 just six years later, combined with a formidable increase in post-surgical cases nursed and the introduction of midwifery (in itself very time-consuming).

Medical cases still represented the highest proportion of the workload, and would probably have also made the heaviest demands on the nurses' time and energy, since general nursing care, such as bed-bathing and care of pressure areas, for these often chronically sick patients would have been especially challenging given the domestic arrangements described earlier. Lack of data against which to compare these figures makes it impossible to claim that this situation was typical nationally, but emphasis on these aspects of nursing care in district nursing handbooks from the 1930s[31] would suggest this was probably the case. This combination of factors would suggest a fairly close working relationship throughout this period between the GPs in Bacup and the district nurses, as well as with the local hospital, with which the district nursing society had direct financial links. It also fits the picture of mutual professional respect, albeit at a distance, that had evolved between GP and QN – although that has been shown elsewhere to have been rather precarious, depending to a considerable extent on the economic situation.

A significant comment was made in the association's minutes in 1925: 'It was resolved that stamped envelopes be provided for the doctors' use, where the communication to the Nurse is of a private character.'[32] This would suggest that, as with many similar-sized district nursing practices, the nurses did not see the GPs on a regular basis, even though their services were well recognised and used by them: in other words, a fairly autonomous mode of practice for both the doctor and district nurse.

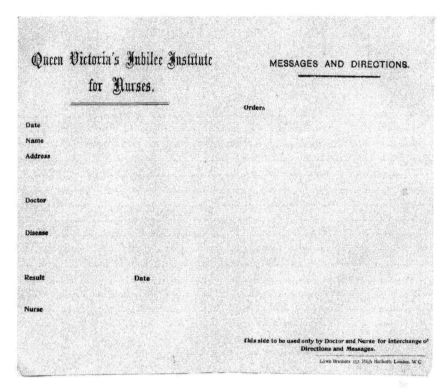

Fig. 6.6QVJN Nurse – Doctor Message Sheet

Inspectors from the Queen's Institute paid regular visits at approximately six-monthly intervals and these are briefly reported in the committee's minutes; their comments always stated that standards of nursing were found to be good, but a subtle change to the previously fairly standard wording was noticeable in the report for January 1927, which may reflect a change of emphasis on the part of the inspector. Alongside observations such as 'the nursing technique was good' and comments about the nurses' books and bags being in good order, it was also noted that 'nursing appliances' were found to be 'correct and tidy'. In November 1929 the inspector noted that 'Sound methods, modern technique and comprehensive individual care characterised all the work seen with the nurses'; and similarly in 1939 nursing care was described as 'comprehensive and skilful'. It seems reasonable to conclude that this change marks an adjustment to the concept of what it meant to be a professional district nurse, representing a move away from the image presented through neat and tidy uniforms, bags and record books towards a more detailed assessment of the techniques of nursing practice and familiarity with modern methods. However, this change in professional emphasis did not appear to extend to the lay committee recognising any responsibility to support the professional development of their nurses, as the January minutes that year also record that 'to attend a 5 day course of lectures in London, N. Bonham was forgoing her usual weekend holidays'. A major concession appears to have been leave of absence granted for the nurses to attend the Jubilee inspection at Buckingham Palace on 16 June 1937. Also, comments were made in the minutes about the off-duty system by which each nurse has one day off each fortnight, taken in alternate weeks in order to provide continuous cover.

In 1935 it was suggested that a telephone might be installed in the nurses' home, as 'hitherto neighbours had kindly conveyed messages to the nurses' but this was now becoming 'rather troublesome' because of the number of calls being made. In the UK, 'widespread adoption [of the telephone] amongst doctors began to occur mainly after 1900'[33] – that is, long before it came to be considered a necessary tool for a district nurse. However, district nurses who worked during the inter-war period described the main method of contact as 'word of mouth', part of living and working within a community. In practice, except where there were larger numbers of district nurses living at a nurses' home staffed during working hours, communication was achieved through a combination of a slate or message board left outside the nurse's front door to say where she could be found, written or verbal messages sent from the patient or doctor, and messages left during the daytime at a central location such as a doctor's surgery, chemist's shop or post office. A QNI-led campaign addressed to the Postmaster General between 1932 and 1935[34] to have telephones provided for district nurses pointed out in its report for 1935: 'It would be possible for the utility of the nurses to be greatly increased by taking advantage of modern inventions.' In their view, the best way of organising district nursing associations was to provide a nurse with a motor car or motor cycle and to install the telephone in her house. It added: 'There was not enough work in some places to keep a nurse fully occupied, but she could not be moved as she must be at hand for midwifery cases.'

The provision of cars and telephones would enable the nurses to be centralised and would reduce the number required. Nevertheless, whatever the means of transport used and whether in town or country, the district nurse of the past was more visible to the public. This was partly due to the fact that, before the nurse's car became ubiquitous, the nurse walked around her area and became widely known and recognisable. The keeping of a tidy uniform worn properly was a factor in this recognition. It was a physical identification with the district nursing service, notably the QNI, and a sign to the public that reinforced the image of the nurse as knowledgeable, authoritative and professional, an image remembered with fondness by district nurses.

Compare this with Hawkshead and District – this is now part of Cumbria, but was included in Lancashire until the boundaries were changed in the 1970s. The district nurses there also covered a particularly large area, recorded in 1924 as '12 square miles' and increased to '25 square miles' in 1934. It was described as a 'country district, rather hilly', adding 'cyclist necessary', but from as early as September 1925 a two-seater Morris Cowley car was provided. A committee which ran a provident system of subscriptions and donations managed the district nursing association, which employed just one QN who covered both general nursing and midwifery. The first stayed from 1919 to 1924 and was paid £75 annually, plus 21s board and laundry weekly and £8 uniform allowance, having 'two furnished rooms with fire, light and attendance provided' – later a furnished cottage was provided.

Interestingly, insurance certificates for the nurses' home for 1930 and 1935 cover two nurses and one domestic servant, and public liability cover included an allowance for claims for 'compensation due to negligence of the nurses', indicating the overlapping of concerns of employment by a lay committee with the professional concerns of the nurses' practice. Back at Bacup, however, the main concerns of the committee at that time appeared to revolve around renovation of the nurses' home – indeed, repairs and renewals for the home account for a considerable amount of discussion at every meeting! A member of the committee responsible for overseeing repairs and renewals regularly inspected the nurses' home, which appears to have been reasonably comfortable according to QNI inspectors' reports, but one is struck in reading these minutes by the lack of privacy and independence accorded the nurses. In fact, in 1940 the nurses requested that a change of the committee's 'visiting day' be arranged so that both nurses could be present when their home was to be inspected.

By 1938 there were very few midwifery cases and deaths were no longer regularly recorded in any detail, although when they were the illnesses concerned remained largely unchanged. The dismissal of the two nurses in May 1938 makes interesting reading and reinforces the concept of [duplicity of professional status]. In April 1938 several special meetings were held to resolve a problem that had occurred concerning the two nurses. The outcome was that both nurses were requested to send in their resignations, receiving one month's pay in lieu of notice – this demand was in fact supported by the QNI county superintendent. At this time Nurse Bonham was seen by the doctor and pronounced unfit whilst Nurse Morgan was away on her annual leave! A subsequent meeting was held with Nurse Morgan who was 'allowed time to consider resignation'. Nurse Bonham's resignation was received a week later, and although she wrote soon afterwards stating that her health was now much better and that she would like to withdraw her offer of resignation and be allowed to return to her post in Bacup, this plea was refused by the committee, and Nurse Morgan's resignation was received at the next meeting (at the end of May). The secretary, having received two report forms from the Queen's Institute regarding Nurse Morgan and Nurse Bonham, was requested to fill these in and return them to the general superintendent for inclusion in their professional records. Both nurses were to be interviewed by Miss Furminger, the county superintendent. I am reliably informed[35] that the main reason for this rather drastic action appears to have been a personal rift between the two nurses caused by a marriage proposal made by the widower of a patient nursed by them both!

Two temporary nurses were provided by the QNI to replace Nurses Morgan and Bonham until new appointments could be made. Following this episode the rules of the association were updated to include a number of restrictive clauses:

The nurse shall not talk over personal matters with patients and their friends

The nurse shall abide by the rulings of the Lancs. County Nursing Association and the Queen's Institute

No pets shall be allowed in the home

The nurses shall take holidays in the regulation manner, a month's holiday at once, and each nurse separately

The nurses shall take duty in alternative districts.

After this incident a considerable amount of renovation work was done to the nurses' home, which appears to have required redecorating and some refurnishing.

Wartime and post-war changes

Although during the war the area apparently suffered only one air raid and minimal war damage, from early 1939 the nurses were required to work with the local Medical Officer of Health Dr McKinney, at the borough first-aid posts as part of the 'Air Raid Precautions Scheme', and they received the necessary training later the same year.[36] The statistics of visits paid and cases nursed for the final two years leading up to the inception of the NHS have survived, and show a rise in medical and surgical cases attended in 1948 despite an actual drop in numbers of visits made. Also, comparing these figures with those for the 1920s shown earlier, the rise in workload is very noticeable, from 5,000 visits per year to 8,000 and from 200–300 cases annually to 300–400. It is evident from this that the district nursing service was not only being fully utilised, but that the nurses were coping with an extremely heavy workload. Nevertheless, 1939 saw an increased effort to raise public awareness of district nursing, firstly through the use of a 10-minute film about district nursing and the district nurses' role. This was shown at the Regal Cinema for the first week of October 1939. Also, it was minuted that the QNI gardens scheme posters advertising participating gardens in Lancashire were to be distributed to local mills and workshops and posted on placards throughout the district;

however, this seems to be more a matter of keeping in line with the county association rather than an attempt to increase the caseload of the nurses. By 1940 holiday relief had become a problem, as war work meant that relief nurses were scarce, and in April 1940 the QNI inspector 'strongly recommended an auto-car or auto-cycle for use on long-distance cases' – after discussion with the nurses this matter was left, but re-emerged soon after the appointment of two new nurses the following year. The hospital committee felt unable to provide funding for this, and money was instead raised by the mayor through public appeal, flag days etc. In the interim, a few local residents voluntarily provided transport on Sundays, when public transport between Bacup and Stackstead did not run.

Bacup after the NHS Act (1946)

The report of the annual general meeting for 1948 notes that the two nurses were continuing to live in the nurses' home for the time being and were sharing a car bought by the society in 1942. However, this had been found to be unreliable, causing the nurses considerable trouble, and a new one had been ordered in 1946, but despite this, 'Medical and Nursing Services are supposed to be endowed with some degree of priority of delivery but this has not worked out in practice.'

The report also notes the continuation of the 'Penny A Week Fund', stating that 'it is regrettable that just at a time when the Society has reached a stage when financial worries have considerably lessened there should be a prospect of having to cease its voluntary work and hand over to a state machine which, though it may be perfectly efficient, it is felt will not provide that personal and knowledgeable contact which a voluntary service can furnish.' This voices fears that must have been felt in many district nursing associations at the prospect of a local authority taking away not only the powers of the local committee, but their distinctive local knowledge and the personal touch of the voluntary committee member.

However, the report of 1949 notes that the transfer of responsibility for district nursing took place 'in principle', but that the society continued its services until 30 September 1948 at the request of the Medical Officer of Health. It records that the nurses' home and two cars (one still pending delivery) are 'still to be paid for – under negotiation'; the money from the sale of these assets was then invested in the newly formed Comforts Guild (see below). A third nurse had also been appointed since the state took over, but her name does not appear in any records. Two articles published in the local press noted the continuation of the QNI's contribution to district nursing in the town, ten years after the NHS Act (1946). The first stated that the two QNs working at Bacup 'have been here for upwards of 15 years . . . The Institute is entirely responsible for the present high standard of nursing amongst those who are proud to wear the title "Queen's" on their uniform, and jealously upholds the qualification and professional integrity of its members.'[37] The second refers to the QNI's Centenary District Nursing appeal for £250,000, 'largely to support training and expansion of QNI's valuable work', and mentions the work of the QNs in Bacup.[38] In fact, despite the fears expressed at the inception of the NHS, the nurses (Nurse Cummings and Nurse John) who were appointed in 1944 remained in post for at least 21 years, presenting a hymn book to the Trinity Baptist Ladies' Fellowship to record this fact in 1965.[39] This is significantly longer than any of their predecessors, and may reflect a happier working relationship. As with most other district nursing associations, the nurses would have been provided with (rented) living accommodation by the local authority, which must have been quite liberating after the somewhat restricted lifestyle of the nurses' home.

From the earliest minutes available there are mentions of regular contributions of bedding and clothing being provided through the East Lancashire Needlework Association. Likewise, larger items such as a waterbed and pillow, bought by the Bacup District Nursing Society in 1924, were provided as nursing aids and patient 'comforts'. Comforts funds are generally associated with the voluntary provision of (usually small) non-essential items during wartime to ease discomfort. For example, the Victoria League of Comforts was established in 1901 to provide 'comforts' for Boer women and children being held in detention camps in South Africa; likewise, comforts funds were established during World War One and World War Two to supply members of the armed services with 'comforts'. However, in some cases comforts funds, possibly with the help of the local Women's Voluntary Service, provided basic material needs such as dressings, clothing and bed-linen for disadvantaged people within the local community, often using the district nurses' knowledge and discretion to distribute these where they were most needed.

However, the Bacup District Nursing Society Patients' Comforts Fund was set up in 1948 following the introduction of the NHS, directly replacing the district nursing association's 'Penny A Week' fund. The annual report of Bacup's nursing association in that year and subsequently refers to the value of the comforts fund to patients. Examples of recipients taken from the records of the society include:

> In 1962: an old lady living alone, who was found to have 'only sheets and a cotton quilt on bed', was provided with blankets from the fund. [40]

> From 1962 to 1964: an 11 year old suffering from Muscular Dystrophy and confined to bed/wheelchair was provided with a bed-table, Mackintosh sheet for the bed, knitting wool, a bed-pan and a mattress.[41]

> In 1965: a young woman with a premature baby detained in Fairfield Hospital for several months whilst her husband was in prison, was provided with blankets and flannelette sheets.[42]

These examples are just three taken from a very extensive and detailed list, to illustrate the wide range of recipients of all ages, some with short-term needs, others needing help over a prolonged period of time. Accounts of the Comforts Guild run through to 1985, with outgoing payments covering clothing and comforts for patients. The aim was the provision of 'Special foods and medicines, medical comforts, extra bedding, fuel and medical and surgical appliances, domestic help, money grants to enable the recipients to obtain such benefits or to defray the expense of convalescence or of obtaining change of air or special protection or treatment including the expense of any necessary transport and of obtaining domestic help during convalescence,' and was intended 'For sick and needy persons resident in the Municipal Borough of Bacup . . . at the recommendation of the District Nurse.'

This was a thriving society, particularly in the 1960s, as may be seen from the annual report's accounts. Receipts at that time range from part-payment of beds and ripple mattresses to Christmas food parcels, bed-rests, commodes, bed-linen, blankets and urinals. From 1950 it was referred to as 'The Borough of Bacup District Nursing Society Comforts Guild', and many of the donations came from grateful patients or their relatives. The deed of constitution for this change was dated 1950 and refers back to the Borough of Bacup District Nursing Society formed in 1897, noting:

> whereas by virtue of the provisions of the National Health Act 1948 and the orders and regulations made thereunder the provision and maintenance of such District Nursing Service has become the responsibility of the Council for the Administrative County of the County Palatine of Lancaster and whereas the assets of the Society have been sold and the proceeds realised by such sales together with the other investments funds moneys and securities of the Society await application in manner hereinafter appearing . . .

The comments on a letter enquiring about the possibility of depositing these records with the Royal College of Nursing's archives note that the Comforts Guild was finally wound up in 1985 because it was felt that 'developments of health care and extension of social services generally have, over the years, rendered the objects and purposes of the Guild increasingly less appropriate or necessary'.[43] The assets were transferred to the local hospice.

Conclusion

This chronologically defined case study has been able to show the complex relationship between district nurse, nursing association and Queen's Institute central and county organisation as this developed through the inter-war period. The study also demonstrates the value of data in establishing statements relating to workload, such as those found in the minute books of the Bacup society. In addition, although it was not possible to obtain first-hand oral histories from the nurses and committee members involved, it has been possible to augment this account with information obtained by personal communications from a number of Bacup residents, which has been invaluable in providing a clearer and hopefully more accurate picture.

The variations in workload and in type of work undertaken have been examined, as to some extent has the relationship with the wider community and its affection for 'their' district nurse(s). Actions ranging from public fundraising and donations to the home for the nurses' comfort, through to generous individual contributions – such as the offers under wartime petrol restrictions to drive the nurse on a Sunday morning's round – all suggest a strong sense of loyalty and affection. Yet the relatively short lengths of stay in post appear somewhat surprising and contradictory until compared with the national picture. It was not until the post-war period that Bacup, as elsewhere, experienced the permanence of district nurses who came and stayed, contradicting one of the many popular stereotypes of district nursing to be explored elsewhere.[44]

Acknowledgements

This chapter was originally presented as a paper presented to the Medical History Society of the University of Manchester School of Medicine, as their Annual Lecture. I would therefore like to thank them for inviting me, for their helpful comments and for encouraging me to publish. I would also like to thank Susan McGann, Archives Manager of the RCN for drawing to my attention the rich resource of the Bacup District Nursing Association material, and to Mr. J.M.D. Hoyle and Mrs Sue Hargreaves and the staff of the Natural History Museum, Bacup for their personal input and for photographic material. I also owe a great debt of gratitude to the Queen's Nursing Institute for use of their library and archives and to the Contemporary Medical Archives Centre, Wellcome Institute for the History of Medicine, London for access to the Queen's Institute's archive.

Endnotes

1   Sweet, H., and Dougal, R., *Community nursing and primary healthcare in Britain, c. 1919–1979*, Routledge, 2007.

2   Drake, M., and Finnegan, R. (eds), *Studying Family and Community History 19th and 20th Centuries. Vol. 4 Sources and Methods: A Handbook*,1994.

3   Baly, Monica E., *A History of the Queen's Nursing Institute: 100 Years 1887–1987*, Croom Helm, 1987, p 93, claims that tuberculosis nursing became a particularly heavy commitment for district nurses during the 1920s and 1930s.

4   Sweet and Dougal, *Community nursing and primary healthcare in Britain*. This aspect of public 'respectability' comes through clearly from biographies, oral histories and obituaries of nurses who worked during the inter-war period, from books, journals and documentary film, and from inter-professional correspondence studied in the preparation of this work and is discussed at greater length than is possible here; see also Baly, *A History of the Queen's Nursing Institute*, p 98, and Stocks, M., *A Hundred Years of District Nursing*, Allen & Unwin, 1960, pp 159–60.

5   Roberts, E.A., *Woman's Place. An Oral History of Working-Class Women 1890–1940*, Basil Blackwell, 1984.

6   Antrobus, A., 'Pioneers Still', *Guardian*, 29 January 1965; Hardy, G., and Lemin, B., 'William Rathbone Staff College: past, present and future', *DN*, 15, 6 (September 1972), pp 120–1.

7   Jones, L., 'Lancashire's Training Experiment', *DN*, 1, 7 (October 1958).

8   Temple, W., *Men without work*, Pilgrim Trust, 1938, p 29.

9   D/N 26, 18/05/00, Oral History: Mrs Elaine Parr (see above).

10 I am indebted to Mr. J.M.D. Hoyle LLB for his helpful comments concerning the town of Bacup and the organisation of the district nursing society to which his mother was honorary secretary for many years, whilst he is the only surviving member of the original trustees of the society's Patients' Comfort Fund which was finally wound up in 1985.

11 ibid, p 85.

12 I am most grateful to Mrs Wendy Lord, photograph librarian at the Natural History Museum, Bacup, and webmaster http://www.bacuptimes.co.uk/, for permission to use this information and a number of related photographs.

13 Bowden, K. F., *The Book of Bacup*,1994, p 86.

14 My thanks to Dr. S. King for sharing his extensive local and demographical knowledge of the area.

15 Bowden, *The Book of Bacup*.

16 ibid, p 47.

17 Personal communication, Mrs Wendy Lord and http://www.bacuptimes.co.uk/

18 Such as Sir Henry and Lady Maden, and Mr Alfred Edmonston.

19 RCN Archives: C444: Bacup District Nursing Association: Comforts Guild, 1915–1943, Monthly reports of Nurses' Work (January 1915–February 1923), (March 1923–July 1931), (September 1931–April 1943).

20 Fox, E., 'Universal Health Care and Self-Help: Paying for District Nursing before the National Health Service', *Twentieth Century British History*, 7, 1 (1996), pp 83–109, notes that the contributory schemes developed in many urban districts 'had much in common with

the contributory schemes that were being developed by voluntary hospitals, sometimes collaborating with them but sometimes competing'.

21 The society's minutes for May 1928 show the grant received from the Hospitals Charities Board for the previous year was £325 and grants applied and received in subsequent years regularly add up to similar amounts.

22 From the early 1930s this had been the preferred system supported by the QNI; A.M. Peterkin explained in 1931 that the urban system differed from the rural provident system of 'Penny A Week' minimum subscriptions from each household, in that it relied more on arrangements with public health authorities, plus charging fees for service given according to means, and 'charitable subscriptions, house-to-house collections or whatever method of raising money is best suited to the particular locality'. See Peterkin, A. M., 'The Scope and Conditions of District Nursing', QNM, XXIV, 5 (1931), pp 128–132. From 1934 a provident organizer was appointed to promote this concept, primarily in urban areas such as Bacup.

23 The original Royal Charter granted to the QNI by Queen Victoria in 1889 was followed by a supplementary Charter granted by King Edward VII in 1904, through which Queen Alexandra became patron. In 1926, following her death, the Queen Alexandra Memorial fund was approved, which raised urgently needed funds ensuring the continuance of the QNI; subsequently, an annual Alexandra Day fundraising appeal was established, with money being raised through the sale of flags and with certain private gardens being opened to the public across the UK.

24 See note 22 above.

25 RCN Archives: C444: Bacup District Nursing Society, 1924–1939, Minutes for Borough of Bacup Sick Nursing Society (January 1924–November 1939), minutes for March 1937.

26 Personal communication, Mr. J.M.D. Hoyle; also mentioned in a letter to Shoe and Slipper Operatives Union Insurance Society in 1937 're. payment for nursing services to their members'.

27 Fox, 'Universal Health Care and Self-Help'.

28 RCN Archives: C444: Bacup District Nursing Association: Comforts Guild, 1915–1943, Monthly reports of Nurses' Work (January 1915–February 1923), (March 1923–July 1931), (September 1931–April 1943).

29 RCN Archives: C444: Bacup District Nursing Society: 1924–1942, Minutes for Borough of Bacup Sick Nursing Society (January 1924–April 1942): Minutes of meeting held May 1926.

30 Nurses Hamilton and Neary

31 See, for example, Merry, E. J., and Irven, I.D., *District Nursing: A Handbook for district nurses*, 1948; and 'Some Queen's Superintendents', 1932 and 1943 editions, *Handbook for Queen's Nurses*.

32 RCN Archives: C444: Bacup District Nursing Society, 1924–1942, Minutes for Borough of Bacup Sick Nursing Society (January 1924–April 1942): Minutes of meeting held January 1924.

33 Digby, A., *The Evolution of British General Practice*, 1999, p 144.

34 SA/QNI Box 81 /H18: Correspondence, Questionnaires, Report of delegations to the Postmaster General, 1932–1935.

35 Personal communication, Mr. J.M.D. Hoyle.

36 RCN Archives: C444: Bacup District Nursing Society, 1924–1942, Minutes for Borough of Bacup Sick Nursing Society (January 1924–April 1942): Minutes of meeting held 6 March 1939.

37 RCN Archives: C444: Bacup District Nursing Society, 1915–1948, Assorted press cuttings, stationery, pre-printed forms and receipts;

'District Nursing – National Appeal: letter from Mrs. E. Hoyle, J.P.', *The [Bacup] Times*, 5 September 1959, p 3.

38 RCN Archives: C444: Bacup District Nursing Society, 1915–1948, Assorted press cuttings, stationery, pre-printed forms and receipts; 'District Nursing Movement is 100 Years Old: Voluntary system still a feature', *The [Bacup] Times*, 5 September 1959, p 4.

39 For this information I am indebted to Mrs Sue Hargreaves, a resident of Bacup.

40 RCN Archives: C444: Bacup District Nursing Association Comforts Guild, 1964–1979, Listings of Comforts Supplied.

41 ibid.

42 ibid.

43 RCN Archives: C444: Bacup District Nursing Association Comforts Guild, 1964–1979, Annual Reports (1964–1979); letter from Mr Michael Hoyle dated 27 November 2001.

44 Sweet and Dougal, *Community nursing and primary healthcare in Britain.*

Section Three: Women and Politics

G race Hadow (1875-1940) provides a bridge between the two movements examined in the last two chapters of this book. She was an active suffragist in Oxford and Cirencester and the first vice president of the Women's Institute between 1916 and 1940. She also provides a link with some of the other women in this book as this short biography illustrates, as well as being an example of a woman who had crossed the boundaries of the private sphere into the public one.

Grace was the only daughter of a clergyman, the Reverend William Hadow and his wife Mary, and was brought up in the Vicarage at South Cerney, near Cirencester. She was educated at home and then obtained a scholarship to Brownshill Court, a girl's school near Stroud, and then attended Truro High School. She went on to study English at Somerville Hall, Oxford (1900-3), where she took a first class degree in English Language and Literature. This was followed by a year as English Reader at Bryn Maur College, Pennsylvania. Whilst at Somerville she participated in the Women's Student's Debating Society. This made her aware of the importance of women's suffrage and of politics more generally. In 1904 she was appointed as an English tutor at Somerville for a year and then appointed English tutor at Lady Margaret Hall. In 1906, after her father's death, she moved to Cirencester to look after her mother but continued her work in Oxford. In Cirencester she formed a branch of the National Union of Women Suffrage Societies. During the First World War, in 1916 she founded the Cirencester Women's Institute, as she had become increasingly aware of the importance of the home production of food. In 1917 she left Cirencester as she was appointed head of a subsection of the Welfare Department of the Ministry of Munitions in London. This experience had enlarged her life and she felt that she could use her skills to develop social services for women. Thus, in 1920 she was appointed Secretary of Barnett House, Oxford, founded as a memorial to Canon Barnett, the founder of Toynbee Hall settlement, London and an active member of the Charity Organisation Society. Here she developed a rural education programme and training courses for social workers. By this time in Oxford she was noted for all her educational work and was appointed principal of the Oxford Society of Home Students (St Anne's College) Oxford, succeeding Miss Burrows. During her period as the principal of a growing women's college she was also an extremely active vice chairman of the Women's Institute, a member of the BBC Advisory Council and of the National Council of Social Services. She also found time to host local and country activities as well as travelling to America and touring the Empire. She was remembered for her administrative skills, as a public speaker and her services to others.

Her life illustrates in many ways the progress that women had made to become independent by utilising their talents and the growing opportunities available to them. In turn she devoted her life to ensure that more women would be able to become more independent and utilised political action to this end.

One of the most important ways in which women crossed the domestic threshold into the public sphere from the mid nineteenth century onwards, was through engaging in politics. By the this period some educated middle class women saw that political action was a means to improving their lives and the lives of their working class sisters. Some of these women had gained experience of working publically through philanthropic organisations, whilst others campaigned on specific issues, such as improving girls' secondary education and ensuring that women were able to receive higher education. As opportunities expanded for women in professional employment and higher education so did women's participation in politics, particularly in the women's suffrage movement. The Women's Institute was also concerned with women's education as well as giving them a voice in the political arena to air their concerns on welfare and health issues.

The first chapter in this section traces the development of the suffrage movement from a local perspective, whilst the second chapter focuses on the Women's Institute from a national perspective. Both represent different aspects of feminism and citizenship. The Oxford women's suffrage societies' ideas were based on liberal democratic ideals, which the Women's Institute then expanded these ideas into a form of discursive democracy. Both were concerned with women's equality, equal opportunities and ensuring that women had the confidence to cross the boundary from the private domestic sphere into the public sphere. In this they were similar to the other women in this book. Indeed many of the suffragists and early members of the Women's Institute were both professional women and/or philanthropists, had benefitted from and were active in higher education, in the church, and in housing and health reform. As chapter 8 illustrates, the two organisations also overlapped in the way in which they were organised. Without the suffrage movement and their experience of campaigning and organising, the Women's Institute might not have been formed in the way in which it was and still is.

Both the Oxford suffrage societies and the Women's Institute were acutely aware of national political issues and had close links with other national movements. They were also concerned with class differences, although their approaches were different. The suffrage women were primarily concerned with women gaining the vote for women on the same basis as men, and realized that they would also have to recruit working class women as they too would eventually have the vote. The Women's Institute was concerned with the plight of rural women, and although many of their leaders came from the middle and upper classes, the individual Institutes were composed of mainly working class women. They also illustrate a way in which women were redefining the boundaries of the public and private, into the personal and the political and ensuring that they made use of their newly won enfranchisement and were seen as an important political force by those in power.

Thus both chapters examine two nationally important organisations. Both have played and play an important part in women's lives today. The Women's Institute still flourishes all over the country and is still involved in local communities and national and local campaigns. The suffrage movement, eventually by 1928, was successful in gaining women the vote and ensuring that women's voices were heard in parliament. Both were in search of an independent voice and status, made their voices heard clearly and influenced a larger public by their actions and activities. Both have left an important legacy and their ideas continue to contribute to women's lives and ideas.

The two chapters also illustrate two different ways of analysing women's history, that is, from a local and national perspective. This has been done in order to illustrate a more intimate view of political women in the period 1870-1939 and to provide an alternative history to that often written about feminism, one that we hope readers can empathize with and will encourage other historians to search the rich material left by similar groups.

CHAPTER 7

'Faith, Perseverance and Patience': the History of the
Women's Suffrage Movement in Oxford, 1870–1918

Katherine Bradley

Some of the workers were busy people already used to
similar work, who could only give a portion of their time;
others were more leisured women, for whom the in-bred
custom of generations made a public agitation of this
character a difficult thing to plunge into; and to these the
campaign itself gave confidence where there had been
timidity, and training in place of inexperience. Then as
time went on enthusiasm waxed, the number of workers
increased, and their work also became more valuable.[1]

In the run-up to the 1910 general election the National Union of Women
Suffrage Societies (NUWSS) organized a special campaign to mobilize
support for women's suffrage. Oxford suffragists contributed to this by
canvassing, collecting signatures for a women's suffrage petition at local
polling booths and holding public meetings. By 1910 many of these
campaigners had been active supporters from at least 1904, when the
Oxford Women's Suffrage Society (OWSS) was formed and gradually
other women had joined them. By this period women had the confidence
to challenge the male political system in the way described above, and
by many other means. Their aim in this campaign was to persuade

the male electorate and politicians to give them the vote. Throughout the decade following 1904 they had been busy organizing meetings, petitions, demonstrations and fundraising events, all of which demanded 'Faith, Perseverance and Patience' (the motto which from 1909 headed the NUWSS weekly paper *Common Cause*). However, some supporters, namely members of the Women's Social and Political Union (WSPU), used additional means to forward the cause and followed their motto of 'Deeds not Words'. Both groups campaigned in Oxford.

So why did so many women and men devote so much energy and time to this campaign in Oxford and elsewhere and what did they hope to gain? This chapter is an attempt to answer this question by providing a snapshot of the women's suffrage movement in Oxford. The analysis is based on examining its links with the London-dominated national movement, its ideas on democracy and feminism, and its strategies, tactics and activities; in addition, a few of the main activists are described.

Finding out about the history of the women's suffrage movement in Oxford, and indeed elsewhere, is not a difficult task, although the surviving information is not only daunting in its extent but requires a certain amount of detective work. The movement is a gift to historians, since suffragists and suffragettes were determined to leave behind a public record of their activities. All their national journals, beginning with *The Women's Suffrage Journal* (1871–1890), recorded local branch activities. As the bibliography illustrates, there is a great deal of material in local and national libraries. This is not just confined to cities such as Oxford, as when I have researched other areas, such as Cornwall, despite being told by librarians and historians that no campaign or campaigns existed, I have instead found a wealth of material.[2]

In Oxford my most exciting discovery was the OWSS minute book (1904–1915), hidden in Lady Margaret Hall's library. These included posters, leaflets, voting papers, newspaper cuttings and other ephemera as well as a diary by a young suffragist, Gemma Bailey. It provided a record of all their meetings and how they planned their campaigns. Their meetings were fully recorded in the three local newspapers together with correspondence and articles. These were particularly interesting since they indicated a high level of support, even though only one paper, the Liberal *Oxford Chronicle*, supported women's suffrage whilst the other two, the Conservative *Oxford*

Times and *Oxford Journal*, were more critical. The one group which proved to be relatively elusive was the local branch of the WSPU, which although recorded in the suffrage journals left no local records, possibly because as militancy increased they became more secretive.

As Jill Liddington[3] points out, an additional aid to research and putting together a local history is a good knowledge of the locality. Here I was helped by the fact that I have lived in Oxford for over 30 years and have taught local history here. By the end of my research I felt that I knew many of the activists fairly intimately and a great deal about the buildings where many of their activities took place.[4]

From its inception in the 1850s until 1928, when it finally achieved its goal, the suffrage movement was not just concerned with gaining women the vote, but with other issues. The vote was perceived as a means to influence all policies concerned with women's rights, for example employment, legal and property rights. It was also part of a wider struggle to broaden the democratic process taking place in the 19th century and early 20th century. This had begun with the earlier political reform groups and the Chartists, and was later pursued by some Liberals, all of whom had developed their ideas against a background of expanding industrialization, urbanization and growing prosperity. In these movements women had already begun to make their voices heard, firstly in a supportive role and then more directly by campaigning specifically on issues such as property rights. By the 1870s, when the movement in Oxford began, women's suffrage was beginning to become part of the liberal democratic discourse concerned with the role of citizenship, and had in addition developed a new discourse – liberal feminism. As Ray Strachey later commented:

> Women's Suffrage was a symbol, a peg on which to hang the whole claim of women to their full share of the things of the world – the good things and the bad things alike, the responsibilities and the pleasures, the toils and the rewards . . . the recognition of their full claim – which was going to change the world for men and women both: it was that which would be the real social revolution, and which would bring the progress towards civilisation for which they strove.[5]

The debate on women's suffrage began in the 1850s with the formation of the Langham Place Group, a ladies' discussion group (1855), the establishment of the National Association for the Promotion of Social Science (1857) and the publication of *The English Woman's Journal* (1858). In 1865 the Kensington Society was formed, which introduced a new way of making women's voices heard, by collecting signatures for the first parliamentary petition for women's suffrage, which included a small number of Oxford women. Like all subsequent petitions and parliamentary bills, it was rejected. However, petitions were an important means of recruiting supporters. In 1869 the Second Reform Act gave the vote to urban working-class householders, but an amendment to include the franchise for women householders was rejected. That year, the publication of John Stuart Mill's book *The Subjection of Women* provided the suffrage movement with a set of intellectual arguments. These were based on the liberal ideals of individual rights, freedom of choice, equality of opportunity and civil liberties. This liberal individualism promised women an equal standing with men.

In 1867, the first national suffrage organization, the National Society for Women's Suffrage, a loose federation of all women's suffrage groups, was formed. By the early 1870s organized groups existed in London and the major provincial cities as well as some smaller towns.[6] Many of the early members were middle-class, often nonconformist, women and men, some of whom had been involved in earlier pressure groups such as the Anti-Corn Law League. They adopted these organizations' campaigning methods, that is, they petitioned and lobbied Parliament and MPs, held public meetings all over Britain and worked together with pro-suffrage MPs. They were law-abiding and non-party.

Suffrage campaigners argued that women should be given the same voting rights as men, which were based on property. However, by 1874 divisions emerged. To begin with, some supporters argued that only single women should be given the vote, whilst others supported voting rights for all women. In the 1880s the argument gathered momentum as a result of the Married Women's Property Act (1882) and the Third Reform Act (1884) – which gave rural male householders the vote – and more new groups were formed, until in 1897 the NUWSS was formed as a federation of the existing societies. This led the campaign until the early 20th century, when the WSPU emerged, followed by other groups such as the Women's Freedom League. The NUWSS and the WSPU dominated the suffrage scene until 1914. The arguments during this period were largely concerned with the tactics to be used to achieve women's suffrage, although the debate about whether to be allied to a political party remained controversial and a minority, mainly members of the Independent Labour Party (ILP) and some trade unionists, supported full adult suffrage. It was against the background of these developments, as well as the formation of party political women's organizations such as the Women's Liberal Federation, that the debate on women's suffrage took place all over Britain, including Oxford.

In Oxford it was members connected to the university who played a pivotal role, ensuring that there was continuity of support and links with the national societies; political support within the city was divided, as Oxford's Conservative MPs were opposed to women's suffrage whereas the mainly Liberal city councillors were sympathetic. According to the census Oxford's population increased from 31,404 in 1871 to 52,979 in 1911. This was because the university had expanded, as had the city's market and county administration.

Support for women's suffrage was primarily middle class; that is, from the wives, daughters and sisters of tradesmen and professional and academic men as well as some of their male relatives. To begin with, like women elsewhere, their main access to public life was through philanthropic work, such as the Charity Organization Society (COS), and areas of local government, namely the Poor Law and School Boards. They were concerned with the health and welfare of the poor. As a result they attended meetings, raised funds and visited the poor and sick. Some were motivated by a strong religious conviction and a sense of moral duty, but others perceived such activities as an antidote to the frustrations and limitations of daily life. All this produced close networks of friends and gave the women access to public life and to the skills needed for campaigning for women's suffrage. It also meant that from the 1870s their activities gradually became legitimized and recognized within the democratic process. In addition, some Oxford women and men campaigned vigorously for women's access to a university education through the Association for Promoting Education for Women (AEW) (1876), which resulted in the formation of the women's halls from 1879 onwards. From the late 1860s, the gradual lifting of the marriage bar for university dons meant that there were a growing number of educated and articulate women – wives and daughters, many of whom lived near each other in the new suburb of north Oxford.[7]

Apart from contributions to the early petitions, it was not until 1873 that the first meeting on women's suffrage took place in Oxford, at the Rector's Lodgings, Lincoln College.[8] It was organized by Emilia Pattison (1840–1904) and her husband Mark (1813–1884), the rector of Lincoln College. It was addressed by Lydia Becker, editor of *The Women's Suffrage Journal*. Those attending included future AEW campaigners such as the Revd T.H. Green, Revd Arthur and Mrs Johnson and Professor Thorold Rogers. Emilia then went on to lead the first women's suffrage deputation to an Oxford MP, the newly elected Conservative A.E. Hall in 1874.[9] She and her husband were members of the General Committee of the Central Committee for the National Society for Women's Suffrage and were friendly with John Stuart Mill and other leading suffragists. In spite of this, it was not until the 1880s that activities really developed, helped by the formation of the Oxford Women's Liberal Association (OWLA) (1888), the only local political organization to debate women's suffrage during this period. Meanwhile, as *The Women's Suffrage Journal* recorded, in the rest of the county visiting suffrage speakers addressed meetings in all the main towns, such as Banbury and Witney, but no groups were formed.

Until 1897, when the NUWSS was formed, Oxford suffragists supported all the different factions within the movement, established close links with these by participating on national committees, contributed to petitions including the 1896 Special Appeal,[10] lobbied the city council and Oxford MPs, and participated in local women's political associations.

An example of a leading Oxford supporter during this period, and of someone who participated in public life, is Eleanor Smith (1823–96). Eleanor, the sister of Professor Henry Smith, Savile Professor of Geometry at Balliol College, attended the first suffrage meeting (she was a close friend of the Pattisons) and continued to support the campaign throughout her busy life by hosting suffrage meetings and signing various petitions. She managed her brother's home and acted as his hostess. This 'plain woman and very badly dressed [woman] . . . direct in speech, caustic of humour . . . had great sincerity and deep-seated tenderness.'[11] Through her brother she had access to university circles. She was involved in philanthropic organizations, such as the Oxford branch of the COS. As early as 1866 she began to agitate for women's access to higher education, eventually becoming a member of the AEW, and she was one of the founders of Somerville Hall in 1879.

Her work for higher education contributed to her appointment as a council member of Bedford College, University of London, in 1891.

In 1871 she entered local political life and was the first woman to be elected on to the Oxford School Board as an Independent, since the local political parties refused to support her. She remained a member until 1883, campaigning unsuccessfully for Oxford elementary schools to become non-denominational and to accept difficult children. She was also involved in the newly established Oxford British Girl's School where she helped to formulate the school's rules of conduct and in 1875 was responsible for the school introducing pupil teachers. This eventually resulted in the establishment of a pupil teacher centre in 1893. From 1875 she was also involved in girls' secondary education and was on the committee of the Oxford Girls' High School, where many future suffragists were educated. As her friend Professor Dicey commented:

> She formed a bridge between the unofficial, unrecognised philanthropic work undertaken by women and the official recognition of women in local government. In Oxford she also provided an inspiration and role model of a woman who could participate with men in public life, when this was relatively rare. [12]

Other Oxford women followed her lead and campaigned for women's suffrage and participated in philanthropic societies: for example, the founders and organizers of the Oxford Sanitary Aid Society, formed in 1902 'for the purposes of improving sanitary and housing conditions and general health in Oxford'.[13] In this, Oxford women were not unique, since similar opportunities for women to play active public roles existed in other cities, thus dispelling the view that women were confined to the domestic sphere during this period. (This is well illustrated in previous chapters of this book.)

In 1897 the NUWSS was formed. It employed the same tactics as previous suffrage societies and campaigned for women's suffrage on the same terms as men. However, it differed in that it was a democratic and hierarchical organization with a constitution. Policies, national campaigns and demonstrations were organized by an annually elected executive committee and council. Formal branches and their members elected delegates and members to these bodies and helped to fund the NUWSS through subscriptions and fundraising events. This model was used by the growing number of local branches. However, it was not until 1904 that an NUWSS branch was formed in Oxford. This rapidly became the largest suffrage society in Oxford, with a membership of 84 in 1904 that by 1914 had risen to over 500.[14]

Six other groups closely linked to the OWSS and with overlapping membership soon emerged. The largest of these was the Oxford Women Students' Society for Women's Suffrage (OWSSWS, 1911–18); this will be discussed later. The Oxford Men's League for Women's Suffrage (1911) and the University Men's League for Women's Suffrage (1912), mainly for undergraduates, were formed to support the OWSS. Men also played an important supporting role as OWSS presidents and vice presidents. In 1910 a branch of the Conservative and Unionist Women's Franchise Association was formed. Their motto of 'Loyalty, Insistency, Moderation' illustrated their discreet campaigning methods. In the same year the Church League for Women's Suffrage was formed by Church of England supporters; the Oxford branch had the blessing of the bishop of Oxford, Charles Gore, and was supported by other leading clergymen. Finally, in the following year the Free Church League for Women's Suffrage formed a branch in Oxford to represent the nonconformists, including Elizabeth Hughes, the second woman to be elected an Oxford city councillor.

Between 1904 and 1916, the OWSS was chaired and dominated by Jessie Payne Margoliouth (1856–1933). In 1904 Mrs Margoliouth was 48, evidently an energetic woman, since as chairman she attended the majority of the OWSS fortnightly committee meetings, spoke at or presided over many public meetings and was the OWSS literature secretary in 1913. She was also an important Arabic scholar.

So who was this dedicated suffragist? She was the daughter of the dean of Canterbury, an Arabic scholar who dedicated his life to compiling a vast *Thesaurus Syriacus*. She was born in Kensington, the second of four daughters, and was brought up in Oxford and Canterbury. Her father taught her Syriac and lexicography. As a result she met her future husband, the Revd David Samuel Margoliouth (1858–1940), another Arabic scholar, fellow of New College and later Laudian Professor of Arabic. Her father apparently instructed her[15] 'to finish the dictionary when I am gone . . . You will need help, and there are only two men in England who would be of any use to you . . . One of them is Mr X, and the other man is Mr Margoliouth.' Mr X died six weeks after the Dean and so it had to be Mr Margoliouth! As a result Jessie came to Oxford to stay with a friend and 'got on with the dictionary and Mr Margoliouth – and with him so well, that by the time the dictionary had reached . . . the letter shin, they were husband and wife'. They were married in 1896 and the book was published in 1901. According to Arnold Toynbee, had it not been for this book, Margoliouth would have remained a 'bachelor'.[16] In 1903 her *Compendious Syriac Dictionary* was published. She was also on the committee of the Archbishop of Canterbury's Mission to the Assyrian Christians based in Turkey and Persia. Its aim was to reinforce their 'faith and religious practice'.[17] In 1901 she and her husband visited the mission. In 1913 she co-edited *Kurds and Christians*, a book about the mission. Both she and her husband continued their support of the Assyrians and Armenians throughout their lives.

Jessie and her husband had contrasting temperaments. She was apparently lively and talkative, with a great many interests, whilst he was quiet and awe-inspiring 'with his snow-white hair and his piercing black eyes and his hat that was a cross between a bowler and a topper'. He also wore a bow tie to signify that he was an Anglican clergyman. She domesticated him and helped him put together a sequel to the *Thesaurus*, a Syriac dictionary.[18] He supported women's suffrage and was a member of the OWSS executive committee (1904–9) and then a vice president until 1918. Both were also active members of the Church League for Women's Suffrage.

The OWSS committee, sometimes helped by nationally paid organizers, held numerous public meetings and activities. For example, in the year 1910–11[19] they held five drawing-room meetings and ten public meetings, organized meetings in the Oxford suburbs and Oxfordshire and Berkshire villages, sent speakers to the Oxford branches of the WLA, the Women's Co-operative Guild, the Young Liberals and the ILP, lobbied municipal and parliamentary candidates as well as joining national demonstrations. The meetings were used to fulfil particular functions. At the annual meetings held in November, the committee was elected and addressed by national speakers such as Millicent Fawcett. There were meetings which focused on specific campaigns, such as the Conciliation Bills (1910–12), and also on specific groups such as teachers. Open-air meetings were held outside women's workplaces or in villages. Informal drawing-room meetings and 'at homes' were held in members' homes. By 1911 the OWSS was in a position to finance an office/shop at 35 Holywell Street (near the centre of Oxford) which it used to hold committee meetings and organize activities. Intermittently the OWSS employed paid organizers: for example, between 1913 and 1914 they employed Miss Helga Gill to help set up events.[20]

The first woman speaking at the Union on November 20, 1908

Fig. 7.1 Millicent Fawcett, President of the National Union for Women's Suffrage Societies addresses the Oxford Union in November, 1908.

Fig. 7.2 The Oxford Women's Suffrage Society Banner illustrating St. Frideswide (patron saint of Oxford) 'bearing the sword of justice, but surrounded with the thorns of prejudice'. (A line drawing, Oxford Times, June, 29, 1908)

RULES.

1. The object of the Society shall be to obtain for Women the right of voting for Members of Parliament on the same conditions as those on which it is or may be granted to Men.

2. The Society shall consist of Men and Women Members, and an Annual Subscription, the amount of which shall be optional, shall constitute Membership.

3. The officers shall be the Chairman of Committee, the Hon. Secretary, the Hon. Vice-Secretary, and the Hon. Treasurer, and shall be elected annually by the Committee.

4. The Committee shall be elected at the Annual General Meeting from among the Members, and shall retire annually and be eligible for re-election. It shall consist of not more than fourteen elected Members, and shall have power to add three to its number. The Vice-Presidents shall be elected by the Committee from time to time.

5. No alteration shall be made in these Rules except at the Yearly General Meeting. Special Business Meetings of the Society may be called by the Committee, and shall be called at any time at the request of not less than ten Members of the Society, notice to be given to the Members at least a fortnight beforehand. Any Member wishing to propose an alteration in the Rules, or to bring forward resolutions on any other subject, shall give notice in writing to the Secretary seven days previous to the Meeting.

6. Nominations for the Committee, with names of proposer and seconder, shall be sent to the Secretary in writing at least seven days previous to the General Meeting.

7. The Report, Balance Sheet and list of Members of the Society, with subscriptions, shall be printed annually as soon as possible after the General Meeting.

8. Members of Committee who do not attend at least one-third of the Committees summoned during the year shall not be eligible for re-election.

Names and subscriptions will be received by the Hon. Vice-Sec., Miss Spencer, 18 Beaumont Street, or the Hon. Treasurer, Mrs. Hughes, Metropolitan Bank House.

Election of Executive Committee, 1913-14.

Please put a Cross opposite 12 Names.

Miss Allen ...

Mrs. Biggs ...

Miss Carter ...

Mrs. Crozier ...

Mrs. Gillett ...

Mrs. Haverfield

Mrs. Hughes...

Miss C. Lewis

Mrs. Lindsay...

Miss Lorimer

Mrs. Margoliouth

Mrs. Phillips ...

Miss E. R. Price

Miss O. Rhys

Miss M. Sidgwick ...

Mrs. Slater ...

Miss M. Venables ...

National Union of Women's Suffrage Societies.

Non-Party.   OXFORD BRANCH.   Non-Militant.

MEMBERSHIP CARD.

For_____191

*Member's Name*_____

*Collector's Name*_____

*Address*_____

*Amount Paid*_____

Fig. 7.3 Oxford Women's Suffrage Society: Rules, Election Paper and Membership Card. (author's own collection)

Fig. 7.4 Oxford Women's Suffrage Society office, 35, Holywell Street, Oxford. (Drawing: Lyn Selwood)

Fig. 7.5 Oxfordshire, Buckinghamshire and Berkshire Federation of Suffrage Societies, banner, 1912. (a 1990s postcard reproduction)

As NUWSS support and activities expanded both locally and nationally, regional federations were formed. The OWSS initiated the Oxford, Berkshire and Buckinghamshire Federation in 1911. This enabled the OWSS to establish groups in Oxfordshire, in the towns of Banbury (1911) and Henley-on-Thames (1913), and in the villages of King's Sutton (1911), Dorchester-on-Thames (1913) and Charlbury (1914). It also helped them to recruit more working-class women so that they eventually formed suffrage circles and offered free membership to 'Friends'.[21] By 1914, 42 branches were affiliated to the Federation.[22]

I will give some examples to illustrate the activities of OWSS as well as its increasing opposition to the WSPU – and the public confusion between the NUWSS and WSPU, which resulted in some hostility. By 1912, in an attempt to avoid this confusion, their literature was clearly headed 'law-abiding' and sported their colours: red, green and white. On 9 March 1912 the OWSS's largest meeting was held at the Town Hall, chaired by Jane Harrison, a leading Cambridge classical archaeologist. The main speakers were Margaret Ashton, a Manchester city councillor, and Lord Haldane, a Liberal peer. The OWSS committee distributed handbills, placed adverts in the local papers, appointed stewards, decorated the hall in NUWSS colours and set the agenda, notice of questions, vote of thanks and resolutions – all standard arrangements for suffragist public meetings. Fifty-eight tickets were sold for the platform (2/6d) and 218 for the hall (1/6d) and 377 free tickets were allocated, a total of 653. Lord Haldane insisted that he would only speak if it was made clear at the beginning of the meeting that the OWSS had no connection to the WSPU and that he would not be questioned. He eventually agreed to reply to three questions. The meeting was a success and 60 new members were recruited, as membership forms were distributed for the first time.[23]

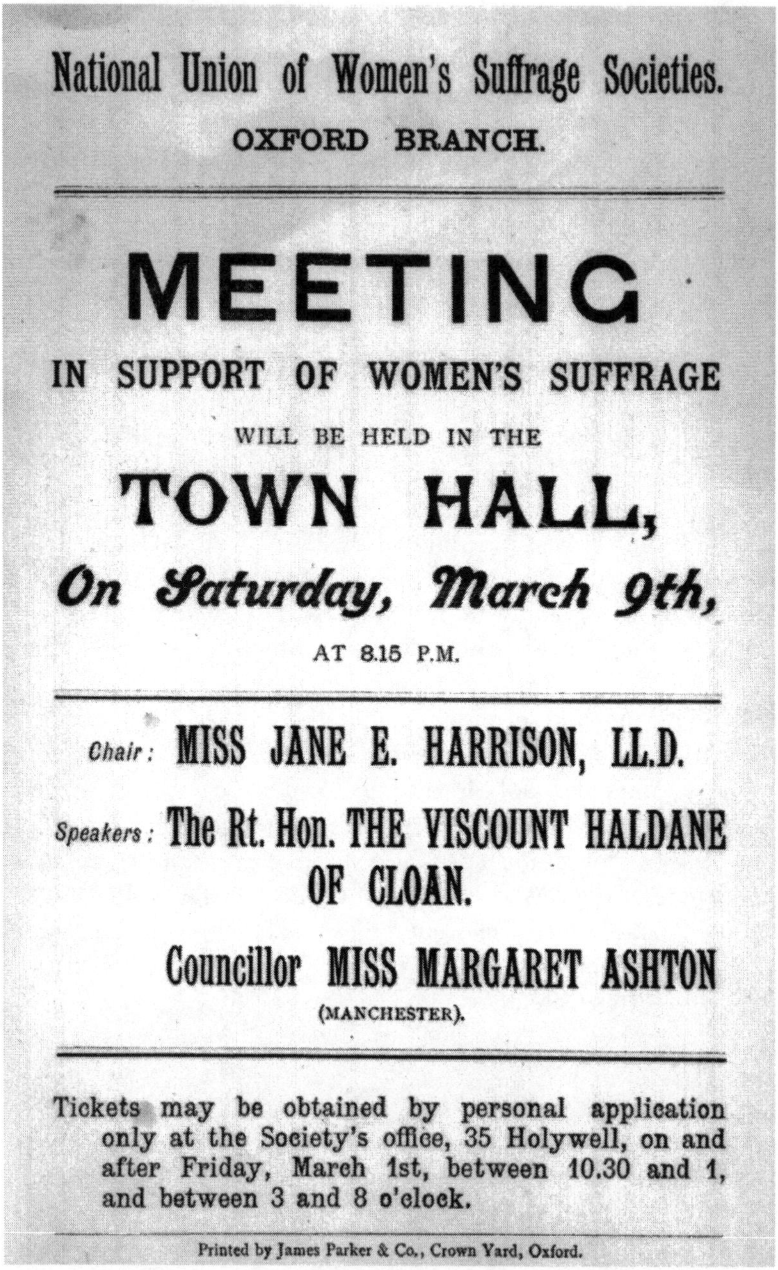

Fig. 7.6 Poster advertising an Oxford Women's Suffrage Society meeting, March 9, 1912. (Centre for Oxfordshire Studies, Oxford)

In December 1912, the OWSS decided to organize a lantern procession from Cowley Place on the eastern edge of the city to St Giles's in the centre, where it would hold an open-air meeting. This took place on 8 January and was supported by all the Oxford non-militant groups. It was a new means to demonstrate their strong support and to counteract the new wave of WSPU militancy (of which more later). Unfortunately it backfired. Each marcher had a lantern and wore a sash in suffragist colours, and the marchers were accompanied by decorated cars. The event was described in detail by the local papers. The *Oxford Chronicle* headlined it 'Women Suffragists Mobbed – Fierce Struggles for Banners – Open Air Meeting broken up' and continued:

> By the time they reached the High, missiles were thrown at them by youths, traffic held up – bad eggs, foul gasses thrown, more jostling, wrenched banners until all banners and lanterns were lowered. Mrs Haverfield [the current OWSS secretary] tried to address the meeting twice, but it was impossible – cat calls, cries of 'Go on home', bicycle bells, howls went up . . . [24]

The *Oxford Times*[25] headline was similar: 'The Battle of the Suffragists. Riotous Scenes at the Martyrs' Memorial. Banners Trampled Underfoot. Leaders Refused a Hearing. ' Eventually the demonstration broke up in disarray, some demonstrators were hurt and two banners were lost. Correspondence raged in the newspapers and all groups condemned the disruption, including the WSPU, but no one took responsibility for it. As a result the OWSS made more strenuous efforts to dissociate itself from the WSPU.

In 1913 the NUWSS organized a nationwide pilgrimage, partly to illustrate to the government the widespread support for women's suffrage and persuade it to pass a Reform Bill which would include women's suffrage, and partly to demonstrate that the majority of supporters were peaceful. In practical terms its aims were to raise funds, to hold meetings at every town and village along the eight major roads in Britain and to lobby MPs. The pilgrimage began on 18 June and concluded at Hyde Park on 25 July, followed by a service at St Paul's Cathedral and a deputation to the prime minister, Mr Asquith.

The strongest and youngest women travelled on foot or by bicycle or on horseback, whilst the older women travelled by cart or car. They wore specially designed NUWSS badges and haversacks in the NUWSS colours. They were advised to wear grey, white, black or blue skirts, coats or dresses and matching or white blouses. Hats were to be simple and only adorned in NUWSS colours.[26] Each Federation appointed a special committee to organize its section of the route. The route which passed through Oxford (Watling Street) had begun in Carlisle. In Oxford a sub-committee of four executive committee members arranged press coverage, hospitality, transport and had 4,000 handbills and posters printed.[27]

The police ensured that the 53 'pilgrims' who entered Oxford from the north on 19 July were peacefully received by a large crowd. This did not, however, prevent a group of men from greeting them with banners which stated 'Women do not want the vote'.[28] After tea, they marched in the early evening to their temporary headquarters, the Lamb and Flag Hotel in St Giles's, and collected money for men thrown out of work by the WSPU arson attack on Rough's boathouse. They then marched to participate in a large public meeting in the Town Hall where they were welcomed by Alderman Hugh Hall. The meeting began with 'The Song of the Suffrage Pilgrims' and was addressed by Malcolm Mitchell, secretary of the Men's League, and Councillor Margaret Ashton, Manchester's first woman councillor and chairman of the Manchester Society for Women's Suffrage. They were both interrupted by people shouting, 'Let women speak! We came to hear the women!' The meeting concluded with a resolution calling for the government to introduce women's suffrage.[29] The next day, following a church service, the pilgrims, now 130 in number, marched towards London, headed by a 'a lady in a khaki riding cross-saddle on horseback, with their flags and banners and supported by the Oxford contingent'.[30]

Although the pilgrimage had passed through Oxford peacefully, elsewhere – for example, in nearby Thame – it met with hostility when men rushed the speakers' platform at an open-air meeting.[31] In spite of such disruptions and the lack of success in persuading the prime minister to listen to their demands, the pilgrimage was partially successful. Hundreds of public meetings were held, attended by thousands of people, £8,000 was collected and many new members recruited.

Fig. 7.7 National Union of Women's Suffrage Pilgrims marching in Oxford High Street. July 21, 1913 (author's own collection)

Fig. 7.8 The Oxford Suffrage Summer School, August 11-18, 1913. (*Common Cause,* August 22, 1913).

Who then were the women who organized Oxford suffrage activities? Between 1904 and 1914 a total of 47 women served on the OWSS executive committee. In some cases little information is available. Those who are known had academic or business family backgrounds. Half were married: 13 to academics, four to businessmen or bankers, one to a clergyman and the rest unknown. Their ages varied, but they were mainly between 20 and 50. Nine had teaching jobs in the university or in secondary schools. Politically many were members of the OWLA until 1912, when some left as a result of the failure of the Conciliation Bills in 1911 and 1912 (which would have given women property owners the vote) and publicly criticized the Liberal prime minister's continued opposition to women's suffrage.

In some cases husbands or wives, or even entire families, were committee members and supporters. One example was the Rhys family: this consisted of Professor John Rhys (1840–1915), his wife Elspeth (1841–1911) and two daughters, Myfanwy (1874–1945) and Olwyn (1876–1953). Professor Rhys had a distinguished career as a linguist and philologist. In 1877 he was appointed professor of Celtic studies, in 1881 fellow of Jesus College and in 1895 its principal. In 1903, he was one of the first fellows to be elected to the British Academy. He was a Liberal and a campaigner for extending national education, particularly in his native Wales. He was an OWSS vice president from 1904 until 1908 and then president until his death. His wife was also a talented linguist and involved in various philanthropic organizations. Although not a member of the OWSS executive committee, she was an active supporter. Both daughters took first-class honours degrees, Myfanwy at the Society of Home Students, Oxford, in 1895 and Olwyn at Cambridge in 1898. Both taught at the Oxford women's halls. Myfanwy played a leading role in the OWSS, as its first secretary until 1907, and continued her support after this. Olwyn was less active, since in 1904 she was appointed assistant examiner on the Welsh Central Board of Education and travelled a great deal.

The support of undergraduates, graduates and academic staff in the new women's colleges was important for the OWSS, enabling it to expand its campaign, particularly between 1911 and 1914 when OWSSW membership grew from 249 to 450. Suffrage as an issue was first debated amongst women undergraduates in the 1890s in their various debating societies. In 1900, in its second debate, the Oxford University Women's

Student Debating Society discussed women's suffrage and a resolution supporting it was overwhelmingly carried. This was repeated in 1905. On the strength of this, members were asked by Mrs Margoliouth to join the OWSS, which some did.[32] From 1907 onwards, students in the individual halls, with the exception of the Society of Home Students, formed their own NUWSS branches. The first, largest and liveliest was formed at Somerville, followed by Lady Margaret Hall and St Hugh's (1908), then St Hilda's (1910). The OWSSWS was formed in 1911. Its president from 1911 to 1915 was Grace Hadow (1875–1940), a former student at Somerville and English tutor at Lady Margaret Hall. Few members joined the WSPU, although they periodically debated both militancy and opposition to women's suffrage. They encountered some opposition from the principals, due to their support over matters such as militancy and inviting male undergraduates to their meetings. OWSSWS members participated in national demonstrations and in 1911 paid for their own banner.[33] They had close links with the NUWSS through their vice presidents, for example Maude Royden and Kathleen Courtney, who were members of the NUWSS executive committee. This ensured that the OWSSWS could make its views known and receive at first hand news of decisions made by the NUWSS executive committee and pass these on to the OWSS.

Fig. 7.9 Oxford Women's Students' Suffrage Society banner, 1911. (reprinted from a 1912 postcard and sold by the Bodleian shop in the 1990s)

In 1903 a group of Manchester women, led by Emmeline Pankhurst and her two daughters Christabel and Sylvia, broke away from the NUWSS, because they felt that only women could campaign for women's suffrage, although men such as the ILP MP Kier Hardie were closely associated. They formed the National Women's Social and Political Union, the WSPU as it became more commonly known. In 1905 they realized that militant action attracted publicity and support. This came as a result of Christabel and her friend Annie Kenney heckling Winston Churchill, an opponent of women's suffrage, at a meeting in the Manchester Free Trade Hall. They were arrested and imprisoned but received much publicity. This led the organization to engage in a continuous search for new tactics. In 1906 the WSPU moved its headquarters to 4 Clement's Inn, London. Here they appointed a central committee, led by the Pankhursts and Frederick and Emmeline Pethick Lawrence. They planned their campaigns during weekly meetings. In 1907 their journal *Votes for Women* was launched, edited by Emmeline Pethick Lawrence and funded by her husband. They also organized fundraising activities to pay for demonstrations, literature and court fines when necessary. As the WSPU became more militant, the organization became more tightly controlled by Emmeline and Christabel Pankhurst, and gradually leading members left to form their own societies: for example, Charlotte Despard, who in 1907 formed the Women's Freedom League.

Although at first closely associated with the ILP, by 1907 the WSPU had become non-party, supporting any political candidate who supported women's suffrage. As it became increasingly frustrated with the lack of parliamentary progress, its activities became more confrontational. This resulted in arrests. In 1909 its campaign took a new direction, when Marion Wallace Dunlop went on hunger strike against the treatment of suffragettes as Second (criminal) Division prisoners, rather than First (political) Division prisoners. This was followed by force-feeding, which in turn was condemned by the whole suffrage movement and much of the general public. This development coincided with increased police brutality at demonstrations. In reaction to this, the leadership, particularly Christabel, perceived the lack of enfranchisement as part of men's oppression of women. In 1913 this perception was further reinforced by the Prisoner's Temporary Discharge for Ill Health Act, the 'Cat and Mouse Act', whereby the police could arrest, imprison and release prisoners at their convenience. From 1911 onwards the suffragettes also introduced new tactics: a campaign against property which began with smashing windows in London department stores and government buildings, and continued with damaging the property of leading opponents, slashing pictures in art galleries, cutting telephone wires, setting pillar boxes alight and finally in 1913 an arson campaign. To begin with, these tactics were a reaction to the failure of the Conciliation Bills, but later became an expression of their frustration with the government's continued opposition to their cause.

The Oxford branch of the WSPU was formed in 1909 by three WSPU members on holiday in the city, who followed WSPU instructions to set up groups in places where none existed. They were successful and organized a joint public meeting with the OWSS at the Corn Exchange. In April 1910 the WSPU branch was officially launched at another joint meeting and a committee established. At first it had an overlapping membership with the OWSS, and its activities were similar to those of OWSS and other WSPU branches, such as public meetings addressed by speakers that included Emmeline Pankhurst in July 1911.

Like the NUWSS, the WSPU formed local branches, but unlike the NUWSS, these branches had no representatives on the central committee, although they had links through centrally appointed paid organizers who either came specifically to help the branch or as public speakers for a number of meetings. The branch committee structure was simpler than that of the OWSS, with no president or vice presidents. The women-only committee had a secretary, treasurer, literature secretary and subscription collectors. They organized participation in national and local demonstrations, public meetings, poster parades, fundraising, writing letters to the press, collecting subscriptions and fundraising activities. They also had a shop for a short time in November 1911 at 55 High Street and then from 1912, for a year, an office and reading room at 49a Cornmarket Street, in central Oxford. They were supported by two branches of the Men's Political Union for Women's Enfranchisement (MPU), formed in 1910 from supporters in the city and the university. These provided speakers and stewards at meetings, as well as organizing their own events.

According to Raeburn,[34] many WSPU members joined out of conviction; they were middle class, young and had no occupation, and were therefore able to devote a great deal of time and energy to the movement as speakers, organizers and voluntary workers. Information about Oxford members is scanty, except for the fact that some were connected to the Society of Home Students (later St Anne's College). A clearer picture emerges of the visiting organizers, since these included leading WSPU members. Firstly there was Charlotte Marsh (1887–1961), who came to the city to launch the Oxford WSPU, a seasoned demonstrator leading WSPU demonstrations as their standard bearer. She was followed by Catherine Margesson, who had given up her career as a sanitary inspector to become a WSPU organizer. She came to Oxford from Reading to ensure that the WSPU branch was viable. This work was then continued by Miss V. Hughes. Finally, Dorothy Pethick (1881–1970), the younger sister of Emmeline Pethick Lawrence and a leading WSPU speaker, came to organize a county-wide campaign in 1912. Both Charlotte Marsh and Dorothy Pethick were arrested numerous times, served prison sentences and went on strike.

Only one Oxford woman was arrested at a WSPU demonstration. This was Miss E.M.S. Graham, the subscription secretary from 1909 to 1914 and branch secretary from 1911 to 1914. She was arrested in London on 'Black Friday', 18 November 1910, together with over a hundred other demonstrators. She was then released. This demonstration was a protest against the shelving of the second Conciliation Bill. Demonstrators were attacked by the police and a battle raged for six hours. She described her experience at a WSPU branch meeting:

> After being chased into the smaller streets leading off the Strand, the banner bearers and their followers found themselves face to face in Whitehall and Parliament streets with lines of police, who had evidently been told to avoid arrests as far as possible and substitute some rough usage as would induce the processionists to surrender and make their escape as early as possible . . . She was hurled by the police into a rough mob, and by the latter again into the ranks of constables. At last in sheer exhaustion and to save herself from falling, she put her hand into a policeman's belt, but her reward was the twisting of her thumb by the policeman in such a brutal manner that for days she suffered excruciating pain. Subsequently she was seized by the throat and on shaking off her assailant, a mounted policeman rode deliberately at her, and when

she seized the horse's bridle to save herself from what appeared a certain death, the rider struck her on the head so violently that she lost her footing and fell into the arms of two constables, who there and then arrested her for 'obstructing mounted policemen!' and escorted her to Bow Street . . . In conclusion . . . the treatment meted out to women who made no attempt to break the law was appalling . . . [35]

From 1911 various events dispel the picture of Oxford as a quiet backwater, for example in March 1911 during a visit by Mr Birrell, Secretary for Ireland and an opponent, who came to address the 'Strangers' debate on Home Rule at the Oxford Union. Both the WSPU and the MPU sent representatives to the Union president, to request an interview with the minister. This was WSPU policy. He refused and so WSPU members waylaid him on his arrival at the railway station and again at his hotel, the Clarendon. The WSPU posted notices on the doors of the Union and 20 colleges; this was regarded by the Union authorities as 'threatening' and it cancelled visitors' passes to the debate. 'For 24 hours Oxford talked of nothing but the suffragettes. Home Rule never had a chance again.' Union members and undergraduates set out on an unsuccessful 'suffragette hunt'. In the evening a visiting WSPU organizer, Ada Flatman, managed to intercept Mr Birrell and confront him. Miss Fripp, the literature secretary, sold *Votes for Women*, an open-air meeting was held at the Martyrs' Memorial and the MPU sent Birrell a telegram: 'Give Home Rule to British women as well as Irish men.' He was accosted again the next day and the debate was cancelled.[36]

By 1912, hostility to WSPU activities was coming to a head nationally and locally, not only from NUWSS supporters, but also from those who opposed women's suffrage, although the force-feeding of suffragette prisoners continued to be condemned. On 21 June 1912, the WSPU encountered its first hostile reception at one of its open-air meetings at the Martyrs' Memorial. The meeting, publicized by a poster parade and a car decorated in WSPU colours, was addressed by leading WSPU organizers and members Dorothy Pethick, Annie Kenney, Sylvia Pankhurst and Rachel Barrett. The speakers spoke from trolleys. On the first, Rachel Barrett was faced with competition from:

rival entertainment in the form of gramophone selections and [students] further amused themselves by throwing sugar from the windows. The first signs of hostility were provided in a disagreeable smell which tainted the atmosphere . . . Men dived into their pockets for pipes, and women and children . . . buried their faces into handkerchiefs. [37]

On the second trolley, Annie Kenney's voice was completely drowned by 'a long prolonged chorus [and] general pandemonium'. This was followed at intervals by shouts of 'We want Christabel'. Annie changed her tone and cried out: 'All the police in London cannot find her, so I don't think you will! . . . and I hope when she comes out to Oxford she will address the students. I think they will never have heard such a speaker in all their lives.'[38] Student disruption was eventually halted by the arrival of a university proctor. Dorothy Pethick and Sylvia Pankhurst continued to speak until a 'noisy element gathered around their platforms, wild scenes of turmoil followed'. Eventually they were forced to escape in hansom cabs. By this time similar scenes were becoming commonplace. In Oxford, this intervention was followed by disruptions at other meetings and demonstrations, including non-militant ones.

As mentioned earlier, from November 1912 onwards the WSPU adopted new methods of campaigning such as damaging property. However, one unofficial earlier attempt near Oxford attracted national attention. This was an attempt to burn down Lewis Harcourt's home, Nuneham House, in the village of Nuneham Courtney:

On July 12th two militants, with cases of inflammable oil, pick-locks and glass cutters, hired a canoe at Abingdon. One of the two, Helen Craggs, who did all the talking at every stage, referred to the other as 'Miss Smyth', but insisted that the boat-keeper should book the name as 'Smith'. At one a.m. next morning a policeman discovered the women crouching among the ivy by the wall of Nuneham House. Helen Craggs said they were camping out, and had come to look round the house, as it was too hot to sleep. Her embarrassment being obvious, he ordered both women to accompany him to the police station. They attempted to run away. Helen Craggs was captured, but her silent companion . . . escaped across the fields . . . a vocal card for Dr. Ethel Smyth's 'March of the Women' was found in a book amongst her luggage in the canoe. Dr Smyth had been arrested for breaking the windows of Harcourt's London house in March . . . She was arrested at Hook Heath [her home], and brought to Oxford for identification. She was able to prove a complete alibi. Moreover the witness obstinately refused to identify her. This was a silent woman – but this! Indeed she was very voluble, very indignant. She wrote to the Press, in high disdain, ridiculing the police for their folly. The alteration of a vowel in one's name seemed to her "one of the less happy devices" for "securing anonymity."Had she desired that, she might have called herself Brown, Jones or Robinson; certainly not Miss Smith. [39]

Miss Smith' was in fact Ethel Smyth's[40] niece Nora, a friend of Helen Craggs and Mrs Pankhurst's chauffeur. Helen and Nora became friends when they were both students at Newnham College, Cambridge. Helen joined the WSPU in 1907 and became a WSPU organizer. She fell in love with Mrs Pankhurst's son, who died in 1909. By the time of the Nuneham Courtney incident, she had already been arrested and imprisoned several times and had just been released from prison. Once arrested in Oxford she had to await trial until 18 October. This enabled the WSPU nationally and locally (with the help of Dorothy Pethick) to publicize her trial and to organize public meetings in her support. Her trial lasted two days and she was sentenced to nine months' hard labour, but was released after ten days, suffering from internal and external bruising as a result of going on hunger strike and being force-fed three times.[41]

Disruptive WSPU activity did not occur again in Oxford until 1913. This included damaging pillar boxes at Carfax (central Oxford) and in north Oxford. Letters were damaged with black printer's ink and green paint or were burnt, and pillar boxes covered with messages painted in green: 'Down with Lloyd George!!!'[42] North Oxford Bowling and Cricket Green was covered with corrosive acid which caused £6,000 damage.[43] Finally, suffragettes burnt down a timber wharf and Rough's boathouse, including some of the boats which would have been used for the Henley regatta. This caused unemployment and at least £3,000 damage. None of the perpetrators were caught, but they left WSPU leaflets and cards.[44] They were probably not local WSPU members, but according to Crawford 'escaped mice'.

By 1914, as militancy increased, many suffrage supporters began to argue that it was destroying public support. However, the actions continued, spreading to the nearby countryside, where empty houses and churches were targeted – such as Wargrave Church, which was almost burnt down.[45] In Oxford other actions were carried out by MPU members. These included disrupting Eights Week and public meetings. [46]

The outbreak of World War One in August 1914 put an end to local WSPU activity. On the other hand, apart from the Church League for Women's Suffrage, which was dissolved, all other Oxford groups survived and the majority supported the country's war effort. They transferred their organizational skills to work with the city council's emergency committee, organized soup kitchens, helped Belgian refugees, sponsored doctors and nurses for the NUWSS-sponsored hospitals and contributed much more.

National political activity by the majority of suffragists and suffragettes was almost totally suspended until 1916, when Parliament sponsored the Speaker's Electoral Committee. As a result, the Representation of the People Bill was passed in February 1918. This gave women householders, wives of householders and graduates who were over the age of 30 the vote. Approximately eight million women could now vote. In November 1918 Parliament approved the Eligibility of Women Bill, which enabled women to stand for Parliament in the coming general election. Seventeen women stood, including Christabel Pankhurst and Emmeline Pethick Lawrence. Only one woman was successful, Constance Markiewicz, a member of Sinn Fein who refused to take her seat. In 1919 the first woman MP to take her seat was the American Nancy Astor. Ironically she was not a suffrage supporter, and was elected to her husband's seat, as he had inherited his father's peerage.

After the war, suffragists continued to campaign for all women over the age of 21 to be given the vote. In Oxford, the OWSS joined the re-formed NUWSS, the National Union of Societies for Equal Citizenship (NUSEC), under the presidency of Eleanor Rathbone, a former student at St Hilda's Hall. NUSEC campaigned not only for suffrage, but also for more women on local councils, for equal opportunities in the workplace, for all professions to be opened to women and much more. In Oxford it helped to ensure that women's degrees were recognized by the university in 1921. In the 1920s some of the former OWSS members were elected as city and county councillors and appointed magistrates. Others joined a variety of new organizations, such as the League of Nations Union and the Women's Institute, including Grace Hadow, who became vice-chairman of the National Federatiion of Women's Institutes 1917 to 1940, and Helga Gill. Finally in 1928 all women over the age of 21 were granted the vote.

The women's suffrage campaign had taken a long time to achieve its goal. This was due to divisions within the political parties and, by the early 1900s, also due to the more formalized opposition provoked by suffragette militancy. In 1908, in Oxford and nationally, the National League for Opposing Women's Suffrage was formed. In Oxford this group was exceptionally well organized and had a membership which was almost the same as that of the OWSS, but that is another story. The suffrage campaign also lasted so long because women had to change their stereotypical image and convince politicians that they were able to participate in the political system and be treated as citizens. As one OWSS supporter, Alys Russell, argued at an OWSS public meeting in March 1907:

> Women had proved by their services on public bodies their
> interest in civic matters and also their worth . . . A true
> democracy must exercise the right of voting. Women were
> told they were citizens, and as far as political work went,
> especially at election times, a great deal was expected of
> them, but they were never given direct responsibility, and
> it was that that had so much to do with educating people
> and bringing out the best in them. But women were not
> educated politically because until they had the vote, they
> were not considered worth educating politically. They did
> not claim that giving women the franchise would make
> them keen politicians at once, but they did claim that it
> would broaden their outlook, and also that a mutual sense
> of citizenship would be a real bond between husband and
> wife and an added tie between mother and child. [47]

To conclude, suffrage supporters contributed a great deal to Oxford political and social life. Although it took over 30 years for the suffragists to become a single-issue pressure group and to make use of the well-established networks which had developed through philanthropy and the AEW, the OWSS became a dynamic organization sustaining a flourishing campaign until World War One. The suffrage movement also influenced a variety of local issues within the city and county, ranging from housing, health and education to participating in local government and political parties. The suffragists also expressed their ideas publicly, through meetings, demonstrations and petitions, by lobbying local MPs and councillors and by writing letters to local newspapers. Like other women in this book they illustrate that many women broke out of the confines of the domestic sphere in the 19th century and early 20th century, in order to make their voices heard on an issue which, once resolved, would ensure that it would be more difficult to keep women away from the public world.

Until recently much of the focus of historians writing about the suffrage movement has been on the suffragettes and the national movement. This is gradually being redressed by historians such as Jill Liddington and Elizabeth Crawford and by a growing number of local histories. The fascination with the WSPU rather than the NUWSS can be explained by the charismatic personalities involved and the way in which their militant tactics destroyed the image of women as frail and weak, incapable of physical force. Many suffragettes, and in Oxford this included visiting speakers and organizers, had a high public profile, which together with their campaigns attracted widespread press coverage, initially sympathetic but eventually almost totally hostile. Suffragettes also caught the public imagination by their femininity, that is, the way in which they dressed. For example, at demonstrations they wore fashionable hats and fitted white dresses adorned with a sash in their colours of purple, green and white. They consciously exploited their femininity in order to combat the notion that serious and politically committed women were dowdy, masculine and ugly. Of equal importance was the way in which they highlighted the unequal distribution of power between women and men and the extremes to which the male establishment was prepared to go in order to safeguard its dominance. They also successfully marketed their ideas by producing posters, photographs of their main supporters and leaders, games, cards, jewellery and other goods, all decorated in their colours, which they sold at meetings and in their shops, such as the one in Oxford. In comparison the suffragists were less exciting and glamorous, their activities more mundane. However, if it had not been for their numerous meetings, petitions and demonstrations, their determination and perseverance in ensuring that the issue did not leave the political agenda, it might possibly have taken longer to achieve their goal. As Sandra Holton comments, the importance of the suffragists was that they served:

> to further the alliance between feminist and progressive politics in the early years of the 20th century by asserting that the possibility of social reform lay only with a feminised polity. The demand for equal votes could, in consequence, be given far greater significance than the simple single-issue campaign among middle-class women it had started out as in the late 1860s. [48]

A history of the women's suffrage movement provides an insight into women's role in society and politics in the last half of the 19th century and the early 20th century. It is also a public history in several senses. [49] Firstly, suffrage activity was and had to be public: that is, suffrage supporters had to both challenge and conform to female stereotypical behaviour and contemporary political ideas. Secondly, they consciously and unconsciously set themselves up as role models, and were used as such, most recently by the Greenham women in the 1980s. Thirdly, their actions and ideas have left us with a democratic system and liberal feminism, which both continue to exercise important influences on contemporary political life.

Local history provides an added dimension to the understanding of the suffrage movement since it illustrates the devotion of a large number of contemporary women and men to this cause. Furthermore, it demonstrates how this one issue touched and influenced many people's lives, it provides an insight into how a movement and its participants operated by illustrating all the mundane tasks activists carried out to ensure the continuation of the campaign, and it shows the importance of formal and informal networks. Thus, without the unremitting 'Faith, Perseverance and Patience' of these many women throughout Britain, it would have taken far longer for women to participate fully in the democratic process. This in turn helped to bring about political, social and economic changes for women. However, it is also important to recognize that every local area is different because of the different individuals who shaped the local political, social and economic environment. Oxford was unique because until the inter-war period it was dominated by the university and a group of highly articulate individuals who were able to combine the struggle for women's enfranchisement with the campaign for women's access to higher education.

Hopefully, future historians will continue to 'discover' suffrage history outside London. The sources exist and are just waiting to be discovered. As Leah Leneman comments:

> The movement was altogether more complex than older histories would have us suppose, and there is plenty of scope for further discoveries, by moving away from the centre and into parts of the country where women fought for the right to vote. [50]

Endnotes

1   *Oxford Chronicle*, 4 December 1910.

2   Bradley, Katherine, *A History of the Women's Suffrage Movement in Cornwall 1870–1914*, Patten Press, 2000.

3   Liddington, Jill, *Rebel Girls: Their Fight for the Vote*, Virago, 2006.

4   Bradley, Katherine, *Women on the March: A Suffrage Walk around Oxford City Centre*, Oxford Women's International Collective, 1996. This information was used to devise a walk which visits the sites of OWSS demonstrations and buildings where meetings and some supporters lived.

5   Strachey, Ray, *Millicent Fawcett*, John Murray, 1931, p 245.

6   See Crawford, Elizabeth, *The Women's Suffrage Movement in Britain and Ireland: A Regional Survey*, Routledge, 2006. This gives examples of suffrage societies in small towns.

7   See Hinchcliffe, Tanis, *North Oxford*, Yale University Press, 1992, for a description of the architecture and life in this area.

8   *Women's Suffrage Journal*, No 4, 1873.

9   *Jackson's Oxford Journal*, 18 April 1874.

10 In 1892 the Central Committee of the National Society for Women's Suffrage organized 'An Appeal from Women of all Parties and Classes'. Books for the collection of signatures were circulated and collected by local committees. By 1896 a total of 257,796 signatures were collected, the largest petition to Parliament since the Chartist ones in the 1840s.

11   Askwith, Betty, *Lady Dilke: A Biography*, Chatto & Windus, 1969, pp 48–9.

12   Professor Dicey (1835–1920), Vinerean Professor of Law, member of Somerville Council and later a prominent anti-suffrage campaigner, wrote Eleanor Smith's obituary for the *Oxford Times*, 19 September 1896.

13   Lettice Fisher (1875–1956), Mabel Prichard (1875–1965), Frances Wells (1875–1925), Mary Smith (1855–1945) were all married to university academics and continued to be active in public life throughout their lives.

14   Membership was recorded by name, address, subscription and donation in the OWSS Annual Reports from 1905 onwards.

15   *Dictionary of National Biography*, Oxford University Press, 2004, pp 661–2.

16   Toynbee, Arnold, *Acquaintances*, Oxford University Press, 1967, pp 43–5.

17   *Dictionary of National Biography*, op cit.

18   Toynbee, op cit.

19   OWSS Seventh Annual Report, 1910-1911

20   Helga Gill (1885–1928), a Norwegian graduate, was an NUWSS organizer who worked all over the country and was in Oxford briefly in 1910 and 1911. Her letter of appointment has survived in the Suffrage Collection, Box 2, John Johnson Collection, New Bodleian Library, Oxford. She was paid an annual salary of £120, in monthly instalments, expenses for travelling, board and maintenance of the office bicycle and given eight weeks' holiday, a weekly half day and one weekend a month off. She had to live in Oxford, make weekly reports to the committee, speak at public meetings and sell *Common Cause*. Just after the war she worked as an ambulance driver in France (obituary, *The Times*, 27 November 1928).

21 Suffrage circles appear to be a uniquely Oxford phenomenon, and were formed all over the city. Suffrage was discussed in an informal setting to attract working-class support. The Friends of Women Suffrage were formed in 1912 by the NUWSS. Friends were supplied with literature and had to pledge their support on a card and would then receive free membership. This was another way of recruiting working-class members and was particularly successful during the Pilgrimage in 1913.

22 NUWSS Oxfordshire, Berkshire and Buckinghamshire Federation Annual Reports.

23 OWSS Minute Book, 31 January, 12 and 28 February, 8 and 13 March, 1912.

24 *Oxford Chronicle*, 10 January 1913.

25 *Oxford Times*, 11 January 1913.

26 *Common Cause*, 13 June 1913.

27 OWSS Minute Book, 8 May 1913, which included a leaflet detailing arrangements.

28 *Oxford Journal*, 23 July 1913.

29 *Oxford Chronicle,* 25 July 1913.

30 This is part of an account written for the *Oxford Times*, 25 July 1913, by Miss Allen, the OWSS press officer.

31 *Oxford Chronicle*, op cit.

32 *Fritillary* (a magazine for women undergraduates), 21 December 1900 and 25 June 1905. OWSS Minute Book, 8 May 1905.

33 The banner was based on a design of *The Towers of Oxford* by the designer and illustrator Edward New. The design cost £3 and the

embroidery £10. Postcards of the banner were printed in 1912 and reprinted recently on mugs and postcards by the Bodleian Library.

34   Raeburn, Antonia, *Militant Suffragettes*, Michael Joseph, 1973, p 42.

35   *Oxford Chronicle*, 6 January 1911.

36   *Votes for Women,* 10 March 1911.

37   See accounts in all the Oxford newspapers, June 1912.

38   Christabel Pankhurst was in Paris in self-imposed exile, so that she could avoid arrest and continue to organize the WSPU.

39   Pankhurst, Sylvia, *The Suffragette Movement*, Virago, 1976, pp 402–3.

40   Ethel Smyth (1858–1944) was a leading WSPU member and well-known composer.

41   *Votes for Women*, 7 and 25 October 1912.

42   *Votes for Women*, 21 February and 15 May 1913; *Oxford Chronicle*, 21 February and 21 November 1913; *Oxford Journal*, 15 May 1913.

43   *Votes for Women*, 30 May 1913.

44   ibid, 6 June 1913; *Oxford Chronicle,* 6 June and 21 November 1913.

45   *Votes for Women*, 10 May 1913. Some people were very angry about this incident: for example, Henry Taunt who wrote an article 'Wargrave Church destroyed by Suffragettes'. Typescript, 1 June 1914 (Centre for Oxfordshire Studies).

46   Crawford, op cit, p 100.

47   *Oxford Times*, 9 March 1907. Alys Russell (1867–1950), a Quaker, was married to Bertrand Russell until 1901 when the marriage collapsed. They still lived together outside Oxford until 1911, with her family,

also suffrage supporters. Alys was a member of the OWSS executive committee from 1905-1911 and one of their main speakers.

48 Holton, Sandra, *Feminism and Democracy: Women's Suffrage and Reform Politics in Britain, 1900-1918,* Oxford University Press, 1986, p 21.

49 See Kean, Hilda, 'Public History and Popular Memory: Issues in the Commemoration of the British Militant Suffrage Campaign', *Women's History Review*, 14, 2005, pp 561–602.

50 Leneman, Leah, 'A Truly National Movement: The View from outside London', in Joannou, Marou and Purvis, June (eds), *The Women's Suffrage Movement: New Feminist Perspectives*, Manchester University Press, 1998, p 48.

CHAPTER 8

Radicalism, Resolve and Resolutions: the Early History
of the National Federation of Women's Institutes, 1915-
1939.

Lesley Wade and Katherine Bradley

E rroneously thought of as a quintessentially English organisation, the
National Federation of Women's Institutes (NFWI) was a Canadian
invention (1897), eventually established in the United Kingdom in
Wales at Llanfairpwll, Anglesey in 1915 and then subsequently in England
and Northern Ireland. From 1917 until 1946 it was managed and chaired
by Gertrude, Lady Denman, the wife of a former Governor-General
of Australia. Celebrating nearly a hundred years, it is an organisation
embedded within the psyche of the British public as a seemingly benign
collection of countrywomen who meet monthly, making jam and singing
the hymn *Jerusalem*. Latterly this image has been punctured by the film
and play *Calendar Girls* (2003 and 2008), television documentaries such
as the one about the Isle of Wight Women's Institute in June, 2007 and
even by the former British Prime Minister, Tony Blair's realisation at
their 2000 Annual General Meeting (AGM), that the Women's Institute
(WI) had important views which had to be taken account of. All this has
illustrated that the WI is far from a provincial sorority of middle aged
women, but is a national treasure that has at its heart radicalism, resolve
and the ability to put forward controversial resolutions that have changed
life not only for those living in rural areas but for all sections of society.

On its ninetieth birthday, *The Guardian* newspaper selected the WI as the tenth most important organisation not only in Britain, but throughout the world.

Providing a sophisticated model of citizenship and engaging for many decades in participatory politics, this chapter will explore the underpinning structures, philosophies and some of the actions of this organisation. 'Action not words' was the philosophy of the WI's first Chairman Lady Denman during the interwar period. At the end of her chairmanship in 1946 she reflected that the NFWI, 'had a knack of getting our own way' through its adroit use of networks, politicians and successful welfare and public health policies.

Thus far from a quixotic group of countrywomen, the WI is an unparalleled and relatively under researched organisation illustrating co-operation, innovation and action. Archival evidence provides testimony to the actual engagement of WI members, their leaders and a particular process of governance employed by their policy-making committee at NFWI headquarters in London. An example of this is how these women supported active rural nursing during the interwar period and how nursing benefited from a sophisticated support system created by this network of WI volunteers. The archives also illustrate how the organisation championed leisure activities, liberal education, astutely made use of technology, produced a particular process of participation and governance and were an early provider of non-state funded health and welfare provision. This chapter will demonstrate that during its early years the organisation purposefully gave a corporate identity to a former disenfranchised minority group, the countrywomen, apparently cutting across class distinctions. Central to the debate is how this new type of citizenship used a complex form of trust as the means by which women during the interwar period could actively change the context of their lives. Maggie Andrews in her excellent study of the WI sees the organisation as a social movement as the title of her book clearly illustrates (*The Acceptable Face of Feminism*). However it can be argued that the WI was and is more than that. In the interwar years it was a highly successful organisation that not only supplemented public health within rural communities but provided a space for the lady bountiful to continue her philanthropic work at the same time as supporting health and social reforms. It also provided a range of social and leisure activities and contributed a great deal to the arts and crafts.

In order to give consideration to such an enduring organisation, it is also pertinent to reflect not only the roots of this organisation's resolve, radicalism and resolution, but also to examine the processes that were used particularly by the early leaders of the WI to sustain development and progress. Thus this chapter considers how a women's organisation designed for a rural environment achieved its popularity without causing excessive antagonism. Did it, as Anne Stamper has argued, rely heavily on its education policy to reduce social barriers, which then enabled it to cross political and professional boundaries? What then was the mechanism employed to facilitate this? As early as 1918 Grace Hadow, the WI's first vice chairman, together with Alice Williams, the editor of the WI's journal *Home and Country* ensured that citizenship and participation were central to the WI.

> ... the essence of the Women's Institute is in their apostolic democracy ... it is for all alike, rich or poor ... each acts as the host to one another, each puts their own practical knowledge at the service of the rest.

As already mentioned the ideas behind the formation of the WI in Britain came from Canada where Women's Institutes had been formed in the 1897. During the 1890s a debate took place all over Canada about the increase in maternal and infant mortality. This debate was taken up by the newly formed National Council of Women. A member of the Council was Adelaide Hoodless. She came from a family with Protestant Irish roots, was a graduate of Guelph Agricultural College in Toronto, married to a farmer and had links with the Canadian Ministry of Agriculture. The skill of Adelaide Hoodless, a conservative pragmatic farmer's wife, to promote a sorority of women within the rural landscape of Ontario, was directed by her personal concern about declining nutritional and domestic skills, during the latter part of the nineteenth century. Thus the foundations of the WI reside in the home of Adelaide Hoodless in Stoney Creek, Ontario, Canada. She was the author of a text on nutrition which was rooted not only within the pragmatism of rural life but was also based on her involvement with the National Council of Women in Canada and her colleagues' political aspirations. Historically she is depicted as a simple homestead mother who when losing her third child, was determined to set up networks and lectures on domestic economics, and saw the WI as the ideal vehicle to educate both family and mother.

In reality in 1890's Canada, the lack of support for, and the rise in maternal and infant mortalities, had created a fierce dialogue all over the country. Adelaide Hoodless' connections with the Agricultural Department and young farmers linked her with Madge Watt, a Vancouver University graduate, Senate member and an advisory board member to the Ministry of Agriculture. She later pioneered WIs in Britain. Another Canadian woman who was also a member and the founder of the National Council of Women had concerns with health care. This was Lady Aberdeen, the wife of the Governor-General of Canada who stated regarding the provision of health in rural and remote areas.

> Many members within the Women's Council told pathetic stories of cases of young mothers and children dying whilst their husbands and fathers travelled miles for medical and nursing help and services ... which may have helped save them.

Lady Aberdeen's solution was to ensure that the British model of district nursing (in Canada the Victorian Order of District Nursing) would focus on remote communities.

> ... In the town she goes from home to home to those many of who cannot afford a trained nurse.... but on the prairie, in the forest, the mining districts everywhere in our brave land amongst our pioneers she goes hither and thither to help our pioneers build this beautiful land amid privation and hardship...

To some extent Lady Aberdeen's nurses predate some of British district nursing dilemmas by two decades, that is, the tensions between town and country, the issue of remuneration and the often real pioneering and heroic nursing whether it was in Ontario or Glamorgan. As will be shown later in this chapter this also influenced the WI and its relationship with district nurses.

Another colonial dominion, Australia, influenced Lady Gertrude Denman. She also listened to the plight of rural women during her unhappy tenure as the wife of the Governor-General of Australia from 1911 until 1914. Lady Denman like her mother, Lady Cowdray, came from an influential Liberal wealthy family. Her mother had been the benefactor to nursing not only in the U.K. but also as far as Mexico, Chile, and Spain, although some nursing factions disliked her, seeing her as nouveau riche.

Meanwhile in Britain in the early twentieth century, concern was expressed for the decline in the number of rural workers. They were moving to the towns where higher wages were paid. The Agricultural Organisation Society (AOS) was formed to help local farmers, smallholders and growers' societies to improve their production. During the First World War rural areas were facing a further crisis as was national food production. In 1915 Major Stapleton-Cotton, chairman of the North Wales AOS met Madge Watt, who was then working for the AOS in Wales and wanted to establish WIs here. He supported her and the first WI was established in Wales and funded by the AOS and later WIs were funded by the Board of Agriculture. Very soon WIs there were three more in Wales as well as Kent, Dorset and Sussex. By 1918 there were 760 WIs and 23,000 members.

The aims of these early WIs were to increase local food production, develop village industries and prepare for post war reconstruction. By 1915 increased food production had become a necessity owing to the German blockade of British ports. In response to this the Board of Agriculture formed the Women's War Agriculture Committees to organize the recruitment of women to work on the land. In February, 1916 the Women's Land Army Corps was established, Agricultural Colleges ran short courses for women and special training centres were also set up. In 1917 the Women's Land Army replaced the Corps. Members wore uniforms and were mobilized to areas which needed them. Most were middle and upper class women. Thus during the War the Board of Agriculture was financing two groups of women. In 1919 the Women's Land Army was disbanded and the WI became independent of government grants.

As can be seen by this short history the formation of the WI was a consequence of the impact of colonial initiatives and the effect of the First World War which resulted in the re-evaluation of women in rural communities. The early success of the WIs therefore could be seen to reside within a culture and climate that was both colonial and transnational.

The WIs were also successful because they offered women an opportunity to earn money and help the rural economy, by selling their handicrafts. The most successful of these throughout the interwar years, was their production of toys and other textile handicrafts. All this was particularly useful in the 1930s depression, enabling women to supplement the family income.

At the end of the war Lady Denman was placed in charge of the fledgling WI by the Board of Agriculture as part of a process of countryside regeneration after the First World War. The Board of Agriculture had been lukewarm about taking up the scheme, but the pilot in Anglesey had proved to be so successful that for example the Rector of Bangor University viewed it as a new experiment in rural sociology. This is illustrated by the appointment of the Voluntary Service Organisers (VSO) who implemented internal education in the early 1920s and who set up WIs and provided them with their own syllabus, educational materials and procedural manuals.

The WI had an eclectic membership whose differing skills were derived from their experiences in the suffrage movement, as Major Stapleton-Cotton acknowledged. Nursing involvement aside, the direction of the locally based WI was run initially by the great and good in rural communities. Cheshire, like other early WIs, usually had an aristocrat as its nominal head. However increasingly during the 1920s the intelligentsia became involved such as Virginia Woolf in Ringmer, or as VSOs helping to set up a WI such as the popular novelist, E.M. Delafield who used her role as a VSO as a background to her novels. Members of the Six Point Group, such as Lady Rhondda who edited their feminist magazine *Time and Tide* where she wrote favourably about the WI, made numerous contributions to lectures and within the WI magazine.

However it was the Liberal Lady Denman who contributed the most to the WI's success. She was, as her secretary recalls, a powerful figure with futuristic ideas. For example she reassured one apprehensive rural member that the great and good of the community did not understand rural needs and it was for its members to bring forward issues and resolutions and commented, 'we walk down those lanes but we do not know what goes on behind those doors... 'This is further illustrated by members' comments such as Alice Freeman's

> Lectures were excellent. We had a sister who did six first aid lectures. We had a lad in the village who broke his arm ... I did everything the nurse told me including using the tourniquet ... the doctor was amazed and asked how I knew what to do ... I thought it odd as it was his sister who was the president of our local WI

Margery Mousey, a Darlington Federation member who served as an ambulance unit driver in the First World War recalled: 'I was forbidden to nurse but I served on our local hospital committee and the Queen's Nursing Committee in 1924'.

Anglicized as it was, Lady Denman, an expert strategist, extracted the very best from the Canadian model including the innovative VSO model and Madge Watt's emphasis on education, which Watt stressed, had brought togetherness in Canada. This is recalled by Alice Freeman, a member from the Warwickshire Federation in an oral history, where she describes the benefits of the WI monthly lectures.

> Welfare reforms and district nursing initiatives could be relied upon to be supported by former nurses and Voluntary Aid Detachment nurses but it was difficult for other members to speak out regarding other public health needs.

Citizenship was another important aspect of the WI, promoted passionately by Grace Hadow, and reflects her suffrage background (see the introduction to this section). In 1918 she wrote of her vision of assisting countrywomen to take up citizenship.

> Interest in their homes tends naturally to interest in housing, sanitation, infant welfare and kindred topics. Members learn to realize their responsibilities towards community and from an interest here they come to see the connection between their own affairs and those of

the nation at large. It would be difficult not to plan a better training for the exercise of the vote, divorced from sectarian policies, based on the actual experience of home life, home needs, educated not to take but to give.

Grace Hadow and Mrs. Nugent Harris, a softly spoken Irish woman, balanced a formidable WI leadership. Mrs. Nugent Harris was adept at reminding Lady Denman that she did not put her own policies forward but those of the WI, '... even if the county Federation make mistakes, let them.'

The WI also relied on its magazine *Home and Country* to keep members informed. These carried regular articles on new maternal, welfare and housing legislation and the readership were kept informed of both national WI policies and government policies. They were also asked to constantly lobby their local authorities.

During the interwar period it is also important to note that although the UK was undergoing a period of regeneration immediately after the First World War, by the late 1920s it was experiencing a period of economic depression which affected agriculture as much as other areas. Indeed with the onset of mechanization in farming from the early nineteenth century onwards, many people were leaving the land and moving to the towns. In the 1920s this was hastened by the use of tractors and other new machinery, all of which required less labour. Agricultural wages were still lower than those in the towns. Thus the countryside was in need of an organisation which would provide it with some form of support. This is what the WI provided. It is therefore unsurprising that the making of 'jam', was seen as symbolic of the WI. It served as a motif for an activity which is now scoffed at or only tolerated. Perhaps this attitude serves as an uncomfortable truth about the enduring British problem with nutrition and food manufacture in general.

Salient to note that by June 1917, at a critical time during the First World War, the Board of Agriculture was facing a state of national emergency, having just three week's supply left to feed the country. As described earlier this was partly a result of German embargos and partly because increasingly throughout the nineteenth century Britain had relied on colonial food imports. The consumption of preserves had been a stable and supplementary diet for both the rural and urban classes. One of the earliest skills of the early WIs was not only to use orchard products, but to process and distribute vitamin rich jams. In doing so the organisation developed sophisticated bottling plants and demonstrated how women could work within a technological environment.

A further enduring misconception is the interpretation of the communal singing of the hymn *Jerusalem*. This uses William Blake's words and Sir Hubert Parry's musical arrangement, which is incorrectly seen as a symbol of jingoistic nationalism. Nearly all the WI's executive opposed the choice of the hymn, recognizing this interpretation. However *Jerusalem* had been adopted by the National Union of Women's Suffrage Societies (NUWSS) and the version used by the WI had been set to new music by Sir Hubert Parry, at the request of Millicent Fawcett, the NUWSS President and played at the Victory dinner in March 1918 to celebrate the passing of the Equal Representation Bill which gave some women the vote (see Chapter 7). In a clear example of democracy the executive's qualms were overruled at the first annual NFWI meeting in London's Albert Hall. Here members selected the hymn as a symbolic gesture of solidarity and community. Both Grace Hadow and Lady Denman were convinced that grassroots members did not in fact grasp the sentiments of the words. However as Madge Watt, the Canadian delegate argued it gave countrywomen a sense of community. It perhaps also reminded women of why it had originally been used.

The goals of the early leaders were to improve health, housing and sanitation. The organisation's active support for these improvements illustrated their ability to work across traditional boundaries. Their philosophy of mutual self help, their careful construction of support structures and their creative use of liberal education provided country women with a new found corporate identity. Citizenship and communication skills were also important, for example the British Broadcasting Company's (BBC) WI wireless broadcasts in 1927, which comprised of six lectures and reached not only a rural female audience but also an intrigued urban and male audience. However ultimately the most enduring image of the WI's activities during this period lies in its focus on nutrition particularly in processing and distributing fruit preserves or jams, as a supplementary but essential part of the diet for both the rural and urban poor.

Ironically it is not the actions or words of the leadership that resonate throughout the archive and memory of the membership, but the letters, meticulous minutes and formal resolutions that demonstrate that the WI uniquely engaged a top down and bottom up approach when it came to helping rural women participate within decision making and engaging fully within the life of its own community. Pat Thane correctly identified that the vote alone was not enough in engaging women to participate within political decision making. Equally other feminist historians have often been critical of a lethargic interwar women's movement that appeared not to actively engage in promoting feminist ideologies. This analysis of the first twenty-five years of the WI hopefully refutes this opinion. In doing so it provides a case history of female citizenship, led by sanguine opinion leaders, many of whom had been involved in the battle for female suffrage at all social levels. It also demonstrates a willingness to engage in political life especially when WI actions could alleviate suffering for both men and women. It is a case history of multifaceted community activity which also used elements of traditional politics when necessary. It is a tour de force of deliberative participation at times democratic and at other times authoritarian. The history of the early WI however is not just about reason and rationality, but about passion and engagement.

During the interwar period WI activity and action, produced complex and radical campaigns. It not only gave a voice to the women living in rural isolation but a direction to a nation undergoing cultural and economic change. Their involvement particularly in relation to health and welfare reforms is testimony to their ability not only to galvanize a previously reticent culture but to live up to Lady Denman's claim that 'action not words' is of prime importance.

The historiography of the WI by its historians, such as Inez Jenkins (1953), Maggie Andrews (1997) and Anne Stamper (2003) seemingly points to an organisation that aims to be innovative yet fails to tell us how those innovations were actually implemented and at what cost. The historical evidence illustrates that it was an international movement which operated across three continents, initiated by women who were both educated, seasoned campaigners, with considerable powers of rhetoric. Equally, they were skilled in the mechanisms of participation whether at local or central government level and it was these precise skills that were used, within the British model of the WI to improve the quality of life for the rural woman. This enabled her to feed her family and to assist her to use her vote effectively by using the latest technology to inform her of relevant public and social issues, avoiding the didactic pitfalls of imposing education pedagogy. Evidence of a third way suggests that engaging in extra parliamentary activities was just as effective particularly within health.

In relation to social issues the WI did not conform to stereotype, since they supported the rural mining areas of the Rhonda and during the 1926 General strike, individual WIs in the South of England twinned with their counterparts in Durham and Jarrow sending food and a Christmas box to every child. As one member of the Sussex Federation recalled, 'learning in the WI was a two way process.' As an affluent, middle class, provincial lady she recalled she gained more from helping her fellow women in Durham, than she had ever done in her earlier life. Indeed by 1939, the WI had 12,000 members, 50% of whom were in mining districts.

James Hinton's recent work on the Women's Voluntary Service of the Second World War shows a contrasting picture of popularity with resistance and tensions within Cheshire, Yorkshire and the coal fields of Durham. Lady Reading's more centralized approach in recruiting and managing this regional voluntary organisation met with opposition particularly if local politics were not understood. By working with female philanthropists rather than against them and by carefully planning an educational strategy that included the practical skills of domesticity the WI.s became a popular phenomena. By 1920 the letter page in *Home and Country* received 3.000 letters per month demonstrating both the immediacy and popularity of the early organisation.

Three activities that exemplify how the WI successfully 'acted and not just talked', a phrase Lady Denman always used, will now be examined. These were lobbying skills and resolutions; wireless (radio) technology; nutrition; public health and nursing. Denman's family involvement with the Royal College of Nursing, allied to the experience of numerous suffrage campaigns, guided by gifted educationalists such as Grace Hadow, ensured that the executive committee of the early WI strategically planned to influence political decision-making. Initially guided by its dynamic leadership, countrywomen at grassroots' level rapidly began to make informed decisions, producing resolutions related to welfare and attending national meetings. This was part of the participatory process that the WI facilitated during the interwar period. However, perhaps as a consequence of their focus on liberal education, the early WI experimented with various forms of media in order to engage countrywomen.

The first activity, lobbying skills and resolutions,. was possible because of the way in which the NFWI was organised. Taking the suffrage democratic model, each Institute elected officers and representatives to the County Federations as well as representatives to the AGM where the executive was elected and policy was debated. Paid staff headed by the General Secretary administered and ensured that the executive committee acted within the WI constitution. The AGM decided on policies based on those voted for by all representatives. These were then implemented by the executive and where possible by at Federation and branch level.

During the interwar period as now, these were wide ranging, demonstrating that the WI was not a single issue pressure group, but an all embracing one. Many of these resolutions mandated the WI to pressurise Ministers, the government and local authorities, and if unsuccessful to continue to do this until they were. (This is demonstrated in the last part of the chapter when discussing the WI's campaigns in improving health.) The resolutions fall roughly into five categories: rural living conditions, welfare, health, education and politics. Some were controversial such as when the executive encouraged WIs to affiliate with the League of Nations Union. There was always an emphasis on improving women's education and participation at all political levels, since this after all was what many women had campaigned for and by 1928 had achieved.

Allied to this and a contributory factor to the WIs popularity and success, was the fact that like the NUWSS it was non sectarian and non party. The latter was proposed in 1918 by Elizabeth Robins, an active suffragette, actress and writer, a founding member of the Henfield WI in Sussex. At the 1918 AGM she proposed that non party should replace non political. This enabled the WI to become a powerful political lobbying organisation.

The second activity, involved the use of wireless technology which was a new means of communication, introduced in 1920 and soon embraced with enthusiasm by the WI. In the spring of 1927 a letter was sent out from Eccelestone Square, WI headquarters, from Lady Denman to all County Federations about an experiment the BBC were thinking of developing.

The BBC's educational committee had co-opted Grace Hadow on to its educational panel and in turn Lady Denman insisted they must have a representative from the Federations on the committee. The letter talked about the project which was to use the wireless as a vehicle to educate and increase the WI's own popularity. Lady Denman whilst agreeing to consider the project rejected the idea of any comments about the use of the wireless. However she did agree for a free wireless to be given out to any WI branch that might want it. Not opposed to this technology she extorted the WIs to, 'Borrow a wireless if you can, wireless is the future key to improve rural life.' Accepting two new wirelesses the plan was to have six lectures specifically for the WI but also to engage town dwellers in the role and function of its organisation. The talks were broadcast in January and March and were so successful that more talks were broadcast in 1928 and 1929.

Archival material illustrates that rather more was hoped for. One of its members was given the research remit of six weeks to review the rural health needs of England. The series directly focused on health, welfare, young offenders, child psychology, citizenship and the democratic right to vote. Lady Denman wrote that it:

> ... will bring money in to support your village nurse and could show how the statutory and voluntary health services in any county if the rate payer wished be covered from the cradle to the grave.

Lady Denman introduced the first series of broadcasts by acknowledging that 4.000 WI members were listening but that she was also talking to town dwellers and church and chapel members:

> We are a friendly organization, we influence, we can give friendly advice, we are practical and we are creative, we write, we take part in drama ... we need to raise money for district nursing and to teach home nursing. We have been successful in poultry farming and can even tackle problems with water supplies by starting our own water company! ... the wise mother, the good teacher, the sensible village nurse these are the foundations of the next generation ... wireless annihilates space and defies imagination.

A university educated WI member, E. Nightingale, broadcast a talk on December 7, 1927 which was based on a six week cycling tour mostly around the south of England with the aim of getting the most up to date feel of rural needs. She reminded her audience that only, '25% of us still live in rural areas, 75% in towns'. She went into particular detail on the nutritional problems in both town and country. She asked listeners to read their local Medical Officers of Health's (MOH) reports, supplementing this by reading Newman on child care. They were also asked to support the school nurse with the medical examinations of children. Advocating clinics for mothers' ante-natal care and infant health, she asked the listeners to challenge their local councils to bring these into effect. Data was also used to discuss maternal health:

> We lose 3,000 mothers per year in childbirth, 70,000 of women have no ante-natal care in 1926, 48,000 babies die in the first year of life ... action is to support local nursing, organise yourself, organise inspection tours of your local clinics, invite your MOH to talk at your WI meetings, tell parents of their worth ... Compare what is actually done with what can be done.

This particular broadcast experiment continued with lectures from Professor Winifred Culiss, Professor of Physiology at the University of London and other eminent health scientists and then moved on to more lighthearted lectures on drama and literature.

The third activity which is clearly linked with the other two activities, was concerned with campaigning on improving nutrition and health. In 1928 Lady Denman, under the auspices of the Board of Agriculture, produced a report on rural education for women. Known as the Denman Report, it advocated better educational opportunities for young women living in the countryside and particularly emphasized domestic science education.

> This would establish an educational institute in which instruction in more technical subjects would be adapted to countrywomen's needs; this would correlate with the diplomas in domestic science.

This was not implemented for another twenty-five years because although nutrition had been seen as a constant health problem, researched and discussed by medical practioners, it was usually based on the simplistic theory of 'scientific motherhood', that is a lack of hygiene, poor mothering, reduced breast feeding and general ignorance. Nursing texts and lectures focused on re-educating the mother, often with no understanding of their lives and the cost of food. However, some forward thinking matrons had in fact proposed a diploma in nursing whose theoretical underpinning was based on nutrition; this would be undertaken at university. Miss Lucy Duff Grant, the Matron of the Manchester Royal Infirmary, even sent her only dietician on a sabbatical to America to develop this programme, which was swiftly rejected by the medical school and University of Manchester in 1936.

As the First World War had illustrated jam making played a useful role in supplementing the diet of the working classes. The technology and distribution of extra nutrients and vitamins from the manufacture of jam was directly and indirectly a result of the WI's knowledge about dietetics and food production (Madge Watt and Adelaide Hoodless both had diplomas and degrees in this and Lady Denman's role in the Women's Land Army also made her conscious of this.) It is therefore unsurprising that the WI campaigned on improving rural diets and the nation's health.

During the 1930s the scientific discussion regarding an appropriate diet demonstrated the anomalies between science, medicine, the Ministry of Health and food production. Issues concerning calorific values were debated by scientists and agricultural experts both in the UK and USA. Values were based on the cal cart scale of manual workers which required the male to have 3,400 calories per day and non manual workers 2,500. However agricultural labourers and their wives were not taken into account in these calculations. Examination of this diet showed that it tended to be particularly low in fats and vitamins. Ironically McDougall's interwar work on rural diets confirmed that these diets tended to be deficient in fresh green vegetables, animal foodstuffs and fruits. Although infants were usually breast fed longer in rural areas, paradoxically deficiencies in the mother's diet and lack of understanding produced underfed children with scurvy, night blindness and rickets.

Most rural families received lower wages than town dwellers, had more children and more working wives and mothers. During the early 1930s, the People's League on Diets demonstrated that in reality families would economize in stages; firstly meat disappeared, then fresh vegetables, then bread with butter. Ultimately people supplemented their diet with JAM.

Greta Jones' work on the social hygiene movement clearly demonstrates that the calculations produced by the British Medical Association and the Ministry of Heath differed by as much as 600 calories per day, and the Ministry tended to underestimate the calories needed. Jane Lewis states that most MOHs neglected this key aspect of health. A report in 1936 from Lancashire and Cumberland stated 'no relationship between employment, wages and deteriorating health standards in these counties'. Canning and distributing jam was therefore important for the majority.

If jam was the pragmatic side of the WI's contribution to a healthier nation, then the attainment of *Jerusalem* is epitomized by the many health and welfare resolutions the WI put before the government and public during the interwar year. These totaled approximately 130. From 1918 onwards numerous maternity and welfare Acts had created the facility, if not the desire for local authorities to improve maternal and child health, prevent infectious diseases and provide financial support to lone mothers and widows. Resolutions cascaded upwards to the AGM and illustrate an assortment of topics which were focused on health and welfare. For example in 1923 Epping District (Essex) WI proposed:

> This meeting viewed with grave concern the fact that since 1902 maternal mortality associated with child bearing has remained stationary, in view of this fact thousands of families have been affected ... this WI urges our members to create an informed public opinion regarding this matter without which no progress can be made.

This was still a matter for concern in 1931 as the following resolution illustrates:

> The matter of maternal welfare concerns us all. We urge county federations to make known health facilities in Local Authorities and further to ascertain:
>
> 1) If pre-natal clinics were available for prospective mothers who so desired them   and
>
> 2) Whether steps were being made by Local Authorities to make sure arrangements with practicing doctors were in place to ensure supervision for women in rural areas where no clinic was available.

Wiltshire went even further by calling for all its members to read the research by the Ministry of Health on maternal and midwifery, which noted that they 'needed improvement.' *Home and Country* proudly announced that, 'we the WI are friends of child welfare'. During the interwar years the WI lobbied continually for improvement centrally and locally for the under-fives including free dental care, and school meals. If this was not forthcoming local WIs sometimes stepped in to supplement the provision of school meals in their village.

Campaigns within other areas of public health demonstrate the wide range of issues that the WI would get involved in. For example in May 1922 the Executive Committee proposed at the AGM

> That the NFWI welcomes the action of the Ministry of Health in setting up a committee of experts representing the National Council for the Combating of Venereal Disease and the National Society for the Prevention of Venereal Disease and urges that questions of public health should be given due weight in education.... [Asking further] whether steps were being made by Local Authorities to make sure arrangements with practicing doctors were in place to ensure supervision for women in rural areas where no clinic was available.

In May 1924 the Oxfordshire Federation proposed:

> This meeting considers it desirable to bring the question of vaccination before WI. meetings with a view to studying it on its merits.

Rural housing was another imperative the WI was keen to lobby on. For example in October 1918, Epping WI proposed:

> That the provision of a sufficient supply of convenient and sanitary houses being of vital importance to the women of this country. The County Federations and Women's Institutes are urged to bring pressure to bear upon the Local Government Board to ensure that full advantage is taken in their districts of the Government scheme for State-aided Housing.

During the 1920s this issue was lobbied and campaigned for yearly, from Durham to Cornwall. By 1924 the Executive stated in its proposal

> Where a local WI has ascertained that their local Housing Committee has failed to deal with the housing shortage ... or practical steps are held up, they must do all in their power to promote the building of small houses as quickly as possible.

By the mid 1930s the WIs recognized the particular needs of the rural elderly. Huntington and West Stoke (West Sussex) for example asked at the 1938 AGM 'that all villages consider improved accommodation for the aged person', even venturing to ask if older people in Institutions were receiving their 2s (10p) a week pocket money.

By the end of the 1920s WIs were focusing on health policies, both in the countryside and nationally. For example, the Berkshire Federation felt that 'the NFWI as a body should frame a policy in regard to public health acting as a guide to those institutions wishing to take part in the health service. The Executive responded in 1928 when they stated:

> The NFWI to take every advantage of existing health services securing further development both practical and educational to help improve the standard of health in the rural population. [They also added] That it be understood that no pressure of any kind is placed upon any individual member or local WI to adopt or submit to any particular method of medical treatment.

Feelings also ran high with regard to rural patients with learning and mental health problems. For example in 1925 the Essex Federation stated in a successful resolution that

> We urge our members to review the facilities for the betterment of the mentally subnormal ... for greater care of them in urban and rural settings. Public opinion should also be sought into their aftercare particularly with regard to marriage.

Apart from the users' perspective, the rural community professional's dilemmas in nursing and medicine were also considered. The issues of recruitment and attrition within nursing itself were debated by the Caernarvonshire Federation in 1938:

> That this meeting welcomes the Government's inquiry into nursing careers and the urgent need for shorter hours, better pay and conditions.

The early waking of patients in hospitals was criticized and the Middlesex hospital praised for the piloting of 'its new nursing policy of not waking patients before 7 am'.

Examination of resolutions brought forward to the NFWI's AGMs during the interwar period demonstrate that there were differences in the health resolutions but a high degree of consistency with concerns relating to housing and child welfare. Many of the exhortations by the WI's founders to 'study and inform themselves' was clearly taking place.

Closely related to public health was the role of the nurse in the countryside. Whilst the WI systematically planned nationally, it always had its power base locally and took cognisance of local culture. In the interwar years nursing had inherited a volatile new professional persona, with a centralised, hierarchical structure. It was also not autonomous, but dominated by medicine and its zeal for its professional project. Nursing consisted of a complicated set of skills as well as a mixture of different types of nurses, midwives, health visitors, village nurses and Poor Law nurses. This profession was in a transitional state and this was exemplified within rural nursing. Here there was a mixed provision of care provided by locally based rural nursing associations, village nurses, midwives and rural doctors who were particularly anxious about losing paying patients. Apart from the overall nursing reforms which restricted and safeguarded those who could be registered and the closure of many rural nursing schools, community nursing in the countryside had its own unique problems. Nursing also included both trained and untrained district nurses and there were tensions between inter and intra professional relationships. It also had an unclear administrative system. Rural nurses were often overseen by a committee of lady administrators. These in turn either worked in tandem or not with the professional district nurses' own professional body, the Queen's Nursing Institute.

The providers of nursing care had to understand the context and local problems. The rural economy was complex and was not just based on agricultural, but also other types of work. The family also often depended on wives and children contributing to the family wage. The fear of the *landflight* of the aspiring female in rural areas, prior to the First World War, was also true in the interwar years as the evidence recorded in hospital training school records of industrial towns illustrates. These nurses did not usually return to the countryside. Compared to the town, social as well as cultural differences were evident. Aristocratic influence might have been arcane, but there was as Carrie Howse and Caitriona Beaumont recognise, a dynastic level of the skilled Lady Bountiful, whose philanthropy supported nursing activity. It was this group that the WI absorbed.

There are a growing number of historical studies re-evaluating this role. Carrie Howse notes in her work on administrators of rural care that the success of district nursing was an important project. She cites for example, that Lady Dent-Brocklehurst of Sudley Castle, Warwickshire paid her district nurse wages for six months herself and provided free accommodation. Beatrix Potter paid a proportion of the new district nurse wages in the Lake District in the 1930s and provided a car but made a proviso that the nurse attended her mother first! Jane Lewis in her review of the history of public health sees the interwar period as one of the most creative in public health but that its creativity came from the periphery, from privately funded initiatives and from independent women's organisations.

Although nurse historians in the past have re-iterated that the interwar period was a type of golden age for community nursing and public health, more recent historians such as Helen Sweet have identified problems regarding professional encroachment, difficulties in funding, the lonely life of the district nurse, the arduous working conditions and the lack of historical understanding of the mix of professional and lay provision. Also identified is whether district nursing activity meant that they were single, or double or triple duty district nurses? If they acted as midwife, heath visitor or district nurse what support was given and was it remunerated? An analysis of *Home and Country* demonstrates that local WIs and Federations raised funds for nurses at bazaars. Some also provided equipment and cars. This must have also affected the nurse's autonomy. Conversely the rural nurse would also find a support network, friendship, influence and gain administrative experience. Promoters of district nursing such as Mrs. Lloyd George, a WI active supporter, defended Queen's Nurses' wages as they rose in relation to the previous village nurse's pay in her own Cricceth community. This was an action which Helen Sweet cites that actively supported the new professional role of the district nurse.

When examining both organisations it should be recognised that comparisons are between a professional and a voluntary organisation. Whilst both had similar aspirations which were concerned with developing the role of women and had a humanitarian perspective, nursing was also a career which provided an occupational livelihood whereas WI members were part of a voluntary organisation. Thus a comparison and appraisal between the two is not simple. District nursing in particular during the interwar period was still re-defining itself. Rural nursing was a veritable smorgasbord of provision both within its material and financial service provision. As a result both groups adopted different approaches.

Whilst nursing adhered to a power coercive model of introducing both reform and regulation, which is well documented by historians of nursing such as Geoffrey Hosking, the WI used a historical framework, based on their ideas of a traditional community and used the concept of Trust as an established and undervalued line of inquiry. Trust is an interesting concept, and as Geoffrey Hosking comments 'brings communities together; it allows them to face together the unknown and it creates within a community a concept of welfare'. At a local level Geoffrey Hosking states communities build up trust by sharing rituals and routines, allowing effort to be given to the unfamiliar. It is a form of social capital which endures and allows for an initial philanthropic largesse which creates a fundamental base in which trust operates. Nursing within rural communities had a difficult pathway in establishing trust. It had to gain trust locally and with individuals as well as adhering to distant professional restrictions and regulations.

Steffan Johansonn's work on voluntary bodies' relationships with governments also demonstrates how the WI could be far more radical than nurses. He identifies several characteristics that either hinder or facilitate voluntary or non- voluntary organisations to move along a continuum between conformity and deviance. Using his characteristics which look at liberal ideology, resource symmetry, membership influence and professionalization, clear differences emerge. Whilst the WI during the interwar period had a critical and challenging ideology, becoming very rapidly independent of governmental resources, highly influenced by its membership, it had a low degree of professionalisation. This in Steffan Johansson's thesis creates a heterogeneity that allows resistance to central governmental pressures. On the other hand nursing during the interwar period shows the opposite, that is a consensus ideology, asymmetrical resources, low grassroots influences and a high degree of professionalisation. Steffan Johansonn would argue from this, that this produces a greater degree of conformity, allows for an initial philanthropic largesse and that this creates a fundamental base in which trust operates.

Independence and trust therefore created the permissive culture that Grace Haddow envisaged would develop within the WI. This would allow it freedom, creativity and the opportunity to actively support rural nursing. Trust within the WI was engendered in a number of ways, for example its formal structure and procedures made it a transparent organisation. This was helped by its magazine which adopted an informal style juxtaposing practical skills with politics. The WI also worked on shared causes with other women's groups and as well as through its local groups (34% of the interwar resolutions were locally driven.) All this facilitated trust. Social activities, communal singing, drama and other leisure activities created a greater cohesion; even if as Maggie Andrews states they appeared not to win major public health battles they often won local ones. All this assisted in creating and maintaining a space for nursing within the rural community.

To conclude, the WI, as stated in the introduction and illustrated by this analysis, was during the interwar period an unparalleled example of co-operation, innovation, and initiator of welfare and public health actions. Through its records it provides a rich source of rural women's lives, their actions and their values. Testimony to an enduring non - militant feminist organisation, it is wise to note its history is that of a movement with an iron fist within a velvet glove.

Sources and Bibliography

All the works cited were published in London unless otherwise stated.

Chapter 2: Movers and Shakers

Primary sources

Comfort for the Poor – Voluntary Information from the people of New South Wales. Collected in that Colony by Mrs Chisholm in 1845/6, John Ollivier, 1847.

The Story of the Life of Mrs Caroline Chisholm, The Emigrant's Friend and her Adventures in Australia, Trelawney Saunders, 1852.

What has Mrs Caroline Chisholm done for the Colony of New South Wales, Sydney: James Cole, 1862.

Colonial Land and Emigration Commissioners, 11th General Report, CO 384/86, 1851.

Passenger Act, CO 384/89, 1852.

Emigration and Transportation Relatively Considered. In a Letter Dedicated by Permission, to Earl Grey by Mrs Chisholm, 3rd Edition, John Ollivier, 1847.

The English Woman's Journal, 1858–64.

The Victoria Magazine, 1863–72.

Female Middle Class Emigration Society, Letter Book, vol 1, 1862–76, GB 106/1//GME/2/1.

The Women's Library Archives

Letter from Miss Rye to Miss Nightingale from Sydney, 21 September 1865.

Maria Rye, ADD MSS letters 45799 ff, 178–207.

Mackenzie, Aeneas, *Memoirs of Mrs Caroline Chisholm and Sketches of her Philanthropic Labours in India, Australia and England*, Webb Millington and Company, 1852.

Rye, Maria, 'On Assisted Emigration', *The English Women's Journal,* vol VIII, March 1862.

'The Colonies and their Requirements', paper read at the meeting of the Association for the Promotion of Social Science held in Dublin, August 1861, reprinted in *The English Women's Journal,* vol VIII, November 1861.

'Female Middle Class Emigration Society', paper read at the meeting of the Association for the Promotion of Social Science held in London, June 1862, reprinted in *The English Women's Journal*, vol X, September 1862.

Swann, Margaret, 'Caroline Chisholm – The Immigrants' Friend', paper read to the Royal Australian Historical Society, Sydney, 1925.

Secondary sources

Anstruther, G. Elliott, *The Emigrant's Friend*, Catholic Truth Society, 1916.

Bogle, Joanna, *Caroline Chisholm: The Emigrant's Friend*, Leominster: Gracewing, 1993.

Carrothers, W.A., *Emigration from the British Isles*, Frank Cass, 1965.

Clark, Manning, *A Short History of Australia*, Heinemann, 1969.

Clarke, Patricia, *The Governesses: Letters from the Colonies 1862–1882*, Hutchinson, 1985.

Darton, J.M., *Famous Girls who have become Illustrious Women of Our Time*, 21st edition, Marshall Brothers, undated.

Diamond, Marion, 'Maria Rye: The Primrose Path' in Orr, Clarissa Campbell (ed.), *Wollstonecraft's Daughters*, Manchester: Manchester University Press, 1996.

Diamond, Marion, *Emigration and the Empire: The Life of Maria S. Rye*, New York: Garland Publishing, 1999.

Fitzpatrick, Brian, *The Australian People 1788–1945*, Melbourne: Melbourne University Press, 1946.

Hughes, Kathryn, *The Victorian Governesses*, Hambledon Press, 1993.

Hughes, Robert, *The Fatal Shore: A History of the Transportation of Convicts to Australia 1787–1868*, Collins Harvill, 1987.

Johnson, Stanley C., *A History of Emigration: From the United Kingdom to North America 1763–1912*, Routledge, 1913.

Kiddle, Margaret, *Caroline Chisholm*, Melbourne: Melbourne University Press, 1950.

Monk, Una, *New Horizons: A Hundred Years of Women's Migration*, HMSO, 1963.

Pratt, Edwin, *Pioneer Women in Victoria's Reign, being Short Histories of Great Movements*, Newnes, 1897.

Summers, Ann, *Damned Whores and God's Police*, Penguin Books Australia, 1994.

Chapter 3: Fram'd and Fashion'd

Primary unpublished sources

Tait Papers, Lambeth Palace Library: all papers and correspondence between AC Tait, Catharine Tait and their family.

Primary published sources

The Holy Bible

The Book of Common Prayer

Benham, William, *Catharine and Craufurd Tait: Wife and son of Archibald Campbell Tait, Archbishop of Canterbury: A Memoir,* 1879.

Davidson, Randall Thomas, and Benham, William, *Life of A. C. Tait, Archbishop of Canterbury,* Macmillan, 1891.

Herbert, George (1632), *The Temple (including The Country Parson),* Washbourne, 1853.

Mills, Mary, and Davidson, Edith, *Edith Davidson of Lambeth*, John Murray, 1938.

Richmond, Legh, *A Memoir of the Rev. Legh Richmond*, 1828.

Wake, Lucy (ed.), *Reminiscences of Charlotte, Lady Wake*, Edinburgh, 1909.

Secondary unpublished sources

Peel, N. J., *The London Episcopate of A. C. Tait*, PhD, King's College London, 1989.

Yamaguchi, Midori, *Unselfish Desires: Daughters of the Anglican Clergy 1830–1914*, PhD, Essex University, 2001.

Secondary published sources

Marsh, P. T., *The Victorian Church in Decline: Archbishop Tait and the Church of England 1868-1882*, Routledge and Kegan Paul, 1969.

Swinton, Georgiana, and Sitwell, Sir Osbert, *Two Generations*, Macmillan, 1940.

Wheeler, Michael, *Heaven, Hell and the Victorians*, Cambridge: Cambridge University Press, 1994.

Chapter 4: Prostitution, Housing and Women's Welfare

Primary sources

Blocklehurst, Revd. Theodore, 'The Economics of Hell', reprinted from the *Spectator*, 24 December 1912, in *The White Slave Traffic*, undated.

Butler, Josephine (ed.), *Women's Work and Women's Culture*, Macmillan, 1869.

Chesterton, Mrs Cecil, *In Darkest London*, Stanley Paul, 1926.

Higgs, Mary, *The Life of Mary Higgs of Oldham*, a memoir written by her daughter, printed for private circulation by Clare, Son and Co Ltd, undated.

Mackirdy, Mrs, and Wallis, M. N., *The White Slave Market*, 1912.

Manchester Guardian, 20 March 1937.

Report on the Proceedings of the National Conference on Lodging House Accommodation for Women, 17 May 1911.

Sellars, Edith, 'Women's Work for the Welfare of Girls', in Baroness Burdett-Coutts (ed.), *Women's Mission: a series of congress papers on the philanthropic work of women by eminent writers*, Sampson Low, 1893.

Stead, William, *The Maiden Tribute to Modern Babylon*, reprinted from the *Pall Mall Gazette*, 1885.

Zimmern, Dorothy M., 'The wages of women in industry', *National Conference on the Prevention of Destitution*, P. S. King and Sons, 1912.

Girls' Friendly Society

Money, Agnes, *The History of the Girls' Friendly Society*, 1897 (revised 1905 and 1913).

Heath-Stubbs, Mary, *Friendship's Highway, being the story of the Girls' Friendly Society 1875–1925*, Girls' Friendly Society, 1926.

The Girls' Friendly Society, pamphlet reprinted from *The Monthly Packet*, 1877.

Townsend, M. E., *An appeal to the mistresses of elementary schools from the Girls' Friendly Society*, Hatchards, 1882.

Townsend, M. E., *Addresses delivered on the aims and objectives of the Girls' Friendly Society*, Hatchards, 1884.

Townsend, M. E., untitled and undated pamphlet, GFS Archive, 4/12.

Mercier, Anne, untitled pamphlet, Hatchards, 1885.

The Need for the Girls' Friendly Society, undated pamphlet.

Minutes and reports

Minutes of the GFS Lodgings Committees.

Minutes of the Committee concerning the proposed amalgamation of Lodges and Homes of Rest into one Department, 3 December 1907, GFS Archive, 1/37.

Annual reports of the Oxford branch of the Girls' Friendly Society, 1891–1908.

Annual Report, GFS Platform, 2005.

Unpublished memoirs

Townsend, M. E., *Memories of a life*, undated.

Townsend, Frederick and Mary, *Sketches and Impressions*, 1901.

Townsend, Mrs, *Some friends of the past*, 1913.

Townend, Kathleen M., *Some memories of Mrs Townsend*, 1923.

Government reports

Census of England and Wales, 1861, PP 1863, 3221, LIII Part 1, 265.

Census of England and Wales, 1911, PP 1914–16, CD 7929 lxxxl, 385.

Census of England and Wales, 1911, PP 1914–16, Cd 8491, xxxv, 483.

Census of England and Wales, 1911, PP 1913, Cd7018, lxxviii, 321.

Report of the Departmental Committee on Vagrancy, 1906, CD 2852, ciii, I.

National Association of Lodging Homes for Women

Higgs, Mary, *Glimpses into the Abyss*, P. S. King and Sons, 1906.

Higgs, Mary, and Hayward, Edward, *Where shall she live? The homelessness of the woman worker*, P. S. King and Sons, 1910.

Higgs, Mary, *How to start a women's lodging house*, National Association of Lodging Homes for Women, P. S. King and Sons Ltd, 1912.

Report for the Year 1912, National Association of Lodging Homes for Women.

Report for the Year 1913, National Association of Lodging Homes for Women.

Revised Handbook of Lodging Homes for Women and Girls, National Association of Lodging Houses for Women, 1913.

Unpublished papers

Girton College Register, 1869–1946.

Annual Report 1909, British Institute for Social Science.

Annual Report 1913, British Institute for Social Science.

Secondary sources

Andrews, Maggie, *The Acceptable Face of Feminism: The Women's Institute as a Social Movement*, Lawrence and Wishart, 1997.

Harrison, Brian, 'For Church, Queen and Family', in *Past and Present*, no 61, November 1963.

Hendessi, Mandana, *4 in 10: Report on young women who become homeless as a result of sexual abuse*, CHAR, 1992.

Keating, Peter (ed.), *Into Unknown England 1866-1913: Selections from the Social Explorers*, Fontana, 1976.

Kelly, Joan, 'The doubled vision of feminist theory', in J. Newton, M. Ryan and J. Walkowitz (eds), *Sex and Class in Women's History*, Routledge and Kegan Paul, 1983.

Prochaska, Frank, *Women and Philanthropy in 19th Century England*, Oxford University Press, 1980.

Rosen, Andrew, *Rise Up Women: The Militant Campaign of the Women's Social and Political Union*, Routledge and Kegan Paul, 1974.

Walkowitz, Judith, *Prostitution and Victorian Society: Women, Class and the State*, Cambridge University Press, 1980.

Watson, S., and Austerberry, H., *Housing and Homelessness: A Feminist Perspective*, Routledge and Kegan Paul, 1986.

Chapter 5: *Festina Lente* – Oxford women's principals 1879–1925

Primary sources: Lady Margaret Hall

Correspondence of Elizabeth Wordsworth, 1879–97.

Correspondence of Elizabeth Wordsworth, 1898–1917.

Henrietta Jex-Blake file.

Helena Deneke file.

Primary sources: Somerville College

Minutes of College Council, 1879–1925

Madeleine Shaw Lefevre file.

Emily Penrose file.

Primary sources: St Anne's College

Delegacy for Women Students Collection.

Johnson Collection.

Oxford Home Students Collection.

Primary sources: St Hilda's College

Chronicle of the Old Students' Association, St Hilda's Hall, 1906–25.

Primary sources: St. Hugh's College

St. Hugh's Club Paper, 1898-1925.

Letters of Ina Brooksbank, 1917–20.

St. Hugh's College Chronicle, 1937.

Primary sources: Bodleian Library

Papers relating to the education of women at Oxford University, 1910–79.

Dep. d. 759, Dep. d. 760, Minute-books of principals' meetings, 1912–41, 1921–33.

Dep. d. 763, Dep. c. 688, Unofficial minute-books of principals' meetings kept by the principal of Lady Margaret Hall, 1910–21, with loose papers from the minute-books.

Dep. d. 765, Dep. c. 689, Unofficial minute-books of principals' meetings probably kept by the principal of St. Hilda's, 1910–20, with loose papers from the minute-books.

Papers of the Association for the Higher Education of Women

Loose Papers Ms. Top. Oxon. c. 817, 117–118, 'Appeal for the Women's Colleges in Oxford.'

Uncatalogued collection, Family correspondence and personal papers of Misses O. H. E. and R. F. Butler 1885–1940.

The Fritillary, 1894–1925.

Private papers of Mrs Anne Milner.

Published sources

'Somerville Hall. Address by Lord Aberdare', *Oxford Chronicle*, 4 June 1881.

Bailey, Gemma, *Diary*, written circa 1904–10, privately printed by Mary Bailey, deposited at Lady Margaret Hall, 1991.

Buchan, John, 'The Dream and the Fact', *The Heritage*, no 1, Trinity Term, 1921.

Byrne, Muriel St. Clair, and Mansfield, Catherine Hope, *Somerville College 1879–1921*, Oxford: Oxford University Press, 1921.

Clough, Blanche Athena, *A Memoir of Anne Jemima Clough*, Edward Arnold, 1897.

Unpublished secondary sources

Keene, Anne, *The Role of an Oxford Women's Principal 1879–1925*, doctoral thesis, Oxford Brookes University, 1998.

Published secondary sources

Anderson, Elizabeth, 'Sex and Mind in Education: A Reply', *Fortnightly Review*, May 1874.

Armytage, W. H. G., *Civic Universities: Aspects of a British Tradition*, 1955.

Battiscombe, Georgina, *Reluctant Pioneer*, Constable, 1978.

Bennett, Daphne, *Emily Davies and the Liberation of Women*, Andre Deutsch, 1990.

Bowerman, Elsie, *Stands There A School*, Brighton: Wycombe Abbey School Seniors, 1965.

Brittain, Vera, *Testament of Youth*, Fontana, 1933.

Brittain, Vera, *The Women at Oxford*, Harrap, 1960.

Burstyn, Joan, *Victorian Education and the Ideal of Womanhood*, Croom Helm, 1980.

Davidson, J., and Cooper, Cary L., *Shattering the Glass Ceiling*, Paul Chapman Publishing, 1992.

Evans, Joan, *Prelude and Fugue: An Autobiography*, Museum Press, 1964.

Farnell, Vera, *A Somervillian Looks Back*, Oxford: Oxford University Press, 1948.

Firth, Catherine B., *Constance Louisa Maynard, Mistress of Westfield College*, Allen and Unwin, 1949.

Griffin, Penny (ed.), *St Hugh's: One Hundred Years of Women's Education in Oxford*, Macmillan, 1986.

Harrison, Brian (ed.), *The History of the University of Oxford: Volume VIII*, Oxford: Oxford University Press, 1994.

Kamm, Josephine, *Indicative Past: A Hundred Years of the Girls' Public Day School Trust,* Allen and Unwin, 1971.

Lodge, Eleanor, *Terms and Vacations*, Oxford: Oxford University Press, 1938.

McWilliams-Tullberg, R., *Women at Cambridge: A Men's University, Though of a Mixed Type*, Gollancz, 1975.

Maudsley, Henry, 'Sex and Mind in Education', *Fortnightly Review*, April 1874.

'Notes and News', *The Oxford Magazine*, 4 February 1926, pp 250–51.

Rayner, Margaret, *The Centenary History of St Hilda's College*, Oxford: Lindsay Ross Publishing, 1993.

Reeves, Marjorie, *St Anne's College, Oxford: An Informal History*, Oxford: St Anne's College, 1979.

Solomon, Barbara, *In the Company of Educated Women*, New Haven and London: Yale University Press, 1985.

Spurling, Hilary, *Secrets of a Woman's Heart*, Hodder and Stoughton, 1984.

Strachey, Ray, *The Cause*, Bell, 1928.

Willson, F. M. G., *A Strong Supporting Cast*, Athlone Press, 1993.

Chapter 6: Town Nurse and Country Nurse: viewing an early twentieth century district nursing landscape

<u>Bodleian Library, Oxford</u>

Temple, W., *Men without work*, Pilgrim Trust, 1938.

<u>RCN Archives, Edinburgh</u>

C444: Bacup District Nursing Association (later 'Comforts Guild'), Bacup, Lancashire: Nurses' records, deeds, minutes, reports, correspondence and assorted press cuttings, 1915–79.

<u>Queen's Institute for District Nursing Library and Archives, London</u>

Queen's Nurses' Magazine, 1904–58.

District Nursing, 1958–73.

Queen's Nursing Journal, 1973–8.

Uncatalogued collection of recruitment leaflets, correspondence, press cuttings, ephemera and photographs.

Contemporary Medical Archives Centre, Wellcome Institute for the History of Medicine, London

SA/QNI The Archives of the Queen's Nursing Institute, England and Wales (c. 1890–1947):

Box 81/H18: Correspondence, questionnaires, report of delegations to the Postmaster General, 1932–5

Box 115 Q6/11-22: Rolls of affiliated branches, England and Wales, c. 1913–39.

Liverpool Central Record Office

ACC3066: Liverpool Queen Victoria District Nursing Association committee minutes, correspondence, annual reports and accounts, 1862–1975. Also correspondence, programmes and circulars for Jubilee Congress of District Nursing held at Liverpool in 1909.

942 BIC 9-10: Private papers of Dr. T. H. Bickerton: Papers for 'A Medical History of Liverpool . . . to the year 1920' (1936).

DDX 1033: Garston and Grassendale District Nursing Association: Minutes, reports and correspondence, 1873–1951.

362WOO: Woolton District Nursing Association: Correspondence, annual reports and accounts, 1925–50.

Unpublished theses and dissertations

Dougall, R., 'Perceptions of change: An oral history of district nursing in Scotland, 1940–1990', PhD thesis, Glasgow Caledonian University, 2002.

Fenne, J. J., '"Every Woman is a nurse": Domestic nurses in nineteenth-century English popular literature (Charles Dickens, Mary Augusta Ward)', PhD thesis, University of Wisconsin-Madison, 2000.

Fox, E. N., 'District Nursing and the work of District Nursing Associations in England and Wales, 1900-48', PhD thesis, University of London, 1993.

Sweet, H., *District Nursing in England and Wales c.1919-1979, in the context of the development of a Community Health Team*, 2003.

Oral histories and personal testimony

D/N 26, 18/05/00, Oral History: Mrs Elaine Parr (see above).

Personal communication, Mr. J. M. D. Hoyle LLB.

Personal communication, Mrs Sue Hargreaves.

Natural History Museum (Bacup) website: http://www.bacuptimes.co.uk/

Secondary sources including local histories, journal articles and book chapters

Antrobus, A., 'Pioneers Still', *Guardian*, 29 January 1965.

Baly, Monica E., *A History of the Queen's Nursing Institute: 100 Years 1887–1987*, Croom Helm, 1987.

Bowden, K. F., *The Book of Bacup*, 1994.

Digby, A., *The Evolution of British General Practice*, Oxford: Oxford University Press, 1999.

Drake, M., and Finnegan, R. (eds), *Studying Family and Community History 19th and 20th Centuries. Vol. 4 Sources and Methods: A Handbook*, 1994.

Fox, E., 'Universal Health Care and Self-Help: Paying for District Nursing before the National Health Service', *Twentieth Century British History*, vol 7, no 1, 1996, pp 83–109.

Hardy, G., and Lemin, B., 'William Rathbone Staff College: past, present and future', *District Nursing*, vol 15, no 6, September 1972, pp 120–1.

Jones, L., 'Lancashire's Training Experiment', *District Nursing*, vol 1, no 7, October 1958.

Merry, E. J., and Irven, I.D., *District Nursing: A Handbook for District Nurses*, 1948.

Merry, E. J., and Irven, I.D., 'Some Queen's Superintendents', *Handbook for Queen's Nurses*, 1932 and 1943 editions.

Peterkin, A. M., 'The Scope and Conditions of District Nursing', *Queen's Nurses' Magazine*, vol XXIV, no 5, 1931, pp 128–132.

Rathbone, E., *Wiliam Rathbone: A Memoir*, Macmillan, 1905.

Rathbone, W., *Organisation of NursinIg. An account of the Liverpool Nurses' Training School, its foundation, progress and operation in hospital, district and private nursing. With an introduction and notes by Florence Nightingale,* Liverpool, 1865.

Rathbone, W., *Sketch of the history and progress of district nursing 1859–1890*, Macmillan, 1890.

Roberts, E. A., *Woman's Place: An Oral History of Working-Class Women 1890–1940*, Basil Blackwell, 1984.

Stocks, M., *A Hundred Years of District Nursing*, Allen and Unwin, 1960.

Sweet, H., and Dougal, R., *Community nursing and primary healthcare in Britain, c. 1919–1979*, Routledge, 2007.

Chapter 7. 'Faith, Perseverance and Patience': the History of the Women's Suffrage Movement in Oxford, 1870–1918

Primary sources

Bodleian Library, Oxford

National Society for Women's Suffrage Society Central Committee Annual Reports, 1884–1897.

National Union of Women's Suffrage Societies: Central and East of England Society for Women's Suffrage Annual Reports, 1898–1902.

John Johnson Collection of Printed Ephemera, New Bodleian Library, Oxford

National Union of Women's Suffrage Societies, Oxford Branch, Annual Reports, 1905–1918.

National Union of Women's Suffrage Societies, Oxfordshire, Berkshire and Buckinghamshire Federation Annual Report, 1912–13.

Miscellaneous material relating to Oxford branches of the Oxford Suffrage and Anti-Suffrage Societies and the Mid Oxfordshire and Oxford Women's Liberal Association; national material of the Church League for Women's Suffrage, the Conservative and Unionist Franchise Association, Women's Liberal Federation and Women's Social and Political Union.

Women's Library.

National Union of Women's Suffrage Societies Annual Reports, 1904–1918.

Museum of London

Suffragette Fellowship Collection.

Lady Margaret Hall Library and Archives

Bailey, Gemma, 'Diaries and Letters, 1906–1939', Typescript.

Lady Margaret Hall Reports, 1900–1918.

Lady Margaret Hall Old Students' Association, 'The Brown Book', 1892–1918.

Deneke Collection, Lady Margaret Hall

Oxford Women's Suffrage Society Minute Books, 1904–1915 (including cards, circulars, handbills, invitations, programmes and leaflets),

St Anne's College Library and Archives

Association for Promoting the Education of Women Annual Reports, 1879-1910.

Society of Oxford Home Students, 'The Ship', 1911–1918; Annual Reports, 1911–1920.

St Hilda's College Library and Archives

St Hilda's Old Student's Association, 'Chronicle', 1905–1918.

St Hilda's Hall Reports, 1900–1918.

St Hugh's College Library

St Hugh's Hall 'Club Paper', 1898–1903, 1910–1919.

St Hugh's Hall Reports, 1891–1914.

Somerville College Library and Archives

Oxford Women Student's Society for Women's Suffrage Central Committee Annual Report, 1914.

Oxford Women's Student Society for Women's Suffrage Inauguration leaflet, 1911.

Somerville Hall Records, 1879–1918.

Somerville Student's Association Reports, 1888–1918.

Centre for Oxfordshire Studies, Oxfordshire County Library, Oxford

Guardians of the Poor within the City of Oxford Annual Reports, 1874–1918.

Jackson's Oxford Journal (renamed *Oxford Journal Illustrated* in 1909).

Oxford Anti-Mendacity and Charity Organization Annual Reports, 1877–1920.

Oxford Sanitary Aid Association Annual Reports, 1908–1910.

Smith, Eleanor, 'Oxford School Board. To the Women of Oxford', undated.

Taunt, Henry, 'Wargrave Church destroyed by the Suffragettes', Typescript, June 1914.

The Oxford Chronicle

The Fritillary

The Oxford Times

Suffrage Journals

Church League for Women's Suffrage Monthly

Common Cause

Conservative and Unionist Women's Franchise Review

Free Church Suffrage Times

The Men's League foe Women's Suffrage Monthly Paper

The Suffragette

The Women's Franchise

The Women's Suffrage Journal

Votes for Women

Secondary sources including English local histories

A. J. R. (ed.), *The Suffrage Annual and Women's Who's Who*, Stanley Paul, 1913.

Askwith, Betty, *Lady Dilke: A Biography*, Chatto and Windus, 1969.

Atkinson, Diana, *The Suffragettes in Pictures*, Museum of London, 1996.

Banks, Olive, *Becoming a Feminist: The Social Origins of 'First-wave' Feminism*, Brighton: Wheatsheaf Books, 1986.

Banks, Olive, *Faces of Feminism*, Oxford: Martin Robertson, 1981.

Barnsby, George J., *Votes for Women: The Struggle for the Vote in the Black Country, 1900–1918*, Wolverhampton: Integrated Publishing Services, 1995.

Bartley, P., *Votes for Women, 1860–1928*, Hodder and Stoughton Educational, 2003.

Bolt, Christine, *The Women's Movements in the United States and Britain from the 1790s to the 1920s*, Hemel Hempstead: Harvester Wheatsheaf, 1993.

Bradley, Katherine, *Friends and Visitors: A History of the Women's Suffrage Movement in Cornwall, 1870–1914*, Newmill, Cornwall: Patten Press, 2000.

Bradley, Katherine, *Women on the March: A Suffrage Walk around Oxford City Centre*, Oxford International Women's Collective, 1996.

Bradley, Katherine, 'Women's Suffrage Souvenirs', in Hitchcock, Michael, and Teague, Ken (eds), *Souvenirs: The Material Culture of Tourism*, Aldershot: Ashgate, 2000.

Brittain, Vera, *The Women at Oxford*, Harrap, 1960.

Caine, Barbara, *Victorian Feminists*, Oxford: Oxford University Press, 1992.

Courtney, Janet E., *An Oxford Portrait Gallery*, Chapman and Hall, 1931.

Courtney, Janet E., *The Women of My Time*, Lovat Dickson, 1934.

Cowman, Krista, *Mrs Brown is a Man and a Brother! Women in Merseyside's Political Organisations, 1890–1920*, Liverpool: Liverpool University Press, 2004.

Cowman, Krista, *Women of the Right Spirit: Paid Organisers of the Women's Social and Political Union (WSPU), 1904–1918*, Manchester: Manchester University Press, 2007.

Crawford, Elizabeth, *From Frederick Street to Winson Green: The Women's Suffrage movement in Birmingham, 1866–1918*, Crawford, 2000.

Crawford, Elizabeth, *The Women's Suffrage Movement in Britain and Ireland: A Reference Guide*, University College London, 1999.

Crawford, Elizabeth, *The Women's Suffrage Movement in Britain and Ireland: A Regional Survey*, Routledge, 2005.

Dictionary of National Biography, Oxford: Oxford University Press, 2004.

Digby, Anne, 'Victorian Values and Women in Public and Private', in Smout, T.C. (ed.), *Victorian Values*, British Academy and Oxford University Press, 1992.

Dobbie, B. M. Willmott, *A Nest of Suffragettes in Somerset: Eagle House, Batheaston*, Bath: The Batheaston Society, 1979.

Dodd, Kathryn (ed.), *A Sylvia Pankhurst Reader*, Manchester: Manchester University Press, 1993.

Dove, I., *Yours in the Cause: Suffragettes in Lewisham, Greenwich and Woolwich*, London, 1988.

Earnshaw, Janet, et al, *Those Misguided Women: A Short History of the Campaign for Votes for Women in Tyndale*, WEA and Newcastle University Adult Education Department, 1984.

Eustance, Claire, Ryan, Joan, and Ugolini, Laura (eds), *A Suffrage Reader: Charting Directions in British Suffrage History*, Leicester: Leicester University Press, 2000.

Fawcett, Millicent Garrett, *Women's Suffrage: A Short History of a Great Movement*, T.C. and E.C. Jack, 1912.

Fawcett, Millicent Garrett, *The Women's Victory and After: Personal Reminiscences, 1911–1918*, Sidgwick and Jackson, 1920.

Garner, Les, *Stepping Stones to Women's Liberty: Feminist Ideas in the Women's Suffrage Movement, 1900 to 1918*, Heinemann Educational, 1984.

Hawtin, Gillian, *Votes for Wimbledon Women*, Gillian Hawtin, 1993.

Heath, G.D., *The Women's Suffrage Movement in and around Richmond and Twickenham*, Borough of Twickenham: History Society Paper No 13, 1968.

Helmond, Marij van, *Votes for Women: The Events on Merseyside, 1870–1928*, National Museums and Galleries on Merseyside, 1992.

Hibbert, Christopher (ed.), *The Encyclopaedia of Oxford*, Yale University Press, 1992.

Hollis, Christopher, *The Oxford Union*, Evans, 1965.

Hollis, Patricia, *Ladies Elect: Women in Local Government, 1865–1914*, Oxford: Clarendon Press, 1987.

Holton, Sandra, *Feminism and Democracy: Women's Suffrage and Reform Politics in Britain, 1900–1918*, Cambridge: Cambridge University Press, 1986.

Holton, Sandra, *Suffrage Days: Stories from the Women's Suffrage Movement*, Routledge, 1996

Joannou, Maroula, and Purvis, June (eds), *The Women's Suffrage Movement: New Feminist Perspectives*, Manchester Manchester University Press, 1998.

John, Angela V., and Eustance, Claire (eds), *The Men's Share? Masculinities, Male Support and Women's Suffrage in Britain, 1890–1920*, Routledge, 1997.

Lacey, Ann Candida (ed.), *Barbara Leigh Bodichon and the Langham Place Group*, Routledge and Kegan Paul, 1986.

Lewis, Jane (ed.), *Before the Vote was Won: Arguments for and against Women's Suffrage, 1864–1896*, Routledge and Kegan Paul, 1987.

Liddington, Jill, *Rebel Girls: Their Fight for the Vote*, Virago, 2006.

Liddington, Jill, and Norris, Jill, *One Hand Tied Behind Us: The Rise of the Women's Suffrage Movement*, Rivers Oram, 2000.

Marcus, Jane (ed.), *Suffrage and the Pankhursts*, Routledge and Kegan Paul, 1987.

Malos, E., *Bristol Women in Action (1839–1919): The Right to Vote and the Need to Earn a Living*, Bristol Broadsides, 1984.

Mayhall, Laura E. Nye, *The Militant Suffrage Movement: Citizenship and Resistance in Britain, 1860–1930*, Oxford: Oxford University Press, 2003.

Mill, John Stuart, *Three Essays: On Liberty; Representative Government; The Subjection of Women*, Oxford: Oxford University Press, 1975.

Morgan, David, *Suffragettes and Liberals: The Politics of Women's Suffrage in Britain*, Oxford: Basil Blackwell, 1975.

Morrell, Caroline, *'Black Friday': Violence against Women in the Suffragette Movement*, Women's Research and Resources Centre Publications, 1981.

Neville, David, *To Make their Mark: The Women's Suffrage Movement in the North East of England, 1906–1914*, Newcastle: Centre for Northern Studies, University of Northumbria, 1997.

Pankhurst, Christabel (1959), *Unshackled: The Story of How We Won the Vote*, Cresset Women's Voices, 1987.

Pankhurst, Emmeline, *My Own Story*, Eveleigh Nash, 1914.

Pankhurst, Sylvia, (1931), *The Suffragette Movement*, Virago, 1978.

Peacock, S., *Votes for Women: The Women's Fight in Portsmouth*, Portsmouth Papers No 39: Libraries, Museums and Arts Historical Publications, 1983.

Pugh, Martin, *The March of the Women: A Revisionist Analysis of the Campaign for Women's Suffrage 1866–1914*, Oxford: Oxford University Press, 2000.

Purvis, June, and Holton, Sandra (eds), *Votes for Women*, Routledge, 2000.

Raeburn, Antonia, *Militant Suffragettes*, Michael Joseph, 1973.

Romero, Patricia W. E., *Sylvia Pankhurst: Portrait of a Radical*, New Haven and London: Yale University Press, 1987.

Rose, Sonya O., *Limited Livelihoods: Gender and Class in Nineteenth Century England*, London: Routledge, 1992.

Rosen, Andrew, *Rise Up Women! The Militant Campaign of the Women's Social and Political Union, 1903–1914*, Routledge and Kegan Paul, 1974.

Rubinstein, David, *Before the Suffragettes: Women's Emancipation in the 1890s*, Brighton: Harvester Press, 1986.

Smethurst, J. B., *The Suffragette Movement in Eccles*, Eccles and District History Society Lectures, 1971–2.

Shiman, Lilian Lewis, *Women and Leadership in Nineteenth Century England*, Macmillan, 1992.

Strachey, Ray (1928), *The Cause: A Short History of the Women's Movement in Great Britain*, Virago, 1978.

Tickner, Lisa, *The Spectacle of Women: Imagery of the Suffrage Campaign*, Chatto and Windus, 1989.

Toynbee, Arnold, *Acquaintances*, Oxford: Oxford University Press, 1967.

Watkins, Clive, *Votes for Women: The Struggle for Women's Suffrage nationally and in and around Beckenham, 1867–1928*, Beckenham Suffragette Centenary Group, 2003.

Journal articles

Holton, Sandra Stanley, 'The Suffragist and the "Average Woman"', *Women's History Review,* vol 1, no 1, 1992, pp 9–24.

Logan, Anne, 'The "New Woman" of Tunbridge Wells: The Suffrage Movement in West Kent, *Journal of Kent History*, no 51, 2000.

Purvis, June, 'Using Primary Sources when Researching Women's History from a Feminist Perspective', *Women's History Review*, vol 1, no 2, 1992, pp 273–306.

Purvis, June (ed.), 'The Suffragette and Women's History', *Women's History Review*, vol 14, nos 3 and 4, 2005.

Unpublished dissertations

Bradley, Katherine, 'Faith, Perseverance and Patience: the History of the Oxford Suffrage and Anti-Suffrage Movements, 1870–1930', Oxford Brookes University, 1997.

Bryan, Susan, 'Women's Suffrage in the Manchester Area, c1890–1906', University of Manchester, 1971.

Leech, Catherine Emmet, 'The Feminist Movement in Manchester, 1903–1914', University of Manchester, 1971.

Walker, Linda, 'The Women's Movement in England in the Late Nineteenth and Early Twentieth Century', University of Manchester, 1984.

Chapter 8 Radicalism, Resolve and Resolutions: the early history of the National Federation of Women's Institutes 1915-1939

Primary Sources

Manchester University, Medical School

Manchester Royal Infirmary Committee Meeting Records, 1936.

Women's Library: National Federation of Women's Institute Archive

Broadcasting Papers, 1922-66 (5FWI/B/12/1/33)

Denman G 1925 (5FWI/B/12/33)

Hadow G. 1922. (5FWI/B2/291)

Freeman A. 1943 (5FWI/B2/29)

Hitchcock M. *Reflections on 25 years of the Federation.* 1944 (5FWW/B/29)

University of Waterloo, Ontario, Canada.

A Catalogue of the Lady Aberdeen Collection, 1897.

Published Primary Sources

Hall D. The Journal of Agriculture 25, 1918.

Yapp. C.S. *Children's Nursing.* Poor Law Publications, 1915.

Secondary Sources

Andrews, Maggie, *The Acceptable Face of Feminism. The Women's Institute as a Social Movement.* Lawrence and Wishart, 1997.

Connell, Linda (ed), *Textile Treasures of the WI.* Southampton: The National Needlework Archive, 2007.

Cordingley, Gill, *Lady Gertrude Denman: 'A Practical Feminist, 18884-1959'* Bengoe WI: Hertfordshire Federation, 2003.

Deneke, Helena, *Grace Hadow.* Oxford University Press, 1946.

Goodenough, Simon,. *Jam and Jerusalem* .Collins, 1977.

Gullace, Nicoletta, *'The Blood of Our Sons': Men, women, and the Renegotiation of British Citizenship During the Great War.* Palgrave Macmillan, 2004.

Hinton, James, *Women, Social Leadership, and the Second World War: Continuities of Class.* Oxford University Press, 2003.

Howes, Ruth, *Adelaide Hoodless: A Woman with a Vision.* Federated Women's Institutes of Canada,1967.

Huxley, Gervas, *Lady Denman G.B.E.* Chatto and Windus,1961.

Jenkins, Inez, *The History of the Women's Institute Movement of England and Wales.* Oxford University Press,1925.

John, Angela V., *Elizabeth Robins* Routledge, 2000.

Jones, Greta, *Social Hygiene in Twentieth Century Britain.* Taylor and Francis, 1986.

Lewis, Jane, *What Price Medicine? The Philosophy, Practice and Politics of Public Health Since 1919.* Wheatsheaf Books Ltd,1986.

Pugh, Martin, *Women and the Women's Movement in Britain 1914-1959* Macmillan, 1992.

Stamper, Anne, *Breaking down Social Barriers: Women's Institutes in England and Wales 1915-35* 2000

Verdon, Nicola, *Rural Women Workers in Nineteenth Century England: Gender, Work and Wages.* Woodbridge: Boydell Press, 2002.

Sweet, Helen, with Dougal, Rona, *Community Nursing and Primary Healthcare in Twentieth Century Britain.* Routledge Studies in the History of Medicine, 2007.

Journal Articles

Barona, J.L., 'Nutrition and Health. The International Context During The Inter-War Crisis.' *Social History of Medicine* 21:1, 2008, 87-105.

Beaumont, C, 'Citizens not feminists: the boundary negotiated between citizenship and feminism by mainstream women's organisations in England, 1918-1939' *Women's History Review* 9:2, 2000, pp. 411-429.

Gibson, Lorna, 'The Women's Institute and Jerusalem's Suffrage Past' *Women's History Review* 15:2, 2006, pp. 323-335.

Hirschfield, Claire, 'Fractured Faith: Liberal Party Women and the Suffrage Movement in Britain, 1892-1914.' *Gender and History* 2:2, 1990, 173-197.

Hosking, G, 'Trust and Distrust : A Suitable Theme for Historians?' *Transactions of the Royal Historical Society* Sixth Series 2006, pp 95 -115.

Howse, Carrie, 'From Lady Bountiful to Lady Administrator: Women and the Administration of Rural district Nursing in England, 1880-1925'. *Women's History Review* 15:3, 2006, 423 - 441.

Johansson, Steffan, 'Independent Movement or Government Sub-Contractor: Strategic Responses of Voluntary Organisations to Institutional Processes' *Financial Accountability and Management* 19:3, 2003.

Mc Dougall, E.J., 'Rural Dietaries in Europe'. *Bulletin Heath Organization* V111, 1939, pp. 470-497.

Stamper, Anne, 'Voluntary Action of Membership Organizations: Countrywomen Organize their own Education.' *The Voluntary Action History Society Occasional Paper*, No 4. 2003.

Stamper, Anne, 'Founding Fathers' *WI Life*. 18, 2009.

Thane, Patricia, 'What Difference did the Vote make? Women in Public and Private Life in Britain since 1918.' *Historical Research*. 76:192, 2003.

General Index